Advances in Intelligent Information Technologies Series (AIIT)

ISBN: Pending

Editor-in-Chief: Vijay Sugumaran, Oakland University, USA

Application of Agents and Intelligent Information Technologies

IGI Publishing • copyright 2007 • 377 pp • H/C (ISBN: 1-59904-265-7) • US $89.96 (our price) • E-Book (ISBN: 1-59904-267-3) • US $68.76 (our price)

Intelligent agent technology is emerging as one of the most important and rapidly advancing areas. Researchers are developing a number of agent-based applications and multi-agent systems in a variety of fields, such as: electronic commerce, supply chain management, resource allocation, intelligent manufacturing, mass customization, industrial control, information retrieval and filtering, collaborative work, mobile commerce, decision support, and computer games. Application of Agents and Intelligent Information Technologies presents an outstanding collection of the latest research associated with intelligent agents and information technologies. Application of Agents and Intelligent Information Technologies provides a comprehensive analysis of issues related to agent design, implementation, integration, deployment, evaluation, and business value. This book presents research results and application of agents and other intelligent information technologies in various domains. Application of Agents and Intelligent Information Technologies offers the intelligent information technologies that will potentially revolutionize the work environment as well as social computing.

Intelligent Information Technologies and Applications

IGI Publishing • copyright 2007 • 300+ pp •H/C (ISBN: 978-1-59904-958-8) • US $99.95 (our price)

With the inundation of emergent online- and Web-centered technologies, there has been an increased focus on intelligent information technologies that are designed to enable users to accomplish complex tasks with relative ease. Intelligent Information Technologies and Applications provides cutting-edge research on the modeling; implementation; and financial, environmental, and organizational implications of this dynamic topic to researchers and practitioners in fields such as information systems, intelligent agents, artificial intelligence, and Web engineering.

The Advances in Intelligent Information Technologies (AIIT) Book Series endeavors to bring together researchers in related fields such as information systems, distributed Artificial Intelligence, intelligent agents, and collaborative work, to explore and discuss various aspects of design and development of intelligent technologies. Intelligent information technologies are being used by a large number of organizations for improving productivity in many roles such as assistants to human operators and autonomous decision-making components of complex systems. While a number of intelligent applications have been developed in various domains, there are still a number of research issues that have to be explored in terms of their design, implementation, integration, and deployment over the Internet or a corporate Intranet. The Advances in Intelligent Information Technologies (AIIT) Book Series aims to create a catalyst for emerging research in this field of growing importance through developing and delivering comprehensive publications for the betterment of intelligent information technologies and their applications. Through the availability of high-quality resources, the series hopes to further the development of this field and build upon the foundation of future implications.

Hershey • New York
Order online at www.igi-global.com or call 717-533-8845 x10 –
Mon-Fri 8:30 am - 5:00 pm (est) or fax 24 hours a day 717-533-8661

Intelligent Information Technologies and Applications

Table of Contents

Section IV:
Semantic Technologies

Preface

In the last few years, we have not only experienced a tremendous explosion in the complexity of technical systems, enterprise structures, supply chains, and customer demands, but also market challenges, balance (and its dynamics) of power between the different stakeholders of companies, environmental and political systems. These trends require us to implement the optimization, adaptation (learning), and the overall behavior of socio-economic systems in a much more decentralized and networked manner, which will encompass more bottom-line oriented approaches than we usually employ today. Besides the necessary cultural changes in our economies (and societies), this will also require new construction principles, architectures, and behaviors for our information technology-based systems.

Intelligent agents are software entities that perform a set of tasks on behalf of a user with some degree of autonomy. They find applications in a variety of domains including: Internet-based information systems, adaptive (customizable) software systems, autonomous mobile and immobile robots, data mining and knowledge discovery, smart systems (smart homes, smart automobiles, etc.), decision support systems, and intelligent design and manufacturing systems. Current research on intelligent agents and multi-agent systems builds on developments in several areas of computer science including: artificial intelligence (especially agent architectures, machine learning, planning, distributed problem-solving), information retrieval, database and knowledge-based systems, and distributed computing.

A multi-agent system (MAS) is defined as a loosely coupled network of problem solvers that work together to solve problems that are beyond the individual capabilities or knowledge of each problem solver. The increasing interest in MAS research is due to significant advantages inherent in such systems, including their ability to solve problems that may be too large for a centralized single agent, provide enhanced speed and reliability and tolerate uncertain data and knowledge. Some of the key research issues related to problem-solving activities of agents in a MAS are in the areas of coordination, negotiation and communication. Coordination is the process by which an agent allocates tasks to other agents and synthesizes the results from these agents to generate an overall output. Negotiation is the process by which agents solve their conflicts and reach a compromise. For coordination and negotiation, they need to communicate with one another and hence the system should provide a general communication mechanism.

Multi-agent technology is one of the enabling technologies that provides appropriate concepts, architectures and protocols for applications with challenging flexibility demands. Based upon the results of the last twenty years of research, a MAS flexibility framework has identified and formalized with six dimensions: qualitative flexibility, quantitative flexibility, problem solving flexibility, economic flexibility, time flexibility and configuration flexibility. These flexibility concepts support the systematic description, analysis, and explanation of MAS flexibility, and they support the design of flexibility profiles into multi-agent system-based applications.

Considerable research has been carried out in the area of intelligent agents and multi-agent systems and a myriad of applications have been built using agents. This book discusses a number of agent-based applications developed in a variety of domains such as e-learning, online auction, Web services, and semantic technologies. The following sections briefly outline the different applications discussed in various chapters of this book.

Book Organization

Section I: Agents and E-Learning

This section presents four chapters that discuss how intelligent agents can be used in e-Learning. Chapter I by Schwingel, Vossen, and Westerkamp titled "Securing the Infrastructure for Service-Based E-Learning Environment" discusses e-learning environments and their system functionalities. The LearnServe system under development at the University of Muenster builds on the assumption that a typical learning system is a collection of activities or processes that interact with learners and suitably chosen content, the latter in the form of Learning Objects. It divides the main functionality of an e-learning system into a number of stand-alone applications or services, thereby giving learners a higher flexibility of choosing content and functionalities to be included in their learning environment. It maintains user identity and data across service and server boundaries. This chapter presents an architecture for implementing user authentication and the manipulation of user data across several Web services. In particular, it demonstrates how to exploit the SPML and SAML standards so that cross-domain single sign-on can be offered to the users of a service-based learning environment.

In Chapter II titled "Intelligent Agents for E-Learning," Bruns and Dunkel propose a software architecture for a new generation of advisory systems using Intelligent Agent and Semantic Web technologies. In the proposed architecture the domain knowledge is semantically modeled by means of XML-based ontology languages such as OWL. Using an inference engine the agents reason on the basis of their knowledge to make decisions or proposals. The agent knowledge consists of different types of data: private data, which has to be protected against unauthorized access, and publicly accessible data spread over different Web sites. Comparable to a real consultancy situation, an agent only reveals sensitive private data if it is indispensable for finding a solution. In addition, depending on the actual consultancy situation each agent dynamically expands its knowledge base by accessing OWL knowledge sources from the Internet. The usefulness of the approach is demonstrated through the implementation of an advisory system whose objective is to develop virtual student advisers that render support to university students in order to successfully organize und perform their studies.

Chapter III titled "Assisting Learners to Dynamically Adjust Learning Processes by Software Agents" by Pan and Hawryszkiewycz, focuses on the application of software agents in assisting learners to dynamically adjust learning processes. Unlike pedagogical agents, the agents in this application do not hold domain knowledge but simply assist learners to get through the learning process by a variety of supportive services. They assist learners to develop personalized preferred learning plans and guide them to dynamically align learning towards their goals. In this chapter, the online learning process is first investigated and an approach to assisting learners to dynamically adjust learning processes is outlined. Then the structure of the UOL (Unit of Learning) database that provides links between a practical learning scenario and the required services is explored. A multi-agent architecture for realizing the services is configured and the roles of the involved agents are described. After that, the related agent algorithms for guiding learners to dynamically adjust learning processes are described.

In Chapter IV by Hamdi, titled "Combating Information Overload by Means of Information Customization Systems," the author argues that the evolution of the Internet into the Global Information Infrastructure has led to an explosion in the amount of available information. The result is the "information overload" of the user, i.e., users have too much information to make a decision or remain informed about a topic. Information customization systems allow users to narrowcast what they are looking for and get information matching their needs. The value proposition of such systems is reducing the time spent looking for information. Hamdi points out that information customization could be best done by combining various artificial intelligence technologies such as collaborative filtering, intelligent interfaces, agents, bots, Web mining, and intermediaries. MASACAD, the system described in this chapter, is an example of an information customization system that combines many of the technologies already mentioned and others to approach information customization and combat information overload.

Section II: Agents and Online Auction

This section contains two chapters that discuss how agents can be implemented within online auctions and another chapter that describes the characteristics of user interface agents. Chapter V titled "An Agent-Oriented Perspective on E-Bidding Systems" by Jureta, Kolp, and Faulkner indicates that a high volume of goods and services is being traded using online auction systems and that the growth in size and complexity of architectures to support online auctions requires the use of distributed and cooperative software techniques. They argue that in this context, the agent software development paradigm is appropriate both for their modeling, development and implementation. This chapter proposes an agent-oriented patterns analysis of best practices for online auction. The patterns are intended to help both IT managers and software engineers during the requirement specification of an online auction system while integrating the benefits of agent software engineering.

Chapter VI titled "Implementing Seller Agent in Multiple Online Auctions" by Anthony points out that very little work has been done on the seller's strategy for online auctions. In any online auction, the final selling price of the item is dependent on several factors such as the number of bidders participating in the auction, how much each bidder is willing to pay for the product, how many online auctions are selling the same item as well as the duration of each auction. Each item to be auctioned off has a reserved price set by the seller. Setting the reserved price too high for the item will result in the item not being sold and setting the price too low may result in profit reduction or even loss. Deciding on the reserved price of an item to be auctioned off is not a straightforward decision. This chapter reports on a preliminary implementation of a seller agent that recommends a reserved price for a given item to be auctioned off by the seller. The seller agent's objective is to suggest a reservation price that guarantees the sale of the item within a given period (as required by the seller) with a profit.

Serenko discusses interface agents in Chapter VII titled "The Importance of Interface Agent Characteristics from the End-User Perspective." Specifically, this chapter reports on an empirical investigation of user perceptions of the importance of several characteristics of interface agents. Interface agents are software entities that are incorporated in various computer applications including electronic mail systems. There are several characteristics of interface agents that require special attention from agent developers. In order to identify the significance of these characteristics, a group of the actual users of an e-mail interface agent was surveyed. The results indicate that information accuracy and the degree of the usefulness of an agent are the most salient factors, followed by user comfort with an agent, the extent of user enjoyment, and visual attractiveness of an agent.

Section III: Agents and Web services

This section discusses intelligent agents and Web services. Chapter VIII by Ramírez and Brena is titled "Multiagent Systems and Web services in Enterprise Environments." It discusses the general aspects related to utilization of multi-agent systems in Enterprise environments with special emphasis on the integration architectures enabled by Web Service technologies. The authors present a decoupled architectural approach that allows Software Agents to interoperate with enterprise systems using Web services. The proposed solution leverages existing technologies and standards in order to reduce time-to-market and increase the adoption of agent-based applications. The authors discuss some case studies of knowledge-oriented Web services that have been designed using their approach and outline some current research and business concerns for the field.

Chapter IX titled "A Service Discovery Model for Mobile-Agent Based Distributed Data Mining" by Li and Song proposes a new model for solving the database service location problem in the domain of mobile agents by implementing a Service Discovery Module based on Search Engine techniques. As a typical interface provided by a mobile agent server, the Service Discovery Module improves the decision ability of mobile agents with respect to information retrieval. This research is part of the IMAGO system—an infrastructure for mobile agent-based data mining applications. This chapter focuses on the design of an independent search engine, IMAGOSearch and discusses how to integrate service discovery into the IMAGO system, thus providing a global scope service location tool for intelligent mobile agents.

In Chapter X, Serhani, Badidi, Benharref, Dssouli and Sahraoui discuss service quality. This chapter titled "Integration of Management of Quality of Web services in Service Oriented Architecture," emphasizes that quality of Web services (QoWS) management has witnessed considerable interest in recent years and that most of the existing works regarding this issue do not provide support for the overall QoWS management operations. Some of these works propose QoWS solutions for only basic Web services while others propose solutions for composite Web services. In this chapter, the authors extend the service oriented architecture (SOA) with a framework for QoWS management in which services may be basic or composite Web services. The framework uses a layered approach to provide support for the most common QoWS management operations, which include QoWS specification, QoWS verification, QoWS negotiation, and QoWS monitoring.

Section IV: Semantic Technologies

This section discusses semantic technologies, Semantic Web, and privacy preserving data mining algorithms. In Chapter XI, titled "Using Semantic Technologies for the Support of Engineering Design Processes," Brandt, Schlüter, and Jarke present a new integrated approach to design process guidance based on capturing the process traces in a Process Data Warehouse (PDW). Both the products to be designed and the corresponding process steps are structured and stored as extended method traces. This trace capture facilitates the processing and subsequent reuse of the information through a process-integrated development environment. The concept of the PDW has been evaluated in several engineering design case studies. One of those, which focuses on the conceptual design of a chemical production plant, is described in detail.

Chapter XII by Cardoso, Fonseca de Souza, and Salgado titled "Using Semantic Web Concepts to Retrieve Specific Domain Information from the Web," points out that the Semantic Web can be described as the Web's future once it introduces a set of new concepts and tools. For instance, ontology is used to insert knowledge into contents of the current WWW to give meaning to such contents. This allows software agents to better understand the Web's content meaning so that such agents can execute more complex and useful tasks to users. This chapter introduces an architecture that uses some Semantic Web concepts allied to Regular Expressions (REGEX) in order to develop a system that retrieves/extracts specific domain information from the Web. A prototype, based on the architecture, has been developed to find information about offers announced on supermarket Web sites.

In Chapter XIII titled "On the Problem of Mining Phrase Definition from Item Descriptions," Nguyen and Davulcu discuss a system for improving the "findability" of products. Most search engines perform their text query and retrieval using keywords. However, vendors cannot anticipate all possible ways in which shoppers search for their products. In fact, many times, there may be no direct keyword match between a search phrase and descriptions of products that are perfect "hits" for the search. A highly automated solution to the problem of bridging the semantic gap between product descriptions and search phrases used by Web shoppers is developed. By using scalable information extraction techniques from Web sources and a frequent item-set mining algorithm, their system can learn how meanings can be ascribed to popular search phrases with dynamic connotations. By annotating the product databases based on the meanings of search phrases mined by our system, catalog owners can boost the findability of their products.

Finally, Chapter XIV discusses privacy preserving data mining algorithms. This chapter is titled "Improved Privacy: Preserving Techniques in Large Databases," and authored by Abumani and Nedunchezhian. They argue that while data mining may help in strategic decision-making as well as many other applications, it also has a few demerits apart from its usefulness. Sensitive information contained in the database may be brought out by the data mining tools. Different approaches are being utilized to hide the sensitive information. The work presented in this chapter applies a novel method to access the generating transactions with minimum effort from the transactional database. It helps in reducing the time complexity of any hiding algorithm. The theoretical and empirical analysis of the algorithm shows that hiding of data using this approach performs association rule hiding quicker than other algorithms.

Effective use of intelligent information technologies becomes a necessary goal for all, and an outstanding collection of latest research associated with intelligent agent applications and Web services is presented in this book. Use of intelligent information technologies will greatly improve productivity and change how we view computing.

Vijayan Sugumaran
Editor-in-Chief

Acknowledgment

The editor would like to acknowledge the help of all involved in the collation and review process of the book, without whose support the project could not have been completed. I wish to thank all the authors for their great insights and excellent contributions to this book. Thanks to the publishing team at IGI Global for their constant support throughout the entire process. In particular, special thanks to Mehdi Khosrow-Pour, Jan Travers, Lynley Lapp, and Kristin Roth for their great help in taking this project to fruition.

Section I

Agents and E-Learning

Chapter I

Securing the Infrastructure for Service-Based E-Learning Environments

Simon Schwingel, busitec GmbH, Germany

Gottfried Vossen, European Research Center
for Information Systems (ERCIS), Germany

Peter Westerkamp, WGZ Bank AG Westdeutsche
Genossenschafts-Zentralbank, Germany

Abstract

E-learning environments and their system functionalities resemble one another to a large extent. Recent standardization efforts in e-learning concentrate on the reuse of learning material only, but not on the reuse of application or system functionalities. The LearnServe system, under development at the University of Muenster, builds on the assumption that a typical learning system is a collection of activities or processes that interact with learners and suitably chosen content, the latter in the form of learning objects. This enables us to divide the main functionality of an e-learning system into a number of stand-alone applications or services. The realization of these applications based on the emerging technical paradigm of Web services then renders a wide reuse of functionality possible, thereby giving learners a higher flexibility of choosing content and functionalities to be included in their learning environment. In such a scenario, it must be possible to maintain user identity and data across service and server boundaries. This chapter presents an architecture for implementing user authentication and the manipulation of user data across several Web services. In particular, it demonstrates how to exploit the SPML and SAML standards so that cross-domain single sign-on can be offered to the users of a service-based learning environment. The chapter also discusses how this is being integrated into LearnServe.

Introduction

E-learning systems and environments have become widespread in recent years, as they are able to offer an improvement of many learning scenarios, independence of time and location for a learner, and availability of content even in remote areas, to name just a few of their advantages. The market for such *learning management systems* (LMS) has grown considerably, and today there is a host of experimental, open-source, and commercial systems around. At the University of Muenster in Germany, one of several systems under research and development is *LearnServe*, which provides e-learning through a service-based architecture.

LearnServe draws upon observations made in vastly different application domains. Indeed, the optimization of processes in a value or production chain is a key factor for the survival of a modern enterprise. To achieve this, more and more organizations concentrate on their core competences by offering those parts of the value chain the respective enterprise has special know-how, technologies, or abilities in and that are most valuable for a customer and not imitable for competitors. By using modern Internet technologies as well as outsourcing and off-shoring, multiple companies are able to combine their abilities to organize production chains very efficiently. As such a joining of forces is not obvious for a customer; these combinations have become known as *virtual companies* (Porter, 1985). Virtual companies are flexible in their configuration and are able to change partners on demand, in order to optimize their output for the customer. In this chapter, we essentially transfer the concept of a virtual company from enterprises to the emerging e-learning domain.

Different from what happens in a virtual company, manufacturers of e-learning systems still concentrate on their core competences in very limited or specialized areas only, and offer common tools and techniques otherwise. As a result, present-day e-learning platforms resemble one another to a large extent in their functionality. In particular, all systems implement a maintenance of user data, a tracking of user actions, ways to display learning content, authoring features, exercise modules, and search mechanisms for the discovery of content, to name just a few of their typical functionalities. However, each platform implements these anew, and a specialization can at best be found for authoring tools that try to build reusable learning objects (see Vossen & Jaeschke, 2002; 2003) to be used within different LMSs and in the offering of learning objects as special add-on packages. For other functionalities the process of offering specialized applications has only just begun (Chen, 2002; Blackmon & Rehak, 2003; Bry et al., 2003).

A problem for learners using this "traditional" form of e-learning or LMS is that these platforms most often realize *closed* communities. The latter leaves no room for an inclusion of additional, possibly personally preferred or for the specific learning situation desirable features. Often learners are not even allowed to upload additional content to be used as new or besides already available learning objects. Some systems enable a simple upload mechanism, but do not provide functionalities to offer this content again for a self-directed learning of other learners in the system. Instead, learners are forced to use what has been allocated by authors, teachers, or tutors and have no flexibility to choose for any form of self-direction—neither with respect to functionality nor to content. But if e-learning providers would concentrate on their core competence and would offer e-learning functionalities as components that can be used via the Internet as a service instead of physical software components, this would lead to several advantages, including the following:

- Providers of services would be able to offer only those parts of a platform they are really experts in. This includes, for example, content in specific fields, advanced search functionalities for content, and so forth. A new organization of company offerings is sketched in Figure 1, which is obviously not exhaustive. Important is the focus on a selected part of a traditional platform instead of an entire system, that is, a shift from a "vertical" integration of functionalities to a "horizontal" service provision.

- Learners get the flexibility to include the services from providers they prefer, for whatever reason. For example, this can be a simulation of a certain fact or special content to be learned in a self-directed way and provided by the author of choice. Obviously learners are then able to choose content of the quality and style they prefer, like, or simply need.

By employing service orientation and using services as indicated in the right portion of Figure 1, "virtual e-learning companies" come into existence. They are able to offer more flexible platforms and environments, considerably going beyond what is offered today. System components as well as learning object content can both be made available as Web services that may be delivered by a host of providers. Since services typically are provided as a particular platform for a user, virtual e-learning companies (and LearnServe) have potentially to be able to connect a user with a multiplicity of platforms during a single learning session. Typically, each platform

Figure 1. Towards a specialization of e-learning providers

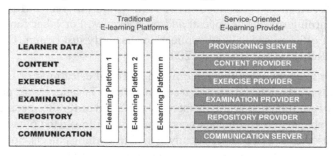

offering services would require a specific user authentication, which is inconvenient in such an environment and should also be hidden from the user. To achieve this, our LearnServe system exploits concepts that have been developed in business-to-business electronic commerce. These concepts are generally known as *provisioning* in that field. In this chapter, we describe how provisioning can be made to work in a distributed e-learning environment.

Clearly, the provision of parts of the e-learning functionalities by different manufacturers leads to new demands in the design of market strategies and pricing mechanisms, since no longer a real software product, but a service will be sold. Technically, the difference is that functionality or content is now offered on demand by remote servers somewhere on the Web. There is no longer a centralized e-learning server and no more centralized content storage. Instead, services with similar or even identical functionalities can even be exchanged on the fly, depending, for example, on availability, pricing, response time, and technical requirements. However, a server to maintain user data, tracking data, and to check authorizations, licenses, and so forth, must still be available in order to ensure the personal aspect of learning. Moreover, the knowledge a learning environment has about a particular user should be available in a single place, and not be spread around the entire system. This is particularly crucial for things like login data, since a user is typically not willing to go through logins several times during a single learning session, just because the underlying platform is switching servers.

This chapter develops an infrastructure for ensuring centralized personalization, authentication, and authorization in a decentralized and distributed, service-oriented platform. It turns out that most related work on the topic of service adaptation to e-learning or on the development of e-learning platforms in general does not care about these aspects (Chen, 2002; Blackmon & Rehak, 2003; Bry et al., 2003). In contrast, this chapter presents a corresponding *external* architecture, that is, an architecture comprising the message flows and the basic interfaces that can be used for a cross-domain-single-sign-on user authentication and the manipulation of user data. Our approach uses standards that already exist in the field of Web services (Casati &

Dayal, 2002; Alonso et al., 2004) as far as possible, in order to ensure a maximum of compatibility. The chapter also explains the use of encryption mechanisms to secure at least parts of the messages passed within the environment.

The organization of the chapter is as follows: The next section describes the fundamentals of Web services. Thereafter, "A Service-Oriented E-Learning Architecture" describes the idea of a service-based e-learning platform and introduces the LearnServe system (Vossen & Westerkamp, 2003a). The fourth section provides background on the service provisioning markup language (SPML) and security assertion markup language (SAML) Web service standards used by us to implement the external provisioning architecture of LearnServe. The architecture itself is explained in the fifth section, where we put an emphasis on security aspects. The final section concludes the chapter with a summary and a generalization of the concepts explained before, since these are not only suitable in an e-learning scenario.

Web Service Basics

As we are aiming at a provision of e-learning features and components as a collection of Web services, we give a basic introduction to that area first. A Web service (see Newcomer, 2002 or Alonso et al., 2004) is essentially a stand-alone software component that has a unique URI (the uniform resource identifier is a unique address), and that operates over the Internet and especially the Web. It builds on the technical idea of a client/server organization where the server implements the service and the client is a software component that is able to use the service. From an economical perspective the basic premise is that Web services have a provider and (hopefully) consumers. The provider has to implement the service and has to write a specification. The latter has to be made available to potential consumers through publication in a directory. The service directory can be queried so that services can be found by potential users. Service clients or users will typically search through such a directory, in order to find a single service that suits their needs, or a collection of services that can be composed appropriately. This scenario, together with the various standards that cover the aforementioned functionality, is shown in Figure 2.

Clearly, Web services need to be interoperable. Moreover, they have to be independent of the operating system they are running on, they should be usable on every Web service engine regardless of their programming language, and they should be able to interact with each other. To achieve these goals, Web services are commonly based on standards as already indicated in Figure 2; currently most used are the XML-based specifications, as listed in Newcomer (2002), simple object access protocol (SOAP), universal description, discovery and integration (UDDI), and Web services description language (WSDL). The Web services flow language (WSFL, see Alonso et al., 2004) was designed by IBM to be part of the Web service technology framework and relies on existing specifications like SOAP, WSDL, and UDDI.

Figure 2. A service provider/consumer scenario

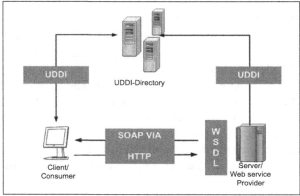

It is an XML-based language for the description of Web service compositions as part of a business process definition. Besides WSFL, there are other specification languages such as Microsoft's XLANG, which has so far made a linkage of different Web services into a business process difficult. To remedy these difficulties, a recent standardization effort has merged WSFL and XLANG into the Business Process Execution Language for Web Services (BPEL4WS, Andrews et al., 2003); it may be expected that this is not the end of the story. BPEL combines the preferences of WSFL (e.g., the support of graph-oriented processes) and XLANG (e.g., the structural constructs for processes).

Essentially, the setting commonly seen for Web services is a generalization of what has previously been envisioned for distributed service platforms such as CORBA. The basic steps for a provider to publish and a consumer to use an implemented software component as a Web service are as following: The provider of a Web service registers the service at a UDDI directory, which acts as a global repository of metadata for all registered services and stores information about a service, but it does not store the service itself. This meta-information includes, for example, the author, the category of service, and technical specifications. UDDI further defines a query language, an authoring authorization, and a replication strategy, since UDDI data is typically stored on several distributed servers. This ensures that a service can efficiently be found in response to a request; a request is answered by delivering information on how to use and call the service at the server of the provider. The communication rules for client and Web service are described in a WSDL file, which is not part of the UDDI directory; it is instead referenced by the information a client obtains from the UDDI directory upon his request. This document describes the conditions for the input and output data and the protocol for the communication. The WSDL document is used to generate a proxy to communicate with the actual Web service via SOAP messages.

Up until now, Web services have mostly been studied and realized in connection with business applications, such as B2B electronic commerce. More recently, Web services have also started to enter the B2C arena, where these services are offered by companies to individual customers. For the future, a reasonable expectation, supported by the host of service platforms recently set up by major vendors, is that more and more service scenarios will be implemented in the form of Web services.

A Service-Oriented E-Learning Architecture

In this section, we review our LearnServe approach to developing and building a service-based e-learning platform (see also Vossen & Westerkamp, 2003a; 2003b; 2004; and Westerkamp, 2006). LearnServe perceives the major activities in a learning environment, both on the learner and on the teacher ends, as *processes*. Taking the latter as a starting point and executing a stepwise subdivision of functionalities in reasonable stand-alone applications leads to an identification of basic e-learning application constituents. The latter can then be realized, implemented, or imported as *services* from appropriate providers. Services in turn can be combined to build new services with more functionality again, for example, by means of the BPEL4WS standard (Business Process Execution Language for Web Services, see Andrews et al., 2003). The overall model of a service-oriented e-learning environment is shown in Figure 3. It can be split into two major parts: client software and Web services provided by a variety of suppliers. The client can be implemented as Web portal or stand-alone application and is the "access point" for users of the learning services. All the rest is based on standards as described before.

Clearly, the use of learning services is not limited to the clients mentioned before, as the implementation of the entire functionality as Web services enables an integration of the e-learning functionality directly into existing business applications to interact with applications, processes, and data. Learning Web services can also be used on mobile devices if there is an appropriate client for that device. They are implemented on distributed servers and in particular include:

1. *Content services* to present the learning material in the form of learning objects, courses, or classes (Vossen & Jaeschke, 2002) in a service-oriented way (Vossen & Westerkamp, 2005).

2. *Discovery services* to be used to search for content as well as to search for additional functionalities that can be included in the system (Vossen & Westerkamp, 2003b).

Figure 3. Architecture of service-oriented e-learning

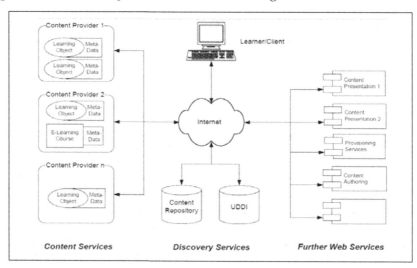

3.   *Further Web services* to implement a variety of other functionalities. This can include typical e-learning activities and third-party services that are worth to be consumed by both learners and teachers. These services also encompass payment, test, examination, and certification services.

The approach of building a decentralized system by combining several Web services in a way intended to achieve the same functionality as a traditional e-learning system has an obvious challenge: It easily leads to problems of managing content for learners and of picking services delivering the desired functionality at the moment of demand. Systems like LearnServe use a UDDI registry to search for Web services as common in the Web services field. However, UDDI is inappropriate for *content* services since the storage of additional metadata about the content is not adequately supported. The discovery process is supported by the LearnServe repository (Vossen & Westerkamp, 2003b) for learning object publication and search and essentially adapts the UDDI framework used for commercial Web services to an e-learning context. It distinguishes itself by the fact that the repository itself contains centralized data about learning objects, that is, all meta-information covered by the IEEE LOM standard (IEEE learning object Metadata, IEEE, 2002), while the actual content that it refers to can be arbitrarily distributed. To improve the search results, ontologies are used within the repository. LearnServe already supports a decentralized annotation of content Web services by means of mechanisms known from the field of the Semantic Web (Vossen & Westerkamp, 2004). However, an automatic selection of content by agents is not implemented owing to a lot of general problems showing up in the area of the Semantic Web. Currently, content and functionality has to be explicitly selected by users on the foundation of presented metadata before it can be used within the LearnServe environment. To utilize some content, the underlying platform calls the desired learning object, which is then executed by a presentation service and delivered to the learner. This presentation service enhances the information about the content as described in the WSRP standard (Kropp et al., 2003) and thus additionally enables an adaptation of presentation information depending on the learner's needs (Vossen & Westerkamp, 2005). Since all WSRP-conform services implement the same interface, content can be included dynamically on demand (see Vossen & Westerkamp, 2005).

All services are described by Web services description language (WSDL) documents and use simple object access protocol (SOAP) messages for their interaction. However, neither WSDL nor SOAP provide the functionality that is necessary to enable a cross-domain-single-sign-on (CDSSO) to the Web service platform and to manipulate user data in a standardized and uniform way. It is also necessary to maintain user profiles in order to be able to offer information on already presented learning material as well as to check *licenses* that allow a learner to use material since e-learning cannot be assumed to be generally free of charge. The central instance that offers these functionalities is the *provisioning server* that is named after its main functionality—the *provision* of data sets that is also needed by a number of other services. The interactions and the authentication-interfaces of this service are explained in the following sections. The provisioning server also implements the tracking interfaces to communicate with content from several providers. These interfaces are based on the well accepted sharable content object reference model (SCORM, see ADL, 2004) and transfer these concepts to a service-oriented environment. Details are beyond the scope of this chapter and can be found in Westerkamp (2006) and Vossen and Westerkamp (2005).

The use of e-learning Web services in an open style on the Web can only be successful if the e-learning community will be able to agree upon a number of realization aspects. The latter particularly include the CDSSO mechanism as well as security aspects described in this chapter, the interfaces of the provisioning server to enable tracking from any other service, and the use of presentation-oriented services, for example, WSRP services. All of the latter is covered in the "L" in Figure 4 by the dark gray-colored layers (with white letters). The "L" gives a general overview of the technologies and providers used in LearnServe and can be seen as a more general model for service-oriented e-learning. If the community will not be able to agree about those aspects, implementation efforts are necessary each time a new provider joins the environment. First approaches to create guidelines for a use of Web services in e-learning have started under the supervision of the IMS in the working group about general Web services (IMS, 2005). Currently, they are working

Figure 4. The LearnServe technology and service model

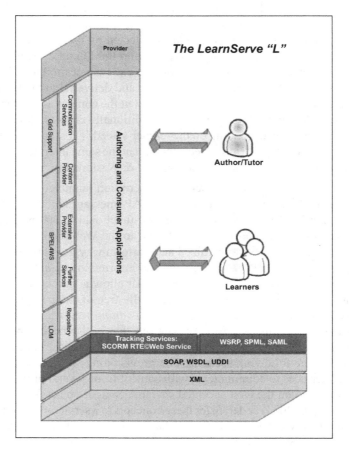

on lower levels of the stack (e.g., versions of SOAP, WSDL, and HTTP), which a peer has to implement in order to establish interoperability. For the higher levels, the LearnServe approach adapts or uses models of existing standardizations that could provide the foundation for the interoperability needed in e-learning.

SPML and SAML

Data about resources (e.g., users, learners, machines) are often stored in *directories*. Directory services in general maintain information that is often read and only rarely written. Nowadays, such services are frequently used to maintain network resources; provisioning servers can be seen as a special type of directory service. Directory services are often organized as trees to allow an efficient discovery of their resources. The objects stored inside such a tree can be defined very flexibly based on the needs of the application domain at hand. Objects can reference one another to model correlations between two or more of them.

Most directory services offer a proprietary interface and query language to execute operations on their resources. To cope with this heterogeneity, the *service provisioning markup language* or "SPML" (Rolls, 2003) has been developed as a framework for executing provisioning requests which in turn manipulate or obtain relevant data from resources called *provisioning service targets (PST)*. The latter can include relational databases, applications, LDAP (lightweight directory access protocol) services, or any other system that may offer relevant information.

For the e-learning scenario we are looking at in this chapter, the relevant PST information particularly includes learner profiles. In the following we will not explain the internal architecture and data model of a directory for user data since this can be implemented in various ways as proposed by competing standards. Instead, we concentrate on the general communication architecture. SPML requests are encoded as XML documents and sent by the *requesting authority* (RA) to the provisioning service that is able to receive and process SPML documents. To execute this, it has to implement an SPML interface called *provisioning service point* (PSP). The request is then executed on the data of the PST.

SPML requests are based on XML schemas that have to be defined by the PSP to publish information about the structure of the resources and objects stored inside the directory. These schemas define object attributes and their data types. Each operation that is requested by an RA is related to a data object defined in a schema. To make a request, the RA must hence be aware of the schema. To obtain relevant schema information, the RA can use the *schemaRequest* operation to ask a PS for the desired schema. In addition to this method the PS has to implement the basic SPML methods, add, modify, delete, and search, and each operation comes with request-response elements to define the communication flow.

To allow operations on the data stored inside the directory and to check access rights of other Web services, it is necessary to have an authentication mechanism to control user rights. The *security assertion markup language* (SAML, see Hallam-Baker & Maler, 2002) offers a way to achieve this by using common Web technologies. SAML defines a protocol that builds on XML-based requests and responses and is a framework for the exchange of security information concerning people or computers. This includes information about authentication, attributes of persons or computers, and access rights to resources defined by an authority. SAML itself is not an authority, but a transport protocol for assertions that cover information about identities, attributes, and access rights. SAML assertions can be combined with other transport protocols, in particular SOAP.

One of the fundamental application domains of SAML is the aforementioned area of cross-domain-single-sign-on (CDSSO). Traditional Web-based e-learning platforms often use cookies for the control of learner sessions. However, as cookies can only be read by the same computer or domain, they are not appropriate in a Web services context since services may be provided by many different servers or institutions. How the SAML standardization can be enhanced to be used within the general Web-service communication processes and in particular in a service-oriented e-learning system to check authentications is presented next.

An External Architecture For
User-Data Provisioning

Following the discussion from the previous section, the basic architecture for a distributed e-learning system as shown in Figure 3 above has to be enhanced by a well-defined mechanism to continuously check user access rights. This concerns, on the one hand, the interfaces of the provisioning server and, on the other hand, the messages that are used for the communication between all protected system

Figure 5. Provisioning architecture of a service-based e-learning environment

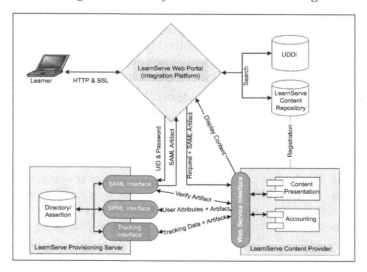

components. The resulting architecture for a CDSSO as well as for the provisioning of additional data is shown in Figure 5. Note that the following descriptions stress the *external* architecture, that is, the functions and message flows of the system. The internal realization of the provisioning server as well as of the processing of user information on all other servers depends on the implementation of the respective service and will not be explained here. Details can be found in Westerkamp (2006). Important are the enhancements and encryptions of the messages sent within the entire system and the implementation of interfaces and functionalities to use SAML and SPML by the services.

As already sketched in Section 2, the user of the system only needs a browser to access any e-learning functionalities. These functionalities are integrated into a portal to let the platform appear as a single Web-based e-learning system. In particular, this means that authentication has to be done only once for all Web services included in the platform. The sample scenario shown in Figures 4 and 5 concentrates on the authentication and a presentation of learning content.

The most important component in this architecture is the *provisioning server* that offers two main functionalities: authentication for all Web services in the system and maintenance of learner records. The provisioning server of the LearnServe system has an SAML, SPML, and tracking interface and keeps all relevant information inside a relational database.

The first step for a person to use the distributed e-learning functionalities is to key in his or her user identification (UID) and password. Both password and UID are transmitted to the *UserLogin* service of the provisioning server for validation (part of the SAML interface; see also the upper part of Figure 6). If the user data is correct, an SAML assertion is created and stored at the provisioning server so that it can later on be used for the CDSSO of other services.

Listing 1 : SAML Assertion

```
<saml:Assertion
    MajorVersion="1"
    MinorVersion="1"
    AssertionID=»6b0d4962-1284-08c9-c0a8-0302faeddd16»
    Issuer=»servername»
    IssueInstant=»2007-01-30T12:50:56.003Z»
    xmlns:saml=»urn:oasis:names:tc:SAML:1.0:assertion»>

 <saml:Conditions
    NotBefore="2007-01-30T12:50:56.003Z"
    NotOnOrAfter="2007-01-30T13:10:56.003Z" />
```

```
<saml:AuthenticationStatement
  AuthenticationMethod="urn:oasis:names:tc:SAML:1.0:am:password"
  AuthenticationInstant="2007-01-30T12:50:56.002Z">
 <saml:Subject>
  <saml:NameIdentifier>learner@provisioning.local</saml:NameIdentifier>

  <saml:SubjectConfirmation>
   <saml:ConfirmationMethod>
    urn:oasis:names:tc:SAML:1.0:cm:artifact
   </saml:ConfirmationMethod>
  </saml:SubjectConfirmation>

 </saml:Subject>
 </saml:AuthenticationStatement>
</saml:Assertion>
```

This assertion is stored inside the relational database. As shown in Listing 1, the minimal required information stored in the assertion is the saml:Subject, which uniquely identifies the user. Additional technical information about the authentication method is needed including version, an internal id, the name of the provisioning server, the saml namespace definition, the authentication method and time limits within which the assertion is valid. It is stored as long as the user is logged into the system or until a time-out occurs. The response of the *UserLogin* service is an SAML artifact referencing the provisioning server and this particular assertion.

Listing 2: SAML artifact

```
<samlp:AssertionArtifact
  xmlns:samlp="urn:oasis:names:tc:SAML:1.0:protocol">
        AgBiSQ1rhBLJCMCoAwL67d0WAAA[...]
</samlp:AssertionArtifact>
```

The artifact shown in Listing 2 consists of one single data block which is encoded for XML representation. It is henceforth used in each Web service call to be able to verify the access rights of the user in question. In the Web services case, the artifact consists of a token and the URI of the provisioning server to announce this address to all other servers that participate in the system. The token can technically be generated, for instance, by a hash-function. However, the way the token is generated does not matter to the interacting services because it has to be interpreted by the provisioning server only. All other servers just have to extract the artifact from the SOAP message, read the URI to connect to the provisioning server and send the token to receive the full assertion or check any user rights. The artifact is added to the optional part of the SOAP header of all messages that are sent inside the system. As a consequence, it can be used by all servers to request the assertion stored on the provisioning server via the SAML interface to check at least the UID and hence to verify the identity of the user. The artifact in combination with its corresponding assertion implements the CDSSO because all services can rely on the first authorization if the referenced assertion for an artifact exists.

In what follows, the use of the artifact in the initialization and content presentation process will be explained. Content presentation is done in several steps, and the entire process needs to contact the provisioning server several times. After a learner has selected the desired learning object, the content provider calls the provisioning server to verify whether the learning objects can indeed be presented. Particularly, the content provider has to check if all requirements concerning the completion of previous contents are met (see center part of Figure 6). The SPML request in Listing 3 to the SPML interface of the provisioning server illustrates how this can be achieved.

Listing 3: SPML query

```
<spml:SearchRequest
    spml:execution="synchronous"
    spml:requestID="70b9417c-1284-08c9-c0a8-030260196f35"
    xmlns:spml="urn:oasis:names:tc:SPML:1:0">

 <spml:searchBase
    spml:type="urn:oasis:names:tc:SPML:1:0#SAMLSubject">

  <saml:Subject
   xmlns:saml="urn:oasis:names:tc:SAML:1.0:asertion">

  <saml:NameIdentifier>
    learner@provisioning.local
  </saml:NameIdentifier>

  <saml:SubjectConfirmation>
   <saml:ConfirmationMethod>
    urn:oasis:names:tc:SAML:1.0:cm:artifact
   </saml:ConfirmationMethod>
```

```
  </saml:SubjectConfirmation>
 </saml:Subject>
</spml:searchBase>

<dsml:attributes xmlns:dsml="urn:oasis:names:tc:DSML:2:0:core">
 <dsml:attribute dsml:name="LearningObject-ID" />
</dsml:attributes>

</spml:SearchRequest>
```

The learner is again identified by means of the artifact contained in the SOAP request. To check the already passed learning objects of the user, the provisioning server queries the learner's profile. To return a list of all successfully completed learning objects to the content provider, the example above filters on the attribute LearningObject-ID of the user. The content provider is then able to verify if the prerequisites of the learning object in question are met by matching them with the list received.

If the prerequisites are satisfied, a second test has to be made in most cases as learning cannot be considered to be free of charge. An *Accounting* functionality is executed that uses the artifact of the learner and the ID of the learning object to call the SPML interface of the provisioning server. This call requests all valid licenses a learner has bought.

The content provider can afterwards verify whether a valid license for the learning object exists. If it exists, the content provider can contact the tracking interface of provisioning server to announce the consumption of the license and to create a tracking data set for the learner. This data set includes at least the information that the learning object is presented. The content provider is now able to do the latter and executes the learning object and transmits the content to the learner.

It should be mentioned at this point that the SPML interface is the overall access point to query information about learners. This interface can be used, for instance, by the content provider to obtain information that may influence the presentation of content. For example, one learner might prefer to learn definitions, whereas another learner likes to use simple exercises and examples to understand a topic to be learned. Two kinds of user data can be used for this type of personalization. On the one hand, it can be data that was explicitly stored by the learner during the creation of his or her profile. On the other hand, an intelligent mechanism inside the provisioning server can extract information from the tracking data stored with the learner's profile. The already mentioned information that a learning object was presented is of course only a very basic one and can be enhanced considerably (see Westerkamp, 2006).

Figure 6. Identity management in a service-based e-learning environment

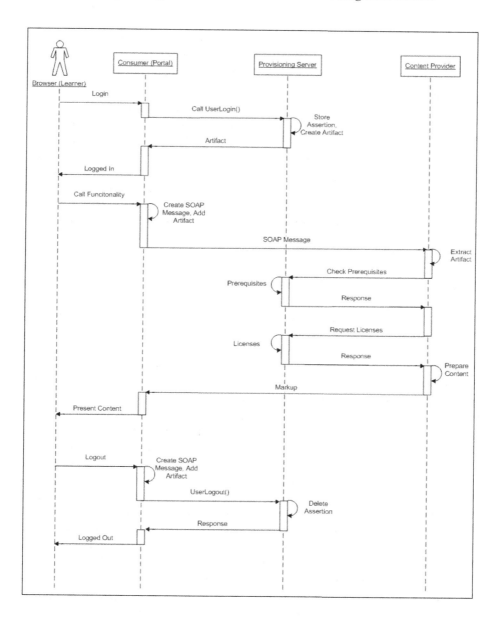

A learning session is terminated by the user by hitting the logout button on the portal page (see lower part of Figure 6). This procedure just sends a SOAP message and deletes the respective assertion on the provisioning server. Afterwards, all requests that reference this assertion fail because it does not exist anymore. Note that in case of an incorrect logout due, for example, to network failures, the assertion can still be deleted by the server after a certain period of time without any user activities.

As the entire communication handles personal data, securing the communication is crucial. The initial part of the authorization process that is not based on SOAP (i.e., the transmission of UID and password from the browser to the portal) has to be secured by the common secure socket layer (SSL) mechanism. For all other messages passed in the system, additional security mechanisms have to be used. Security concerns are not covered by SOAP to be as flexible as possible. However, several SOAP messages passed between consumers and providers in the service-oriented e-learning system may contain data that has to be protected against a tapping of the line or against other adversaries. In particular, data that has to be protected includes all payment information like credit card numbers. In addition, authentication information like usernames, identification tokens for the CDSSO, and passwords as well as tracking and profiling data about a learner have to be secured. Security aspects are roughly explained in the following.

The use of SOAP via hypertext transfer protocol (HTTP) is very common. As there is the de facto standard *secure socket layer* (SSL) for the use of secure HTTP (HTTPS for short), it makes also sense to use these concepts with SOAP via HTTP. Conceptually, SSL secures the message while it is transported on the Internet starting from the fourth layer (HTTP) of the ISO open systems interconnection (ISO/OSI) reference model. Although the use of SSL ensures a secure transportation of a SOAP message, the entire message is encrypted and routed by means of the transmission control protocol (TCP) header, not by means of the SOAP header. This results from the fact that the SOAP header is also encrypted and cannot be read by intermediaries. As the processing of SOAP messages is also designed to allow intermediaries to process parts of the message if necessary, SSL is not able to secure these messages and is thus not the best choice. Instead, messages still have to be able to process for intermediaries, at least to some extent. The Web service security (WSS, OASIS, 2004) standard addresses this problem. It enhances SOAP by adding encryption and digital signatures (DS) and only secures the security-relevant information of a SOAP message. Other parts of the message can still be read by the intermediaries. The standard is based on the concepts of XML digital signature (W3C, 2001) and XML encryption (W3C, 2002).

XML digital signature ensures that certain parts of a SOAP message have really been created by the sender of the message and that the sender is really the peer it pretends to be. It is based on public-key encryption approaches such as RSA (the algorithm developed by Ron Rivest, Adi Shamir, and Len Adleman; see Rivest et al., 1978). They are based on the assumption that users have a pair of keys: one private key only known by themselves, and a key publicly available for everybody. The function of the digital signature is to encrypt a message with the private key of the sender. The receiver can only decrypt this message with the public one of the sender. Two aspects are ensured by this approach:

- The receiver of the message can be sure that the message has indeed been created by the sender because only the sender is able to encrypt the message with the private key corresponding to the public key known by the receiver.
- The message has not been changed by intermediaries. If somebody had changed the message, the decryption would no longer work correctly.

The sender can digitally sign only parts of a SOAP message that are specified in the security header of the message. For these parts a checksum is calculated that is afterwards added to the message and signed digitally. The receiver of the message decrypts the encrypted checksum and calculates it again based on the data received. If the checksums are identical, the receiver can be sure that these parts of the message were sent by the original sender and that they were not changed by intermediaries.

Intermediaries as well as other adversaries are still able to read all the information contained in the SOAP message. XML Encryption also uses the public key approaches to encrypt parts of a SOAP message to protect them. This time, the public key of the receiver is used to encrypt the information by the sender, and only the receiver is able to decrypt the data with her or his private key. The elements of the SOAP message that have been encrypted are listed in the SOAP header as well as the algorithms used. In principle, each element can be encrypted by a different algorithm.

It is worth mentioning that WSS does not specify how to exchange the keys between the partners. This can be coped with by employing approaches like the key-exchange defined by Diffie and Hellmann. Details can be found, for example, in Tanenbaum and Steen (2002).

Figure 7 illustrates the use of security standards for a service-oriented system, where the consumer as integration platform for the Web services is implemented as Web portal. This concept is not only usable in the e-learning case, but is more general and can be used for several application scenarios. The learner or user employs a common Web browser to access the Web portal, and security is implemented via HTTPS as it is common on the Web. The back-end security for the Web services communication with the portal uses XML Digital Signature and XML Encryption.

Figure 7. Security mechanisms in a service-based e-learning environment

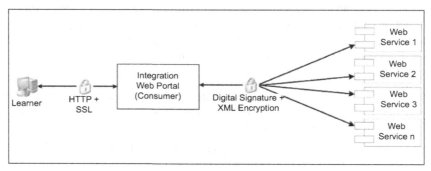

Figure 8. A physical architecture for a provisioning server

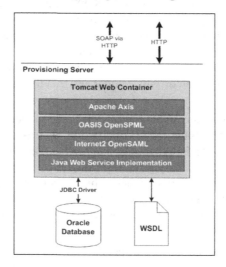

Physical Architecture

Figure 8 shows the physical architecture used for the LearnServe provisioning server. It is centered around open source implementations of the most important building blocks necessary to implement the specified interfaces of the LearnServe provisioning server. The most important part of the server is the Apache AXIS implementation that is an open source implementation of the SOAP specification. Apache AXIS is integrated in form of servlets into a servlet container like Apache Tomcat. Tomcat offers an HTTP server that receives and sends SOAP messages and serves additional requests, for example, the download of WSDL documents that describe the interfaces of the LearnServe provisioning server.

The SAML and SPML interfaces use open source implementations offered on the Web in form of Java programs. The profile API and the RTE API are implemented in form of Java programs that interact with an Oracle 9i database via a JDBC connection.

Conclusion

The concept of a central *provisioning server* has been introduced in this chapter as an important means to free users of an e-learning environment from repeated logins while they move around service providers to incorporate, for example, new content or switch from a content object to an exam server. However, this concept can only work successfully if it is implemented by a trustworthy third party, since each server that requests a SAML assertion via a corresponding artifact has to rely on that information. This particularly includes the identity and authentication of a user. Learners storing personal data on such a provisioning server want to be sure that their data cannot be publicly accessed and then misused. Technically, all peers participating in the system have to be able to understand the SOAP. This concerns, on the one hand, the SAML extension, and on the other hand, mechanisms to cope with encryption and decryption. If the peers want to use licensing and tracking functionalities, they have to be also able to invoke the tracking and SPML interface on the provisioning server. We have implemented a first prototype of the LearnServe system. Currently, the concept is used to integrate all e-learning platforms of the University of Muenster to offer all 40,000 students a single point of entry to all systems. The concepts of CDSSO and the requests of profile data build the foundation for all services that interact inside the system. Later, we expect LearnServe to even be able to handle virtual-university learning scenarios that incorporate services from all over the world.

We mention that there is no official recommendation yet on how to use SAML together with Web services, although a SOAP binding has already been introduced for SAML. The presented mechanism based on SAML artifacts in the SOAP header introduced in this chapter bridges this gap and can be seen as a consequent variation of the OASIS browser-artifact profiles. In combination with the presented security mechanisms, SAML can now provide the functionality needed to implement a reliable communication infrastructure. Although the chapter presents the concepts of the CDSSO and the provisioning of user data in the field of an e-learning application, the overall concepts are, of course, more general and can be used in any kind of service-oriented scenario. Our hope is that these concepts help melt down currently existing doubts concerning the security of Web services.

Although the overall architecture of a service-based e-learning environment seems to be very complicated, the strict usage of Web service standards enables a reduction of e-learning standards and fosters the interoperability of platforms. To give a rough feeling of this, we mention some e-learning specifications or standards that can be simplified or are even obsolete in the service-oriented implementation (for more details on this, see Westerkamp, 2006):

- *IMS simple sequencing* is replaced by BPEL4WS course definitions. Owing to the nature of service-based content, courses can better be compiled by BPEL and corresponding BPEL tools. Internal representations of course structures do not have an effect on other platform implementations as they are included as services.

- *IMS content packaging* to distribute content between e-learning platforms is not needed anymore because content is not reused in a physical form, but as a Web service.

- *IMS question and test interoperability specification* (IMS, 2004) is used to exchange definitions of tests and examinations. Both of them are offered in the new organization as Web services. There is no need to exchange files with test definitions.

- *IMS learner information packaging* (IMS, 2001b) is not needed since learner information can be accessed on the remote system via mechanisms explained in this chapter if a Web service front-end is available.

- *IMS sharable state persistence* addresses the storage of state information by a content object. As they are handled on the content provider machine, information can be stored after each Web-service-call in a proprietary way.

- Specifications like *ULF* (universal learning format, Saba, 2000) that are based on IMS specifications can be made simpler or are obsolete.

The SCORM philosophy to combine the best standards still gives hope to choose the best standardization when implementing a platform or server. However, SCORM can now be made simpler because it uses some of the standardizations mentioned above.

The e-learning community has only recently launched an initiative to establish service-oriented e-learning architectures. The e-learning framework (ELF, Hoel et al., 2005) project has begun its work by providing a service-oriented framework for modular, Web-services-based e-learning services. ELF does not make any assumptions about the implementation of services. The framework is intended as a starting point for discussion. Some partners have just started to implement services, but the core functionalities like tracking, CDSSO, and provisioning as proposed in this chapter, and a plug-and-play content integration, are not implemented. The

LearnServe services could be published under the shield of the ELF framework. Of course, ELF services could also be used in LearnServe as soon as they are available. Hopefully, ELF will be able to define high-level specifications within the e-learning community for the reuse of existing standardizations like WSRP, SAML, SPML, and for those parts that have to be newly defined like tracking interfaces.

References

Advanced Distributed Learning (ADL). (2004). *Overview. Sharable content object reference model (SCORM)* (2nd ed.). Retrieved September 26, 2007, from http://www.adlnet. gov/downloads/AuthNotReqd.aspx?FileName=SCORM2004.zip&ID=236

Alonso, G., Casati, F., Kuno, H., & Machiraju, V. (2004). *Web services. Concepts, architectures and applications.* Berlin: Springer Verlag.

Andrews, T., Curbera, F., Dholakia, H., Goland, Y., Klein, J., Leymann, F., Liu, K., Roller, D., Smith, D., Thatte, S., Trickovic, I., & Weerawarana, S. (2003). *Specification: Business Process Execution Language for Web Services Version 1.1.*

Blackmon, W.H., & Rehak, D. R. (2003, June). Customized learning: A Web services approach. In *Proceedings of Ed-Media.*

Bry, F., Eisinger, N., & Schneemeyer, G. (2003, June). Web services for teaching: A case study. In *Proceedings of the First International Conference on Web Services (ICWS'03)*, Las Vegas.

Casati, F. & Dayal, U., (Eds.). (2002, December). Special issue on Web services. *IEEE Bulletin of the Technical Committee on Data Engineering, 25*(4).

Chen, W. (2002, December). Web services: What do they mean to Web based education? In *Proceedings of the International Conference on Computers in Education* (pp.707-708). Auckland, New Zealand.

Hallam-Baker, P. & Maler, E. (2002). *Assertions and protocol for the OASIS Security Assertion Markup Language (SAML).* Retrieved July 7, 2004, from http://www.oasis-open. org/committees/security/docs/cs-sstc-core-01.pdf

Hoel, T., Campbell, L., Arnaud, M., & Pawlowski, J. (2005, January). *A service oriented approach to learning in Europe: The need for a common framework.* Position paper to the CEN/ISSS WS-LT, Oslo.

IEEE, The IEEE Learning Technology Standards Committee (LTSC). (2002, July). *Draft Standard for learning object meta-data.* IEEE 1484.12.1-2002.

Kropp, A., Leue, C., & Thompson, R. (2003, August). *Web services for remote portlets specification.* OASIS Standard Version 1.0. Retrieved September 26, 2007, from http://www.oasis-open.org/committees/download.php/3343/oasis-200304-wsrp-specification-1.0.pdf

Newcomer, E. (2002). *Understanding Web services: XML, WSDL, SOAP, and UDDI.* Boston: Addison-Wesley.

OASIS (Organization for the Advancement of Structured Information Standards). (2004, March). *Web services security: SOAP Message Security 1.0* (WS-Security 2004) OASIS Standard 200401.

Porter M. E. (1985). *Competitive advantage.* London: Collier Macmillan.

Rivest, R., Shamir, A., & Adleman, L. (1978). A method for obtaining digital signatures and public-key cryptosystems. *Communications of the ACM, 21*(2), 120-126.

Rolls, D. (2003). Service Provisioning Markup Language (SPML) Version 1.0. *OASIS.* Retrieved from http://www.oasis-open.org/committees/download.php/4137/os-pstc-spml-core-1.0.pdf

Schwingel, S. (2004). *Provisioning in Web service based e-learning applications.* Unpublished master's thesis, University of Muenster, Germany.

Tanenbaum, A. S., & Steen, M. van (2002). *Distributed systems: Principles and paradigms* (1st ed.). Munich: Prentice Hall.

Vossen, G., & Jaeschke, P. (2002, July). Towards a uniform and flexible data model for learning objects. In *Proceedings of the 30th Annual Conference of the International Business School Computing Association (IBSCA)* (pp. 99-129). Savannah, Georgia.

Vossen, G., & Jaeschke, P. (2003). Learning objects as a uniform foundation for e-learning platforms. In *Proceedings of the 7th International Conference on Database Engineering and Applications (IDEAS),* Hong Kong, China (pp. 278-289). IEEE Computer Society Press.

Vossen, G. & Westerkamp, P. (2003a). E-learning as a Web service (extended abstract). In *Proceedings of the 7th International Conference on Database Engineering and Applications (IDEAS),* Hong Kong, China (pp. 242-249). IEEE Computer Society Press.

Vossen, G., & Westerkamp, P. (2003b, November). UDDI for e-learning: A repository for distributed learning objects. In *Proceedings of the 2nd International Conference on Information and Knowledge Sharing (IKS2003),* Scottsdale, AZ (pp. 101-106).

Vossen, G., & Westerkamp, P. (2004, December). Intelligent content discovery within e-learning Web services. In B. Trezzini, P. Lambe, & S. Hawamdeh (Eds.), *People, knowledge, and technology: What have we learnt so far? Proceedings of the 1st International Conference on Knowledge Management (ICKM),* Singapore (pp. 365-375).

Vossen, G., & Westerkamp, P. (2005). Turning learning objects into Web services. *Learning objects and Learning Design, 1*(1), 15-28.

W3C, World Wide Web Consortium. (2001). *SOAP security extensions: Digital signature.* W3C Note, February 2001. Retrieved September 26, 2007, from http://www.w3.org/TR/SOAP-dsig/

W3C, World Wide Web Consortium. (2002). *XML encryption syntax and processing.* W3C Recommendation, December 2002. Retrieved September 26, 2007, from http://www.www3.org/TR/xmlenc-core/

Westerkamp, P. (2006). *Flexible e-learning platforms: A service-oriented approach.* Unpublished doctoral dissertation, Logos-Verlag Berlin, Germany.

Chapter II

Intelligent Agents for E-Learning

Ralf Bruns, Hanover University of Applied Sciences, Germany

Jürgen Dunkel, Hanover University of Applied Sciences, Germany

Abstract

We propose the software architecture of a new generation of advisory systems using Intelligent Agent and Semantic Web technologies. Multi-agent systems provide a well-suited paradigm to implement negotiation processes in consultancy situations. Intelligent software agents act as clients and advisors using their knowledge in order to assist human users. In the proposed architecture, the domain knowledge is semantically modeled by means of XML-based ontology languages such as OWL. Using an inference engine, the agents reason on the base of their knowledge to make decisions or proposals. The agent knowledge consists of different types of data: on the one hand private data, which has to be protected against unauthorized access, and on the other hand publicly accessible data spread over different Web sites. Comparable to a real consultancy situation, an agent only reveals sensitive private data if it is indispensable for finding a solution. In addition, depending on the actual consultancy situation, each agent dynamically expands its knowledge base by accessing OWL knowledge sources from the Internet. The usefulness of our approach is proved by the implementation of an advisory system whose objective is to develop virtual student advisers that render support to university students in order to successfully organize und perform their studies.

Introduction

E-learning has started to play a significant role in the learning and teaching activities at institutions of higher education worldwide (Hamdi, 2006). The students perform major parts of their study activities decentralized via the Internet. The main focus of current e-learning systems is to provide an appropriate technical infrastructure for content engineering and information exchange. The emerged individual ways of study are location- and time-independent, consequently requiring a permanently available and direct support to answer questions and give advice. A recent comparison of modern e-learning environments (CCTT, 2004) revealed that intelligent advisory agents are not applied so far in e-learning systems.

The aim of the semantic e-learning agent project (Dunkel, 2004; 2005) is to develop virtual student advisers that render support to university students, assisting them to successfully organize und perform their studies. The experiences of human course advisers show that most students have similar problems and questions. The advisory agents should help to resolve these problems. Typical questions concern the regulations of study (e.g., does a student possess all requirements to participate in an examination or a course?) or organizing student mobility. In order to achieve these goals, we propose a software architecture of an advisory system where virtual student advisers are developed with novel concepts from Semantic Web (Berners-Lee, 2001; Horrocks, 2002) and Intelligent Agent (Wooldrige, 1995) technologies.

The **Semantic Web** can be defined as an "extension of the current web in which information is given well-defined meaning" (Berners-Lee, 2001). The basic idea is to represent domain data and its structure in a well-defined and machine interpretable way. For this purpose, ontology languages based on XML and RDF/ RDF Schema (W3C-RDF, 2004) are defined. The W3C consortium announced the standard ontology language OWL (Web ontology language) (W3C-OWL, 2004). Ontology languages allow the explicit formal specification of the entities in a domain and the relations among them. They can encode the knowledge accessible on different Web sites making it understandable for computer programs.

One essential aspect of our proposed software architecture is to model the structure of the e-learning domain by means of ontologies, and to represent it by XML-based ontology languages. Software agents apply the knowledge represented in the ontologies during their intelligent decision-making process. We claim that this is a promising approach because e-learning systems that successfully support students in organizing their studies are still to come. This chapter reports on the experiences gained from the development of an advisory system architecture that effectively integrates both Semantic Web and Intelligent Agent technologies. The first use case that has been implemented reflects the counseling situation where a student intends to study a semester abroad within the European Socrates/Erasmus exchange program. Together with the international coordinator, the student has to choose the foreign university and the foreign study program that matches best her/his personal interests and her/his individual situation of study. Subsequently, a study plan for the semester at the host university must be determined that corresponds to the home university syllabus. This study plan constitutes the so-called Socrates Learning Agreement.

The chapter is structured as follows: In the next section the employed knowledge representation techniques and the developed knowledge models are presented. The third section shows how automated inference can be carried out on the knowledge models. Subsequently, the software architecture of the agent-based advisory system is outlined. Finally, the last section summarizes the most significant features of the approach and provides a brief outlook to future lines of research.

Knowledge Engineering

The key concept of a semantic advisory system is the semantic modeling of the domain knowledge (e.g., university organization, degree requirements, course descriptions, examination regulations) as well as an individual user model, which reflects the current situation of study (e.g., passed exams, registered courses). The fundamental structures of the available domain knowledge as well as the basic facts (e.g., offered courses) are defined in appropriate models.

In our architecture, the structural part of the knowledge base is modeled by means of **ontologies**, which formally define domain entities and the relations among them. For this purpose, we apply Semantic Web technology using the W3C standard ontology language OWL to model the knowledge required in the advisory system. Software agents employ this information as the basis for their reasoning and negotiation process. Due to the standardization of these technologies, knowledge models can easily be shared and reused via the Internet. Thus, the developed ontologies can serve as standardized and open interfaces for the interoperability of different advisory systems.

Ontology Modeling

In order to implement the counseling situation of the Socrates/Erasmus exchange program, information is necessary about the possible exchange universities and their offered degree programs. In addition, further information about the living conditions of a particular university city and its urban infrastructure may influence the decision. Several interrelated ontologies have been developed for our advisory agents: Two central ontologies describe the organizational structure of a university and the offered courses in a semester. To facilitate the comparison of different study places and course contents, two subordinated ontologies are used. Furthermore, the individual study situation of a specific student is represented by a separate ontology.

Dividing the knowledge base of the advisory architecture into several different ontologies is crucial to yield a coherent scope of each ontology and to facilitate the reuse of existing ontologies (Noy, 2001). In the following, we describe the responsibilities of the employed ontologies in more details.

University Ontology

The university ontology is the core knowledge base of the case study. It models the essential parts of the organizational structure of a particular university and the departments with the different programs of study. Its main domain concepts are: university, department, degree program, and offered degrees. The following example shows an excerpt of an instance of the university ontology.

```
<uni:DegreeProgram rdf:ID="FHH_Master_CS">
  ...
  <uni:numberOfStudents rdf:datatype="http://.../XMLSchema#int">
    547
  </uni:numberOfStudents>
  <uni:hasContent rdf:resource= "http://../subject.owl#softwareEng"/>
  <uni:hasContent rdf:resource="http://../subject.owl#compGraph"/>
  ...
</uni:DegreeProgram>
```

At first, a degree program instance with ID FHH_Master_CS is created. The property numberOfStudents specifies how many students are enrolled and has the XML schema data type int. The property hasContent describes the contents of the degree program and refers to a computer science instance of the subject area ontology specified by the URI.

Course Ontology

The course ontology models the courses per semester for a degree program. This information changes each semester and can only be provided by the responsible department. Several properties describe an individual course, for example, course name, teaching language, number of credit points, keywords describing the course content, and the semester when the course takes place. This knowledge will be used in the second step of our sample use case when open courses of the home syllabus are matched with courses at the exchange university.

Each university that participates in the Socrates exchange program should build its own instances of these ontologies. Furthermore, for our counseling scenario we need further information that is provided by two additional ontologies.

Regional Ontology

The regional ontology models the relevant properties of a study place, for example, in which country, state, and region it is located, its number of inhabitants, which infrastructure is available (e.g., airport, station, or theatre). Each study place is represented by an instance of this ontology, thus allowing a comparison due to the students living preferences. It is expected that for many cities this information will be available on the Semantic Web in the near future.

Subject Area Ontology

To determine an appropriate study plan at the exchange university, home and foreign courses must be compared based on their contents. A simplified taxonomy is modeled in the subject area ontology, for example, one instance for computer science, one instance for mechanical engineering, and so forth.

The presented ontologies define some transitive properties that are used for inference and reduce the number of facts significantly. An example for transitivity is the property isLocatedIn of the regional ontology.

```
<owl:TransitiveProperty rdf:ID="isLocatedIn">
<rdfs:domain rdf:resource="#region"/>
<rdfs:range rdf:resource="#region"/>
</owl:TransitiveProperty>
```

For example, from the two facts, that Hannover is located in Lower Saxony, and that Lower Saxony is located in Germany, it can be concluded that Hannover is located in Germany. In a similar way a hierarchy of subtopics is modeled in the subject area ontology. In contrast to these ontologies, which model public accessible information, the user ontology serves as the knowledge model of a particular user, for example, student or faculty member and, consequently, contains confidential information.

User Ontology

The major classes of this ontology are Student and Faculty. Relevant information of a student are, for example, login name, student ID, current semester, passed/failed courses and so forth. Every student owns her/his own instance file of this ontology, reflecting her/his individual progress of study. This information allows the adviser to give a personalized advice considering the individual situation of a student.

Note that the different ontologies are not isolated, but related to each other. So, for example, a student instance of the user ontology is related to a course instance of the university ontology via the property isEnrolledIn. Figure 1 sketches the structure of the ontologies with the interrelating properties and some of their classes.

In a Semantic Web infrastructure the knowledge is spread over the Internet in form of different OWL files. We can distinguish two types: OWL schemas and OWL instances.

1. **OWL schema files** introduce the essential domain concepts and define how they are structured and interrelated. This knowledge is rather data-centric and application-independent. Usually, OWL schemas do not change often and are

Figure 1. Structure of ontologies for sample case study

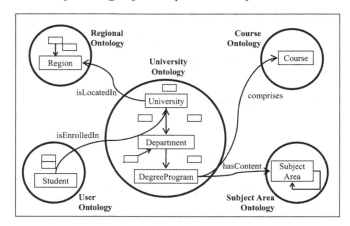

very stable. Because OWL schema files do not contain any instance data, they are normally publicly accessible.

2.   **OWL instance files** contain the domain object data. The OWL instances apply to the concepts defined in the OWL schemas and refer also to other objects specified in OWL instances. All the references are determined in form of URIs, as shown in the examples.

In our advisory system, there are five different OWL schema files, each containing just one of the ontologies described above. However, the OWL instance files are created and maintained locally. It is crucial that the OWL instances conform to the language specification defined in the OWL schemas and refer also to other instances.

Ontology Development

The previous section described the knowledge base, that is, the ontologies and their corresponding facts, from a logical point of view. To make the knowledge usable for the advisory agents, internally or via the Internet, they must be defined in a formal ontology language suitable for automatic reasoning. For this purpose, we applied the W3C standard ontology language OWL (Web ontology language) (W3C-OWL, 2004) based on XML and RDF/ RDF Schema (W3C-RDF, 2004). The expressiveness of OWL-DL was sufficient to model our domain knowledge. Only a few shortcomings of OWL came up, which we resolved within the inference engine, as described in the next section.

To develop complex ontologies, an adequate tool support is indispensable. OWL is intended for the usage of software programs and cumbersome for humans, as the short OWL example in the previous section illustrates. In our project, we used the well-known Protégé Version 2.1 with the OWL Plugin (Protégé, 2007) for ontology development. Except for some smaller technical problems, we made good experiences with this tool. It allowed us to specify ontologies with a graphical user interface and to generate the corresponding OWL files, avoiding a potentially error prone "manual" OWL coding. Furthermore, facts in form of OWL instances were created on the base of these ontologies.

Inference

The semantic advisory agents should act similar to human advisers according to their knowledge modeled in the ontologies. This is achieved by using the rule-based

inference engine JESS (Java expert system shell) (Friedman-Hill, 2003) to carry out the automated inferences entailed by the semantics of OWL. JESS provides a convenient way to integrate reasoning capabilities into Java programs.

OWL Transformation

JESS was initially developed as a Java version of CLIPS (C Language Integrated Productions System). With the JESS language, complex rules and queries can be specified. To make use of the knowledge modeled in an ontology, the OWL semantics must be mapped into facts and rules of an inference engine. Because JESS does not provide an interface to import an OWL ontology, we employed an appropriate tool named OWL Engine to load OWL ontologies and OWL instances into a JESS knowledge base (OWL Engine, 2007), which provides an XSLT-based transformation process. The OWL inference engine consists of three different parts. One file contains JESS rules describing the OWL meta model, that is, the OWL built-in rules. Two XSLT style sheets transform files with OWL schemata or with OWL instances into JESS assertions. A major advantage of the XSLT style sheets approach is that the style sheets can be easily adjusted to individual requirements. In our project we extended the transformation rules for the owl:transitiveProperty and the owl:UnionOf OWL constructs.

Ontology Reasoning

Mainly, the advisory agents reason on the basis of the OWL knowledge model loaded into the JESS knowledge base. In our case study, the semantic expressiveness of OWL is nearly sufficient. But to express more sophisticated expert knowledge, for example, complex examination regulations, domain-specific rules must be developed. Inference engines such as JESS provide their own languages to specify complex rules for developing rule-based systems. A simple example for a domain-specific rule, out of the scope of OWL, is a JESS rule that categories cities according to their size. The data modeled in OWL is usually domain specific, but independent of a certain application. The OWL properties define rules, which represent the general structure of the knowledge. They are mainly data-oriented, and therefore usage-in-dependent and applicable to different applications. The rules additionally specified in an inference engine are process-oriented; they specify the reasoning capabilities of an advisory system and are tailored to a specific use case.

Agent Architecture

To develop the software architecture of an advisory system, it is useful to analyze real-life consultancy situations, since the main components of the software architecture must implement the capabilities and responsibilities of the human participants. Advisory situations are characterized by two different participants: a client and an advisor, who interchange information and proposals to solve a problem of the client. Both participants need different kinds of information: some information is private, for example, the study situation of a student looking for an exchange semester, other information is publicly available on the Internet, for example, the course descriptions of an exchange university. Depending on the actual status of the consultancy situation, clients and advisors use their private knowledge, but collect also knowledge from publicly available sources. Clients as well as advisors reason on their knowledge to make proposals or decisions. The participants negotiate to reach an agreement, which depends on their intents and how the consultancy situation develops.

The multi-**agent** software paradigm offers a direct way to implement negotiation processes between the consultancy participants and to express their personal intents (Jennings, 2000). Figure 2 shows the main components of an agent-based advisory system, corresponding directly to the described consultancy situation. Multi-agent systems provide an architectural pattern that fits well to the described situation (Woolridge, 2002; Sun, 2006). The advisory system can be viewed in terms of au-

Figure 2. Components of the agent-based advisory system

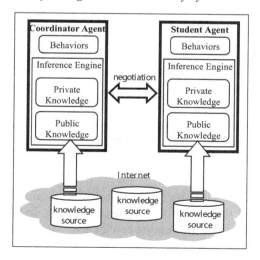

tonomous agents of two different types: student agents and international coordinator agents. The two agent types are conceptually identical. These agents interact to find an exchange university and a suitable study plan. Multi-agent technology provides the right level of abstraction to model a negotiation process between independent partners (Jennings, 2000; Kraus, 1997) and, consequently, is well-suited for our purposes.

The software architecture of an advisory system should reflect the situation of a real counseling interview. In our use case, a student intends to study abroad for one semester and consults the international coordinator of the department to get advice. Together, they first search for an appropriate exchange university and, in a second step, for a study plan, which fits best with the course program at the home institute. All students are characterized by their personal situation and intents; the international coordinators give their advice on the base of a profound knowledge of the study regulations and the different exchange programs.

Each agent type uses an inference engine to reason on its knowledge base that consists of private and public information. An agent can dynamically expand its knowledge base by collecting further knowledge from different Internet sources. Both agents exchange information in a problem-specific negotiation process to re-solve a specific problem. Each agent acts according to its particular behavior which reflects its intents and desires.

Semantic Web Architecture

In a **Semantic Web** architecture all information is spread over the Internet (Hor-rocks, 2001) in form of different OWL schemas and instance files. It is crucial that we can distinguish different protection levels for instance data.

- Private data has to be protected against unauthorized access. For example, a student agent protects the confidential information of its human owner. As in a real consultancy an agent only reveals sensitive private data, if it is indispens-able for finding a solution.

- On the other hand there is some publicly accessible knowledge spread over different Web sites. In our example application, each university participating in the Socrates/Erasmus exchange program should build its own instances of the ontologies and make them available on its Web site.

Of course, additional protection levels are possible: Typically, there exists infor-mation not indented for the public, but for trusted partners. In this case agents are acting as trustworthy partners exchanging confidential data.

Figure 3. Distributed knowledge sources in the Semantic Web

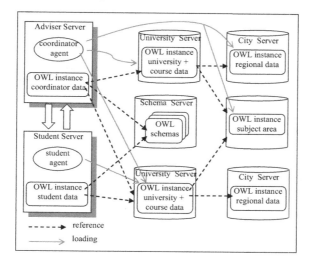

Figure 3 shows a possible situation for our advisory system. There are five different OWL schema files existing on a central OWL schema server. The OWL instances describing, for example, the department structure and the offered courses are located at each university Web site, where they are also maintained. The client and the adviser agents reside on different servers, where their private knowledge is stored in corresponding OWL instance files. Human participants in a counseling interview use their personal knowledge, but acquire also publicly available knowledge, depending on the actual consultancy situation. The client and adviser agents should act in a similar way: As in reality, the knowledge of the agents is not static, but increasing during the counseling interview. Depending on the state of the interview, agents acquire dynamically useful knowledge from different sources in the Semantic Web and integrate it in their personal knowledge base.

To build up its knowledge base, each agent has to process the following steps:

1. According to the status of the interview, the agent determines the required information for the actual counseling context.

2. If the information is publicly available, the agent locates the corresponding OWL files in the Internet.

3. It downloads the OWL instances, transforms them and imports them into JESS using OWL Engine.

The international coordinator agent requires information about all exchange universities and their course contents. To gain this knowledge, it can dynamically expand its knowledge base by accessing the locally stored OWL files of the universities registered in the advisory system. Beyond the information the coordinator agent collects in the Internet, it can hold some private knowledge. For example, it may know about all exchange agreements of its university or the utilization of the courses in its department. The student agent is characterized by its individual study situation, which can be described by the study year, the attended lectures, and the passed exams. Of course, this information is confidential and, therefore, it is represented in a personal OWL instance file, which is protected against unauthorized access. Furthermore, each agent can have more sophisticated reasoning capabilities expressed by some further JESS rules, as explained above.

Agent Interaction and Negotiation

In a real counseling situation a problem is resolved by a communication and negotiation process, which is characterized by an information exchange among the different dialog partners. In a **multi-agent system** the communication between the agents reflects this negotiation process between clients and advisers. Depending on how the consultancy is developing, different information is exchanged between the agents. The agent behaviors implement the negotiation protocol determining the rules that govern the interaction (Jennings, 2000; Ossowski, 2002).

The negotiation protocol is specific to the application domain and the problem type. However, in general the agents behave during the negotiation process according to the different stages shown in Figure 4. Each negotiation state is analyzed and evaluated by the agents. The negotiation process stops if a final agreement between all agents (see step 5) can be achieved. Otherwise the agents iterate the following steps.

1. **Information procurement:** The agent determines the information required for the next negotiation step. In principal, an agent has to know which kind of information it needs, but not necessarily the physical location of the information. It can be advantageous to delegate the administration or brokering of the different information sources to an own so-called middle-agent as described in the next section.

2. **Knowledge loading:** The agent accesses the knowledge stored in OWL schema and instance files and dynamically loads it into the knowledge base of its inference engine. If necessary, the agent uses a tool to transform the OWL

descriptions into facts and rules of the inference engine, for example, with the tool OWL Engine.

3. **Reasoning:** Using the inference engine the agents reason on base of their knowledge to make decisions or proposals. Especially the adviser agents usually own application-specific rules to provide more sophisticated reasoning. The expressiveness of the languages incorporated in the inference engines is normally much more powerful than of OWL.

4. **Negotiation:** The information exchanged between the agents is application-specific and determined by the negotiation state and their interpretation of the situation (Jennings, 2001). After passing general information, more details are necessary when a solution is narrowing. Each agent has its own desires and eventually conflicting interests. In our example, the student agent is interested in certain subjects or prefers studying at a specific location. Also the advisers may have some intentions, for example, they could be interested in sending students to particular universities or accepting only students with suitable skills and precognitions.

5. **Agreement:** Depending on the issues over which an agreement has to be reached, all participating agents must accept a certain negotiation state. An agreement can be achieved by the agents or delegated to their human owners. In our example, both agents must agree on a certain exchange university and a corresponding study program, which constitutes the Socrates Learning Agreement. In the sample implementation the adviser agent has no own intentions, that is, it leaves all decisions about the exchange program to the student agent, who again delegates them to its human user.

Figure 4. Activity chain of agent behavior

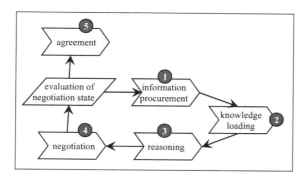

There are a lot of different approaches for negotiation protocols and decision making models, which usually are highly depending on the application domain. A good overview can be found in Kraus (1997).

Agent Behavior in the E-Learning Case Study

The following steps illustrate in more detail how the agents interact in our chosen exemplary **e-learning** use case:

1. A student starts his/her personal student agent (SA) to search for a suitable exchange semester, and logs in.

2. The SA loads the OWL user ontology and the OWL instance data representing the students specific study situation into its JESS knowledge base.

3. The student can enter some preferences regarding the exchange university (e.g., the subject of study, the teaching language, desired location). The SA extracts the specified parameters and queries further personal data (e.g., the aimed degree) from the knowledge base. Then the SA sends a request to the international coordinator agent (ICA).

4. The ICA collects instance data about all universities registered in the system as well as about the study places and loads them in its knowledge base. During its initialization, the ICA has already loaded all ontology schema files.

5. Then the ICA reasons on the knowledge base, aggregates the results and sends a ranked list of appropriate foreign degree programs to the SA.

6. The SA receives the result and presents it to the student, who chooses his/her favorite exchange university and degree program. The student's decision and further user instance data are sent to the ICA (e.g., the study program based on the passed exams).

7. The ICA accesses the OWL course instance data of the selected foreign degree program via the Internet, and loads it into its knowledge base. Usually the courses information is maintained in each exchange university separately. On the basis of the expanded knowledge base, the ICA suggests the foreign courses that are fitting best to the study program of the home university; see Figure 5.

8. The SA receives the results from the ICA and the student chooses manually the desired course plan out of the different suggested options. Finally, the SA generates a formal document, called Socrates Learning Agreement, determining the personalized exchange study plan.

Figure 5. Study plan proposal of the coordinator agent

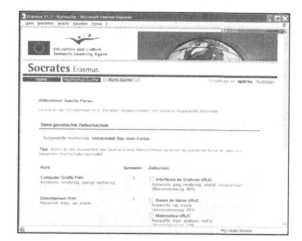

The student agent protects the confidential information of its human owner. Similar to a real consultancy situation, it only reveals sensitive private data, if it is necessary for finding a solution. The knowledge of the student agent is rather restricted; it mainly knows the personal situation of its owner. The international coordinator agent has a much broader knowledge, which it dynamically expands in the Semantic Web. Of course, the behavior of both agents could implement personal desires and intentions. For example, the coordinator agent could present only a selection of possible exchange universities, depending on the exchange agreements or the number of applicants.

Middle-Agents

During the negotiation process, the agents have to know where the publicly accessible OWL schema and instance information is located. Of course the contents and their location can change dynamically. In our university example, new exchange universities or new study programs should be continuously integrated into the informational base of the system. Especially new network architectures, as peer-to-peer systems foster spontaneous ad-hoc networks, where nodes continually join and leave the network. To cope with this situation, an adequate mechanism for the notification of new information sources in the Internet is needed (Carzanagia, 2000). In agent systems, so-called middle-agents assist in locating and connecting information providers with information or service requesters. Middle-agents can be implemented according to different designs as shown in-depths in Wong (2000).

In advisory systems, each adviser agent can register at the middle-agent, which provides a decentralized service for information procurement. Furthermore, middle-agents can act as mediators to set up consultancies between different client and adviser agents.

Implementation Issues

Powerful agent development frameworks facilitate the development of multi-agent systems. The semantic advisory agents are developed with JADE (Java Agent Development Framework) (Bellifemine, 2006), which complies with the FIPA (Foundation of Intelligent Physical Agents) standards (FIPA, 2007). JADE includes two main components: a FIPA-compliant agent platform and a framework to develop Java agents. The core part of the FIPA architecture is a standard for agent communication, that is, its ACL (Agent Communication Language). The interaction between the student and the international coordinator agent is based on the exchange of ACL messages. To avoid a situation in which a user has to install the student agent on her/his computer, we chose a Web architecture: the user agent resides on a central server and has a Web interface implemented with JavaServer Pages.

Conclusion

We described how Semantic Web and Agent Technology can be integrated to build an intelligent advisory system for an e-learning environment. Our goal is to create and deploy semantic advisory agents capable of supporting university students in successfully organizing and performing their studies. The first issue of our architecture is to model the knowledge used in advisory systems by means of the Semantic Web. Ontology languages like OWL can express the domain concepts, its structure and interrelations. In a Semantic Web architecture, all information is spread over the Internet in the form of different OWL instance and schema files. As in reality, the knowledge of the agents is not static, but expanding during the counseling interview. Depending on the state of the interview, agents dynamically collect their knowledge from different sources in the Semantic Web and integrate it in their personal knowledge bases of the inference engine. Additionally, each agent possesses private data, which has to be protected against unauthorized access. As in a real consultancy, an agent only reveals sensitive private data, if it is crucial for finding a solution.

Furthermore, we showed the principal stages of the negotiation process between the agents. There are a lot of different approaches for negotiation protocols and decision-making models, which usually are highly dependent on the application domain. In our future work, we will improve the negotiation process between the agents, especially their decision-making process. The major difficulty encountered was the integration of the different concepts—on the one hand the knowledge bases written in RDF and OWL, on the other hand the inference engine JESS and the agent environment JADE. We implemented a prototype system, where the agents were able to reason upon the knowledge base in the desired manner. Our experiences show that the employed technologies are mature and well-suited for the implementation of advisory systems.

In our future work, we will implement more use cases for the Semantic E-learning Agent project. For example, advisers should be able to announce new opportunities for students who are looking for suitable thesis subjects and to answer questions regarding the regulations of study.

References

Bellifemine, F, Giovanni, C., Trucco, T., & Rimassa, G. (2006). JADE Programmers's Guide. Retrieved January, 2007, from http://jade.tilab.com/doc/programmersguide.pdf

Berners-Lee, T., Hendler, J., & Lassila, O. (2001). The Semantic Web. *Scientific American, 284*(5), 34-43.

CCTT—Center for Curriculum, Transfer and Technology. (2004). Retrieved August 25, 2004, from http://www.edutools.info/course/compare/all.jsp

Carzaniga, A., Rosenblum, D.S., & Wolf, A.L. (2000). Achieving scalability and expressiveness in an internet-scale notification service. In *Proceedings of the 19th ACM Symposium on Principles of Distributed Computing* (pp. 219-227).

Dunkel, J., Bruns, R., & Ossowski, S. (2004). Semantic e-Learning agents. In *Proceedings of the Sixth International Conference on Enterprise Information Systems ICEIS 2004*, Porto, Portugal (pp. 271-278).

Dunkel, J., & Bruns, R. (2005). Software architecture of advisory systems using agent and Semantic Web technologies. In *Proceedings of the IEEE/ACM International Conference on Web Intelligence*, Compiégne, France (pp. 418-421).

FIPA - Foundation of Intelligent Physical Agents. (2007). Retrieved January, 2007, from http://www.fipa.org

Friedman-Hill, E. (2003). *JESS in action: Java rule-based systems*. Greenwich, CT: Manning.

Hamdi, M.S. (2006). MASCAD: A multi-agent system for academic advising. *International Journal of Intelligent Information Technologies, 2*(1), 1-20.

Horrocks, I., & Hendler, J. (Eds.). (2002). The Semantic Web. *First International Semantic Web Conference.* New York: Springer.

Jennings, N., Faratin, P., Lomuscio A., Parson, S., Sierra, C., &Wooldridge, M. (2001). Automated negotiation: Prospects, methods and challenges. *International Journal of Group Decision and Negotiation, 1*(2), 199-215.

Jennings, N.R., Parsons, S., Sierra, C., & Faratin, P. (2000). Automated negotiation. In *Proceedings of the 5ᵗʰ International Conference On Practical Application and Intelligent Agents and Multi-Agent Systems*, Manchester, UK (pp. 23-30).

Kraus, S. (1997). Negotiation and cooperation in multi-agent environments. *Artificial Intelligence, 94*(1-2), 79-98.

Noy, N.F., & McGuiness, D.L. (2001). *Ontology development 101, A guide to creating your first ontology.* Stanford Knowledge Systems Laboratory Technical Report KSL-01-05.

Ossowski, S.& Omicini, A. (2002). Coordination knowledge engineering. *The Knowledge Engineering Review, 17*(4), 309-316.

OWL Inference Engine. Retrieved January 2007, from http://www.cs.cmu.edu/~sadeh/My-CampusMirror/OWLEngine.html

Sun, R. (Ed.). (2006). *Cognition and multi-agent interaction: From cognitive modeling to social simulation.* Cambridge University Press.

The Protégé Project. Retrieved January, 2007, from http://protege.stanford.edu/

Wong, H.C., & Sycara, K. (2000). A taxonomy of middle-agents for the internet. In *Proceedings of 4ᵗʰ International Conference on Multi Agent Systems (ICMAS-2000)*, Boston (pp. 465-466).

Wooldridge, M., & Jennings, N. (1995). Intelligent agents: Theory and practice. *Knowledge Engineering Review, 10*(2), 115-152.

Woolridge, M. (2002). *An introduction to multiagent systems.* New York: Wiley.

W3C—The World Wide Web Consortium. RDF Primer—W3C Recommendation. Retrieved January, 2007, from http://www.w3.org/TR/rdf-primer/

W3C—The World Wide Web Consortium. OWL Web Ontology Language Reference—W3C Recommendation. Retrieved January, 2007, from http://www.w3.org/TR/owl-ref/

Chapter III

Assisting Learners to Dynamically Adjust Learning Processes by Software Agents

Weidong Pan, University of Technology, Sydney, Australia

Igor Hawryszkiewycz, University of Technology, Sydney, Australia

Abstract

In order to make online learning more productive, software agent technology has been applied to provide services for learners to assist them to construct knowledge in constructivist ways. This chapter is focused on the application of software agents in assisting learners to dynamically adjust learning processes. Unlike pedagogical agents, the agents in this application do not hold domain knowledge but simply assist learners to get through the learning process by a variety of supportive services. They assist learners to develop personalized preferred learning plans and guide them to dynamically align learning towards their goals. In this chapter, the online learning process is first investigated and an approach to assisting learners to dynamically adjust learning processes is outlined. Then the structure of the UOL (unit of learning) database that provides links between a practical learning scenario and the required services is explored. A multi-agent architecture for realizing the services is configured and the roles of the involved agents are described. After that, the related agent algorithms for guiding learners to dynamically adjust learning processes are described.

Introduction

Constructivist learning is being recognized by more and more people as a productive learning method. Although there are diverse constructivist paradigms, they share commonly epistemological assumptions for learning (Fosnot, 1996). The fundamental epistemological assumption is that knowledge cannot be transmitted to learners but must be individually constructed and socially co-constructed by learners (Jonassen, 1999). Because constructivist learning focuses on actively constructing meaningful understandings of the study theme, it can generate more significant learning outcomes than other methods such as the objectivist ones (Wilson et al., 1995).

According to constructivist theories for learning, learners are *active* knowledge-constructors, whereas teachers are cognitive guides who provide guidance and scaffolds to support the construction (Mayer, 1999). Unfortunately, most current online instructional systems have not really taken such roles. Mostly they just simply deliver online course materials over the Internet without providing effective guidance on how to use these materials to build knowledge. As a result, learners only passively receive information from the presented materials. They have not been engaged in *actively* constructing meaningful understandings of the study theme. This research is aimed, by incorporating software agents into online learning, to *actively* assist learners to build knowledge by using constructivist methods.

The research into software agents has been a rapidly developing area of research. Already a lot of agent-based systems have been proposed ranging from comparatively small systems such as e-mail filters to large, complex, mission critical systems such as air-traffic control (Jennings et al., 1998). In particular, pedagogical agents have been developed to take the role as a virtual tutor or a virtual learning partner, and so forth. The agents we are developing facilitate online learning through comprehensive applications of the properties agents exhibit, for example, autonomy, learning, cooperation, reactivity, and goal-driven. They work together cooperatively to facilitate effective construction of knowledge by individual learners. They assist learners to build knowledge not through understanding the academic content of subjects, but rather through providing a wide range of services. These services include: (1) providing access to appropriate learning resources and learning strategies; (2) fostering meaningful interactions with content, teachers, and fellow learners; (3) supporting personalized learning for individual learners; (4) promoting collaborative learning among learners in groups; and (5) aiding to evaluate learning achievements in a timely and accurate manner (Pan & Hawryszkiewycz, 2004a).

This chapter is focused on showing how software agents are applied to assisting learners to dynamically adjust learning processes. This includes: (1) guiding them to develop personalized preferred learning plans that satisfy their learning needs and match their particular learning styles; and (2) assisting them to align learning according to the actual progress of learning. The purpose of such services is to engage learners in knowledge construction and promote its success through providing guidance for learners to solve the problems pertaining to learning strategies which they often meet with in online learning.

Dynamically Adjusting Learning Processes

Online Learning and the Learning Process

Online learning takes place in many environments rather than just at institutions for education and training. Learners in institutions usually follow a particular instruction program. Other learners, however, build their knowledge through a continuous and guided process of identifying learning project goals, discussing and trying ideas and evaluating learning outputs. Such a process, as shown in Figure 1, is initiated and driven by a learning goal. After a goal is constituted based on a project, a case, or a problem, learners go through a guided process to reach it. The first step is to *build a plan* to achieve the goal. This includes defining the learning activities to be taken and designing the methods to conduct these activities based on their particular cognitive features and learning history. Then, learners *carry out the plan* to construct their own understanding of the study theme. They follow the learning steps in sequence as defined in the plan. Each learning step is a particular learning activity, for example, accessing learning resources, discussing with others, doing assignment, doing self-assessment, requesting assistance from others, and so forth. As the learning proceeds, learners *manage the plan* to align learning towards their goal. They record the learning activities they conducted, evaluate their outcomes, and then revise the current plan based on the evaluation. The updated plan will immediately affect the learning process; the relevant activities or sequences will be adjusted. The learning based on the updated plan will be evaluated again, which may further result in a new plan revision. An online learning process evolves in this way until the evaluation shows that the learning goal has been achieved.

General Framework for Supporting Online Learning

As described above, the major challenges for learners to take part in online learning include: (1) building an appropriate learning plan to achieve their learning goal; and (2) timely and accurately adjusting learning towards the goal based on the actual progress of learning. It will significantly benefit learners to continue their pursuits for the goal if the online instructional system can provide assistance for them to tackle these challenges. This is because *not* all learners are equally capable of adequately addressing these challenges on their own (Britain, 2004). Some may lack the necessary *prior* knowledge or abilities to independently determine the needed learning activities and choose a proper method to conduct them. Some may have no idea of how to evaluate the learning outcomes and vary plans according to the actual learning progress.

What degree of the assistance is suitable for helping learners to deal with these problems? Is it suitable to take a full control of the learning by the online instructional system? Most intelligent tutoring systems (ITS) adopt this mode. They *pre-design* all learning routes for learners based on a variety of learner models, expert models and tutorial models. Learners can only *follow* these routes precisely. The problem is that these models cannot possibly specify all possible ways in which learners may go about trying to solve a problem (Jonassen, 2000). This is because learners never learn using the same way due to their different backgrounds, interests, styles, motivations, and capabilities. It is even more true for online learning because most of the online learners are adult learners. As a result, learners in those systems are

Figure 1. An online learning process

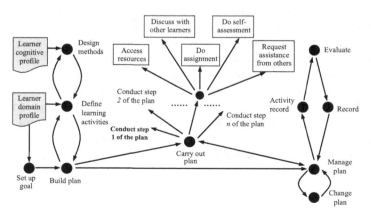

often forced down the *pre-set* learning routes that do not suit them, or even limit the development of their cognitive abilities.

In order to provide personalized learning experiences for individual learners and make the learning process optimal, learners must assume responsibility for some decisions in the process (Kay, 2001). *Active learning* must be encouraged because learners construct knowledge only by active learning (Akhras & Self, 2000). Therefore, an innovative strategy has been applied in our work, where learners are encouraged to actively construct knowledge and meanwhile the system provides them with services to shape and scaffold the learning process. Those services are directly aimed to solve the problems that may emerge in the learning process. They are customized to the personalized needs of learners according to their unique learning characteristics.

In the proposed instructional system, learners are not imposed to take any learning activities. They can thus independently develop and explore their own learning plans for the study themes and actively build meaningful understandings of the themes. Their autonomy in learning has been sufficiently supported and encouraged. Meanwhile, the system offers suggestions or advice to guide or assist them to develop learning plans and align learning while they have difficulties with these things. This contrasts with most current online instructional systems, which just present course materials and leave learners themselves to determine how to achieve their learning goals. This also contrasts with those ITSs where learners can only *passively* follow a pre-designed learning plan chosen by the system.

Approach for Dynamically Adjusting Learning

In order for the online instructional system to provide services to meet an individual learner's *just in time* needs or even *just for me* needs in online learning, knowledge about the learning activities being conducted, the actual learning progress and the learner's learning styles is necessary. Moreover, the rules regarding *what* supportive services should be provided for *which* learners at *what* moment in a learning process are required. A UOL (unit of learning) database is being used to provide such rules.

A UOL is a learning unit that satisfies one or more learning objectives. It may correspond to a course, a lesson, a module, or even a single learning activity such as a discussion to elaborate on some topic (IMS, 2003). The UOL database contains a collection of UOLs, each of which is an outcome of learning design (Koper & Tattersall, 2005), where not only the reference of learning objects is specified but also the relevant learning activities, conduct sequences, assessments, and corresponding supportive services for various types of learners are defined as well.

Furthermore, the customized services suggest the requirements for the dynamic interaction and communication between different components in the system. Those require communications between distributed components, sensing and monitoring the environment, and autonomous reactions. The application of software agents into the realization of these services is quite appropriate since software agents can act as human agents on behalf of their clients. They can easily perform sequences of complex operations based on the messages they receive, their own internal beliefs and the overall goals and objectives (Garro & Palopoli, 2002). Therefore, software agents have been developed to realize these services. They are responsible for providing suggestions or advice according to the actual learning progress and unique learner characteristics of individual learners.

Figure 2 depicts the overall system architecture. The agents work independently of learners, observe and monitor the learning of individual learners, and offer suggestions and advice to them when necessary. The learning activities taken by the individuals are detected by the agents. The learning progress of individual learners is evaluated through evaluating the detected events. The learner profiles are built and updated timely through collecting the detected events and inducing from them. The agents take an actual learning scenario and a learner's profiles as input and generate a suggestion or advice for the learner. The suggestion is on what the learner should do next, which is mainly based on the knowledge extracted from the UOL database by matching the input to the learning scenario in the UOL database.

The *activity list* and the *checklist* are for managing individual learner's learning. When a learner initiates the learning for a unit, the unit, its learning goal, and the adopted learning plan for the goal are together put into the *activity list*. Meanwhile, all the learning tasks of the unit are put into the *checklist*. When a learner has completed all the tasks of a unit, the unit in the *checklist* will be checked. The two lists are dynamically updated and maintained by the agents according to the actual learning progress of individual learners. With the two lists, the agents can keep track on individual

Figure 2. The overall architecture of the online learning system

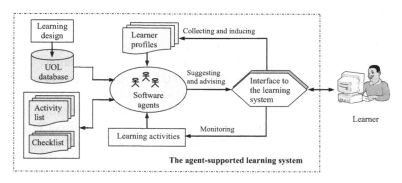

learning and suggest learning adjustment when it is necessary. For example, when a learner starts learning a new unit, the agents can judge if he or she has completed all the units planned to learn *prior* to the one he/she is going to study through the two lists. If not, the agents will advise the learner to adjust learning.

The major components in Figure 2 and their roles in assisting learners to dynamically adjust learning processes will be explored in the following sections.

The UOL Database

The purpose of developing a UOL database is to provide software agents with the knowledge regarding *what* supportive services they should provide for *which* learners at *what* moment in a learning process. Figure 3 provides an overall vision of the major elements in a UOL and their mutual links. The specific structure of a UOL provides a framework to describe learning activities and processes and the related supportive services. It is developed based on the earlier work in the descriptions of learning activities, particularly the educational modeling language (EML) (Koper, 2001). The principal development is extending and adapting the object parameters of the EML in ways that they can be flexibly combined to describe and specify learning activities, learning processes and the corresponding supportive services that facilitate individual learners to accomplish these learning activities (Pan & Hawryszkiewycz, 2004b).

As shown in Figure 3, a UOL describes the learning activities for a particular objective and the corresponding supportive services using seven compound elements: *metadata, roles, content, methods, assessments, cases,* and *learning plans.* Each of them contains more elementary elements, constructing a complex hierarchical structure. The major fields and their roles in implementing the services that facilitate construction of knowledge by individual learners are outlined below.

The *metadata* field is for providing the meta-information of the UOL, including the title, the prerequisites, the learning objectives, and so forth. Each objective has a brief description and a corresponding category, for example, skill, knowledge, and so forth. The *keywords* field is to store the key words extracted from the objective descriptions which are used to match with the learning goals of the learner.

The *roles* field is for specifying the intended users of the UOL. Users can of course be learner, but also instructor or tutor. The intended learners can be further classified into different categories through the *property* field. In the current system prototype, learners are categorized based on their cognitive ability levels, and so the *property* field of a learner denotes the cognitive ability level of the learner. This design is to enable software agents to provide services according to the unique learning characteristics of individual learners.

Figure 3. The major elements of a UOL

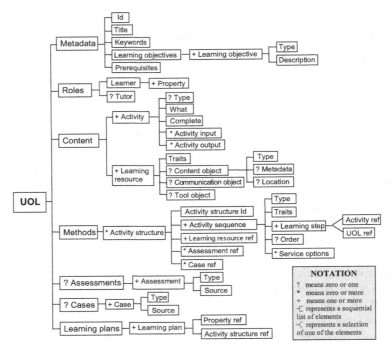

The *content* field is for storing the description of all the learning resources and all the learning activities related to the UOL. Every *activity* field describes a learning activity. Its *complete* field specifies the progress status of learning while the activity is completed. Its *activity output* field specifies the artifact files the activity will produce, which is used for evaluating the outcomes of learning. Every *learning resource* field describes a resource available for the UOL. Its *traits* field specifies the specific features of the learning resource, *content object* indicates the medium type of the resource and its exact location, *communication object* represents the requirements for the communication facilities, and *tool object* specifies the prerequisite tools and facilities for using the resource.

The *methods* field is for defining all the dynamics of the learning process to achieve the objectives of the UOL. They are categorized based on the learning characteristics of their targeted learners and divided into different groups accordingly. Each group is put into an *activity structure* field. This implies that an *activity structure* field stores all the possible methods suitable for a particular category of learners to achieve the learning objectives defined in the UOL. Within an *activity structure* there are multiple *activity sequence* fields each of which defines a particular *"learning flow"* in which a sequence of learning activities is performed during the learning process. This design enables software agents to assist a learner with optional activity sequences that suit his or her learning characteristics. Each activity sequence can be associated with more than one learning resource, ensuring that an activity sequence can be conducted by using different learning resources. Each activity sequence can be associated with multiple assessment approaches, multiple related case materials, ensuring an activity sequence can be evaluated through alternative methods and be scaffolded by alternative case materials respectively.

Within the description of a particular activity sequence, a learning step can be a reference to a learning activity defined in the UOL or a reference to another UOL. In the latter case, other UOL is referenced to implement a learning step of the UOL. This way can ensure a hierarchical architecture of a module, or a subject can be constructed. The *type* field is to specify the pedagogical methodology category of the activity sequence, for example, knowledge-acquisition, problem-based, project-based, learning by designing, discovery learning, and so forth. *Service options* declare the computer supported collaborative tools that are required in the learning activities, for example learning spaces, discussion forums, and so forth. *Traits* indicate the particular features of the sequence: if it can accommodate a learning style then the style will be put into the field.

The *assessments* field and the *cases* field are respectively for describing the assessment approaches and the case materials related to the UOL. The *type* specifies the category, and the *source* indicates where to find it.

The *learning plans* field provides the link between a learning method and its targeted learner category. It is composed of a number of *learning plan* fields, each of which contains a pair of *property ref* and *activity structure ref*. The former is an ID of the property defined in the *roles* field whereas the latter is an ID of the activity structure defined in the *methods* field. This enables software agents to specify the learning methods for a learner based on the category that he/she belongs to. This field is crucial to dynamically determine a specific learning mode for individual learners and provide associated supportive services for different learning needs.

The Multi-Agent Architecture

Agents and Their Roles

The agents we have developed to realize the services to facilitate construction of knowledge by learners are a series of individual agents with specific expertise, which construct a multi-agent architecture. In this chapter, we only concentrate on the agents involved in assisting learners to dynamically adjust learning processes. These agents include the following three categories:

- **Personal assistant agent (PAA):** An agent associating with an individual learner that aims to help the learner with his or her learning activities. It continuously observes the behaviors of the learner in order to maintain a profile. The profile covers many facets that can be relevant in the learning process. The PAA updates the profile as the learning proceeds, and provides this information to other agents when being requested.

- **Planning agent (PA):** An agent particular for the work relevant to the learning plans of the learners. Its tasks include designing the learning plans for a particular goal and for a particular learner, and adjusting a learning plan under a certain condition. All of these are accomplished based on the actual learning scenarios and the unique learning characteristics of individual learners.

- **Managing agent (MA):** An agent responsible for managing the learning for a particular UOL. Each UOL has an agent and its task is to provide personal assistance for individual learners to learn the unit and manage the learning based on the plan being adopted. It delegates work to learning activities according to the plan. The MA keeps track on the progress in the learning activity for the UOL and provides assistance for learners in revising the learning plan accordingly. It includes monitoring the submission of the artifact file for the UOL, evaluating the artifact file or asking a field expert to evaluate it and then receiving the evaluation result from the expert.

Working Modes of the Agents

The agents use a hybrid architecture that combines a reactive reasoning and a BDI-based proactive reasoning (Wooldridge, 2002). They autonomously monitor the learning requirement, observe and react to the events in the learning environment. When a learner sets up a learning goal, the PAA for the learner perceives the event. It requests the PA to provide learning plans for that goal. The PA, based on the goal and the learning characteristics of the learner provided by his/her PAA, designs learning plans for that goal. These learning plans are provided for the learner for making a decision. While the learner initiates the learning for a unit, a MA is created for assisting him or her in the completion of the learning activities in that unit. The MA manages his/her learning of the unit by following the plan being adopted. It, based on the sequence of the learning activities scheduled in the plan, delegates a learning activity, creates an agent (another MA) for the learning activity as well. The agent for the activity further creates agents to assist the learner in conducting related actions in the activity and reports the progress to the MA. The MA delegates another learning activity after it receives the report from the activity agent on the completion of the activity it is associated with. It reports the progress of the learning plan to the PA, and the latter revises the plan when it is necessary.

Implementation Approaches for Adjusting Learning Processes

Developing Personalized Preferred Learning Plans

Assisting learners to develop personalized preferred learning plans is realized through advising them several plans they can follow to achieve their goals. These plans are the methods to conduct learning, including relevant learning activities to be taken and their sequence. They are extracted from the UOL database based on the actual learning scenario and the specific learning characteristics of the learner. As shown in Figure 4, the agent first determines a UOL by matching an individual learner's goals to the objectives of a UOL in the UOL database. Then it captures all the learning methods for the UOL from the database. These are the ones that can be adopted for learning the unit, but only some suit the learner; and some do not suit the learner in terms of learning characteristics. Accordingly, at the next, the suitable ones will be chosen from them based on the learner's profiles. At the first, the ones that suit the learner in terms of the cognitive ability level are chosen. Then the remaining ones

Figure 4. Assisting learners to develop personalized preferred learning plans

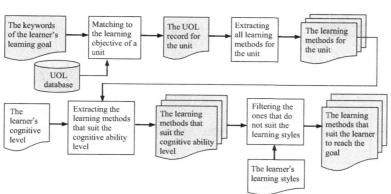

are further filtered based on the learner's learning styles. Only the learning methods whose traits most match the learner's learning styles are left. Finally these methods are presented to the learner as the recommended learning plans.

In the filtering, the agent identifies if a particular learning method is suitable for a learner through measuring the degrees it fits the learner in terms of learning styles. The learning styles of a learner, stored in his or her cognitive profile, are characterized by a set $P = \{p_1, p_2, ..., p_n\}$, where p_i is one of his/her preferred styles in learning, for example, like to study together with other learners, like to work through concrete experiences, and so forth. Every learning method for a UOL stored in the UOL database includes a set $M = \{m_1, m_2, ..., m_m\}$ to describe its traits, where m_i is a style that the method can accommodate. The agent recognizes if a method is suitable for a learner by comparing set M with P. The fit degree is calculated by summing the numbers where the learner's favored styles are met by a method, namely $V_{fit} = \sum (p_i$ in $M)$. A learning method is recognized as an appropriate one for a learner if its V_{fit} is larger than a designated threshold value. A learning method is considered as the optimal one if it has a larger V_{fit} than other methods.

In order to promote active learning, the agents do not force a learner to accept any of the learning plans they have designed for him or her. Instead, they present these plans as a suggestion for the learner to make his or her own decisions. Figure 5 shows a typical scene, where the PA, based on the cognitive profile and domain profile of a learner, has generated three plans for the learner to study unit *database design*, and the learner's PAA is presenting the three plans for the learner. The learner is free to accept any one of them or reject them building his or her own plan. If the

Figure 5. Presenting learners with appropriate learning plans

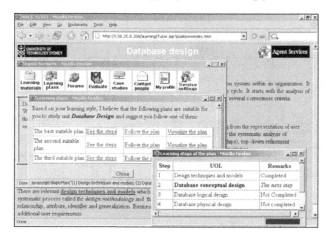

learner wants to accept a plan recommended by the PAA, he or she only needs to click on the "*Follow the plan*" in the plan line. The learner will then be forwarded to the learning step defined in the plan. The learner may also want to look at the detailed learning steps of a plan before making a decision. If so, he or she can click the "*See the steps*" in the plan line. If the learner wants to inspect and analyze a plan in depth, he or she can click on "*Visualize the plan*" in the plan line. The learner will be presented with an interactive visual interface where he or she can inspect the learning steps and view their hierarchical architecture (Pan & Huang, 2006).

Dynamically Aligning Learning

Guiding learners to dynamically align learning towards their goals is implemented through managing individual learners' learning. The agents perform this work with the aid of two lists, *activity list* and *checklist*.

The *activity list* stores the units that a learner has started learning but has not completed yet. Its principal fields are shown in Table 1. Each record stores the information about a unit that a learner has started learning, the goal of the unit and the used plan to reach the goal. The last field indicates the current status of learning for the unit by using the plan, which provides information for the revision of the learning plans for the goal.

The *checklist* stores all the tasks in a unit a learner has started to study, namely all the tasks the learner has to accomplish in order to achieve the objectives of the unit. Its principal fields are shown in Table 2. Each record is a task that the learner has

Table 1. Principal fields of the activity list

Field	Meaning
stu	the ID of a learner
unit	the ID of a unit the learner has started learning
goalunit	the ID of the goal unit that the unit is for
plan	the ID of the plan to achieve the goal unit
status	the status of learning for the unit by using the plan, proceed or suspended

Table 2. Principal fields of the checklist

Field	Meaning
stu	the ID of a learner
unit	the ID of a unit that the learner has started learning
task	a task that should be accomplished in the unit
checked	if the task is accomplished, yes; otherwise no

Figure 6. Recognizing the requirement for learning adjustment

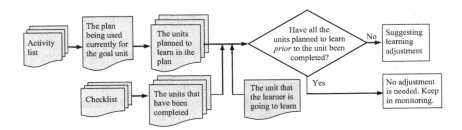

to accomplish in the unit he/she has started learning. The last field indicates if the learner has completed the task or not.

The requirements for aligning learning recognized by the agents take place mainly in two scenarios: (1) when a learner starts learning a new unit but has not completed all the units planned to learn *prior* to the one he or she is going to study; and (2) when a learner is not able to achieve the objectives of the unit. Figure 6 depicts the recognition of the first scenario. The agent first retrieves the learning plan from the *activity list* that the learner is adopting for the goal unit. It then compares the *checklist* against the learning tasks scheduled in the plan to see if all the units planned to learn *prior* to the one he or she is going to study are checked in the *checklist*. If it does not, the agent will suggest adjusting learning. The second scenario is recognized by keeping track of the execution of the units in the *activity list* and evaluating the artifacts submitted by the learner for those units. If a learner fails to submit the desired artifacts of a unit for a long time after starting it, the agent will suggest adjusting learning. If the evaluation of an artifact indicates that a learner is not able to achieve the objectives of a unit, the agent will also suggest adjusting learning.

As to the approaches to aligning learning, two kinds of adjustment are usually recommended by the agents: (1) to keep the learning plans being carried out unchanged and select another unit to learn; or (2) to revise one of the plans being carried out. The agent can generate a suggestion for the first kind of adjustment through examining the current plan and the *checklist*, since it can identify the unit that should be learned *next* by comparing the learning tasks scheduled in the current plan against the ones that have been checked in the *checklist*. It is a challenging task to generate a suggestion for the second kind of adjustment as it needs a complicated search procedure. As it can be seen, a unit with a larger grain (e.g., a subject or a chapter) may have a number of learning paths with a complicated hierarchical structure. Accordingly, there are very complicated relationships between the plans being carried out and the ones that can be adopted after some adjustment. To search for a suitable plan in the hierarchical architecture, the agent has to examine the plans from the current unit to higher level units level by level. That is, the agent first checks if there is any other plan to reach the current unit's objectives, and if not, it will further check to see if there is any possible plan suitable for the objectives of the higher level units. In this way, the agent checks the plans for the units level by level until it finds a suitable plan or attains another reasonable result.

Figure 7 shows two examples of the suggestions offered by the agents for learning alignment. In the one on the left, the agent suggests the learner study another unit *first*, because, based on the current plan being adopted, the learner should learn it *prior* to the one he/she is going to study. In the right one, the agent suggests the learner revise the current learning plan, because the evaluation illustrates that the learner is not able to achieve the objectives of the unit by using the plan.

Figure 7. Two examples that the agents suggest learning align

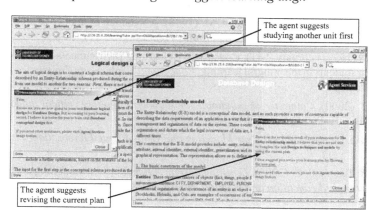

Summary and Further Work

A prototype of the multi-agent architecture to facilitate construction of knowledge by learners has been developed and the services to assist them to dynamically adjust learning processes have been implemented. This research has illustrated that software agents are effective in assisting learners to dynamically adjust learning processes. They can efficiently solve various problems that learners often face in online learning and can promote deeper cognitive engagement for them. Our future work involves further refining and extending the UOL database and the agent services so that they can assist learners to adjust learning processes in effective, efficient, and attractive ways. A systematic evaluation of the approach would also be carried out to demonstrate the usefulness of the system to a wide range of online learners.

References

Akhras, F. N., & Self, J. A. (2000). System intelligence in constructivist learning. *International Journal of Artificial Intelligence in Education, 2000*(11), 348-376.

Britain, S., & Liber, O. (1999). A framework for pedagogical evaluation of virtual learning environments. *Report to JISC Technology Applications Programme.* Retrieved from http://www.jisc.ac.uk/uploaded_documents/jtap-041.doc (10/04/2006)

Fosnot, C. (1996). *Constructivism: Theory, perspectives, and practice.* New York: Teachers College Press.

Garro, A., & Palopoli, L. (2002, October 8-10). An XML multi-agent system for e-learning and skill management. *Third International Symposium on Multi-Agent Systems, Large Complex Systems, and E-Businesses (MALCEB2002)*, Erfurt, Thuringia, Germany.

IMS. (2003). *IMS Learning Design Specification V1.0.* Retrieved October 2004, from http://www.imsglobal.org /learningdesign/index.cfm

Jennings, N., Sycara, K., & Wooldridge, M. (1998). A roadmap of agent research and development. *Autonomous Agents and Multi-Agent System, 1*(1), 7-38.

Jonassen, D. (1999, February 9-11). Constructivist learning rnvironments on the Web: Engaging students in meaningful learning. *Educational Technology Conference (EdTech 99)*, Singapore.

Jonassen, D. (2000). *Computer as mindtools for schools: Engaging critical thinking.* Columbus, OH: Prentice-Hall.

Kay, J. (2001). Learner control. *User Modeling and User-Adapted Interaction, 11*(1), 111-127.

Koper, R., & Tattersall, C. (2005). *Learning design: A handbook on modelling and delivering networked education and training.* New York: Springer.

Koper, R. (2001). *Modeling units of study from a pedagogical perspective: The pedagogical model behind EML.* Retrieved October 12, 2004, from http://eml.ou.nl

Mayer, R. E. (1999). Designing instruction for constructivist learning. In C. M. Reigeluth (Ed.), *Instructional design theories and models: A new paradigm of instructional theory.* MahWah: Lawrence Erlbaum Associates.

Pan, W., & Huang, M. L. (2006). A visual interface to assist learners to inspect learning plans. *AACE World Conference on Educational Multimedia, Hypermedia & Telecommunications (ED-MEDIA 2006)*, Orlando, FL (pp. 703-710).

Pan, W., & Hawryszkiewycz, I. (2004a). To develop constructivist learning environments on the Web using software agent technology. *The 7th IASTED International Conference on Computers and Advanced Technology in Education (CATE 2004)*, Kauai, Hawaii (pp. 236-241).

Pan, W., & Hawryszkiewycz, I. (2004b). A method of defining learning processes. In R. Atkinson, C. McBeath, D. Jonas-Dwyer, & R. Phillips (Eds.), *Beyond the Comfort Zone: Proceedings of the 21st ASCILITE Conference*, Perth, Australia (pp. 734-742).

Wilson, B. G., Teslow, J., & Osman-Jourchoux, R. (1995). The impact of constructivism (and postmodernism) on instructional design fundamentals. In B. B. Seels (Ed.), *Instructional design fundamentals: A review and reconsideration.* Englewood Cliffs, NJ: Educational Technology Publications.

Wooldridge, M. (2002). *An introduction to multiagent systems.* New York: John Wiley & Sons.

Chapter IV

Combating Information Overload by Means of Information Customization Systems

Mohamed Salah Hamdi, University of Qatar, Qatar

Abstract

The evolution of the Internet into the global information infrastructure has led to an explosion in the amount of available information. The result is the "information overload" of the user, that is, users have too much information to make a decision or remain informed about a topic. Information customization systems are supposed to be the answer for information overload. They allow users to narrowcast what they are looking for and get information matching their needs. Information customization systems are also a bargain of consummate efficiency. The value proposition of such systems is reducing the time spent looking for information. We hold the view that information customization could be best done by combining various artificial intelligence technologies such as collaborative filtering, intelligent interfaces, agents, bots, Web mining, and intermediaries. MASACAD, the system described in this chapter, is an example of an information customization system that combines many of the technologies already mentioned and others to approach information customization and combat information overload.

Introduction

The Problem of Information Overload

Historically, more information has almost always been a good thing. However, as the ability to collect information grew, the ability to process that information did not keep up. Today, we have large amounts of available information and a high rate of new information being added, but contradictions in the available information, a low signal-to-noise ratio (proportion of useful information found to all information found), and inefficient methods for comparing and processing different kinds of information characterize the situation. The result is the "information overload" of the user, that is, users have too much information to make a decision or remain informed about a topic.

One interesting solution to this problem may be obtained by reversing the conventional ways we find information. Instead of users investing significant effort to find the right information, the right information should find the users. This approach will, of course, require the development of appropriate software. Such software is expected to do more for us today, in more situations, than we ever expected in the past. This is the challenge of complex environments. The complexity comes from many dimensions. There is a variety of users (professional/naive, techie/financial/clerical, etc.). There is a variety of systems and interactions among them (Win/Mac/Unix, Client/Server, Portable, etc.). There is a variety of resources and goals (earlier, programmers had only to trade off time versus space; now, they also have to worry about bandwidth, security, money, completeness of results, quality of information, etc.).

Information Customization Systems

To cope with such complex environments, the promise of information customization (IC) systems (Hamdi, 2006a, 2006b, 2006c, 2007a) is becoming highly attractive. IC systems customize information to the needs and interests of the user. They function proactively (take the initiative), continuously scan appropriate resources, analyze and compare content, select relevant information, and present it as visualizations or in a pruned format (Figure 1).

IC systems are different from conventional search engines or database systems. When using a search engine, for example, not all information is easy to find because it is difficult for people to articulate what they want using a limited set of keywords. The words might not match exactly and hence nothing is returned, or much more common, is that too many URLs are returned by the search engine. Even when the relevant information is easy to find, it will be perhaps boring and time-consuming for the user to perform this task. The search engine is not able to identify and present the information with little or no user intervention. Furthermore, each query is independent of the previous one and no attempt is made to customize the responses to a particular individual. A search engine receives millions of queries per day, and as a result, the CPU cycles devoted to satisfying each individual query are sharply curtailed. There is no time for intelligence. The search engine is also not able to inform the user when new information becomes available. The user should continually observe the resources since they may change.

IC systems, however, do not preclude users from self-directed information finding, such as browsing and searching. They often combine user-directed functions with proactive search functions to meet the user's demands. They can also rely on existing information services (like search engines) that do the resource-intensive part of the work. Consequently, they can be sufficiently lightweight, reside and run on an individual user's machine, and serve as personal assistants. In this way, there is no need to turn down intelligence and information customization becomes possible.

An IC system, in order to work properly and in order to be accepted, must/may exhibit some or all of the following characteristics. IC systems tend, by their very nature, to be distributed. The IC system developer must therefore plan for problems of distributed systems. IC systems are often expected to be adaptive. A system is adaptive when it is able to adapt, with little or no intervention by a programmer, to changes in the environment in which it runs. It is also adaptive when it is able to use feedback to improve its performance or when it is able to change its behavior based on its previous experience. IC systems are also expected to be autonomous, that is, able to act even if all the details are not specified, or when the situation changes. Of course, an IC system must be robust (a working system, accessible all the time) and

Figure 1. Information customization

fast (begins transmitting useful information within seconds). Other considerations such as pro-activeness (the program does not simply react in response to the environment) and mobility (where does the program run?) are also of importance.

Information customization is achieved by observing the needs of the user and providing the referred information based on user needs. In an IC system, information access is enhanced by optimizing the percentage of relevant information exposed to the user. There may be varying forms or degrees of customization, but they all share a similar methodology and cycle. First, user data is collected and used to create user profiles. These profiles can either be for individual users or groups of users. Second, content is selected from the content repository that matches the profile of the user. Third, the selected content is delivered/published to the designated user in the desired format.

We hold the view that information customization could be best done by combining various artificial intelligence (AI) technologies such as collaborative filtering, intelligent interfaces, agents, bots, Web mining, and intermediaries.

MASACAD, the system described in the following, is an example of an IC system that combines many of the technologies mentioned above and others to approach information customization.

Achieving IC Through Combining Various AI Techniques: A Case Study

In previous work (Hamdi, 2005), we presented an e-learning system that provides a service to a student that checks whether lecturers are offering information that matches the profile of the student and informs the student of the information found. The student is registered in many courses and seeks course materials from the sites of the different lecturers. These diverse resources can be physically distributed. They are also dynamic so that course materials can be added, updated or deleted. The student profile, that includes the courses currently attended and possibly much more information, changes also over time because the student can leave a course or register in a new one. All of this means that the customized presentation of information for the student should be updated continuously as new information becomes available. This happens with no user intervention using an autonomous multi-agent system.

In the case study described in the framework of this chapter, following the same long-term objective of providing a complete e-learning environment for students and aiming for the more general goal of information customization, we focus on MASACAD (Multi-Agent System for ACademic ADvising; "MASACAD" is also the Arabic word for "courses"), a multi-agent system that advises students by adopting a machine learning paradigm. The decision for employing the multi-agent approach combined with machine learning (and other AI techniques) is supported by the following general arguments (more specific arguments are discussed later):

Humans often deal with problem complexity by organizing teams and cooperating in the search for solutions. Group problem solving techniques have evolved into powerful strategies in areas where any single individual would simply be overwhelmed. AI research has paralleled this approach by developing the distributed problem-solving paradigm. Problem-solving systems can distribute among them the processes needed to accomplish a given task.

Given the amount of problems that can be approached through distributed processing, AI has directed significant effort towards exploring possibilities to develop specialized problem-solving systems that can interact in their search for a solution. One way to embody this approach is represented by the multi-agent system paradigm.

An agent is a collection of knowledge and methods that are intended to embody a well defined functionality. Agents cooperate in solving a problem by contributing various parts of the problem-solving process. Agents can be modified independently and they are well focused on their tasks. Such subsystems are often easier to design, develop and validate, than their counterparts that combine the equivalent functionality within one system.

Because it is not possible to account for all the aspects of multi-agent problem-solving at development time, a good problem-solver has to be able to autonomously compensate for the dynamic and unpredictable aspects of its execution environment through adaptation. Adaptation is reached by letting the system learn from experience.

In the following, we first briefly overview the many AI techniques combined to realize the IC system subject of the case study, namely, MASACAD. Then we introduce the problem of academic advising and argue that a multi-agent system would be a good approach for addressing this problem. The chapter then presents the architecture of the proposed system and discusses in detail its individual components. The following section discusses the student evaluation of the system and provides preliminary evidence that it is helpful. Benefits and limitations of MASACAD, future improvements and extensions of MASACAD, related work on the topic of academic advising, and challenges of IC systems in general are discussed respectively in each of the next sections. The final section presents a short summary of the chapter.

Enabling Technologies for IC Deployed in MASACAD

The MASACAD system is related to and makes use of a wide range of technologies. These are briefly discussed in the following.

E-Learning

E-learning is a valuable extension of the distance education paraphernalia, enabled by the new information and communication technologies. Distance education normally occurs in a different place from teaching and as a result requires special techniques of course design, special instructional techniques, special methods of communication, as well as special organizational and administrative arrangements (Moore, 1996). E-learning is often described as the use of network technology, namely the Internet, to design, deliver, select, administer and extend learning.

Due to the flexibility provided to students and teachers, both in space and time, e-learning may be a source of great joy to its users and an important source of financial resources for many organizations. E-learning is based on the cooperation of geographically distributed participants, and many of the activities the participants are supposed to perform do not have strict time schedules, but do have time constraints that must be respected. If these constraints are not fulfilled, severe problems may occur and the success of a specific task or action may be in jeopardy. These kinds of problems are very difficult to handle and solve, because of the distributed nature of the resources and participants of an e-learning environment.

One key issue in e-learning is communication between participants, for which there are two basic types of technological solutions: asynchronous and synchronous. In the asynchronous approach, the interaction between parties does not require them to be engaged at the same point in time. In synchronous communications, the interaction between participants requires simultaneous engagement of the participants. Examples of technologies for asynchronous communications are hypertext publication (namely WWW), e-mail, mailing lists, newsgroups/bulletin boards and file download (ftp). For synchronous communications, the more often used technologies are: chat/IRC, whiteboard, audio/video streaming and videoconference. The existing e-learning platforms, such as WebCT, Lotus Learning Space, Blackboard, Centra, and so forth, incorporate both models, and corresponding services, in different ways.

Online education is today a reality in many sectors of the society, especially in educational centers such as colleges and universities, increasingly high schools, and also professional groups demanding continuous access to education. Several years ago, this new educational method was considered as an experimental approach with more disadvantages than advantages. However, today it should be considered not only a complementary educational resource but also a serious alternative that competes to conventional and now classical methods. Both methods will coexist and the logical initial inertia to ignore the new opportunities provided by the new media should be reduced and be faced sooner better than later in the same manner in which many other areas were modified throughout history.

Obviously, the adaptation to the new features and services of the e-learning environment is not immediate and requires experience, time, investment, pedagogical and technical resources, and government or campus administration support. At the UAE University, there exits enormous interest in the area of online education. Rigorous steps are taken towards the creation of the technological infrastructure (hardware, software, and communications) and the academic infrastructure (course materials, teacher-student communication) for the improvement of teaching and learning. MASACAD, the academic advising system described in this chapter, is to be understood as a tool that uses network technology to support learning and as part of the e-learning environment at the university. We use it to demonstrate the capability of exploiting the digital infrastructure, enabled by the online mode of teaching and learning, to extract and infer useful knowledge and to point out the potential of computational intelligence in the area of intelligent Web-based education.

User Modeling

An IC system is software that acts, in accordance with a user's preferences, in an environment. To realize an IC system acting in accordance with a user's preferences, user modeling is needed. User modeling (Kobsa, 1990) comes in two varieties, behavioral and knowledge-based. Knowledge-based user modeling is typically the result of questionnaires and studies of users, hand-crafted into a set of heuristics. Behavioral models are generally the result of monitoring the user during an activity. Stereotypes (Rich, 1979) can be applied to both cases, classifying the users into groups (or stereotypes), with the aim of applying generalizations to people in those groups.

The typical user profiling approach for IC systems is therefore behavior-based, using a binary or a multi-class behavioral model representing what users find interesting and uninteresting. Machine learning techniques are then used to access potential items of interest in respect to the behavioral model. There are a lot of effective machine learning algorithms based on two classes (see, e.g., Sebastiani (2002) for a survey). Ali and Smith (2006) present a method for learning algorithm selection for classification.

Systems based on behavioral models and employing a learning technology are classified according to the type of information required by the learning technique and the way the user model is represented. Algorithms requiring an explicit training set employ supervised learning, while those without a training set use unsupervised learning techniques (Mitchell, 1997). There are three general ways to learn about the user: monitor the user, ask for feedback, or allow explicit programming by the user. Monitoring the user's behavior produces unlabelled data, suitable for unsupervised learning techniques. This is generally the hardest way to learn, but is also the least intrusive. If the monitored behavior is assumed to be an example of what the user wants, a positive example can be inferred. Asking the user for feedback, be it on a case-by-case basis or via an initial training set, produces labeled training data. Supervised learning techniques can thus be employed, which usually outperform unsupervised learning. The disadvantage is that feedback must be provided, requiring an investment of an often significant effort in the system by the user. User programming involves the user changing the system explicitly. Programming can be performed in a variety of ways, from complex programming languages to the specification of simple cause/effect graphs. Explicit programming requires significant effort by the user.

User profiles are of great importance for information extraction and information customization since they are essential for deciding what kind of information is needed, where this information can be found, how this information can be retrieved, and how this information should be presented to the user. User profiles will therefore have a great influence on the solution to be adopted for implementing an IC system. In our case, they will have a strong impact on the multi-agent system to be created.

Agent Approach

A convenient metaphor for building software to interact with the range and diversity of online resources is that of an agent. An agent is a person that performs some task on your behalf. We would like to have a program that navigates the online resources to find the specific information that is strongly suspected to be there. You care about the result, and are happy to delegate the process to an assistant. You expect an agent to act even if all the details are not specified, or the situation changes. You expect an agent to communicate effectively with other agents.

Agents can be viewed as a new model for developing software to interact over a network. This view has emerged because of the predominance of networks in the world. Information, knowledge, and electronic resources in general, are distributed across a network and programs and methods are needed to access them and present them in a customized manner. Using agents adds a layer of abstraction that localizes decisions about dealing with local peculiarities of format, knowledge conventions, and so forth, and thus helps to understand and manage complexity. Agents should therefore be seen as an abstraction that appears to provide a powerful way of conceptualizing, designing, and implementing a particularly complex class of software systems.

Multi-agent systems are systems composed of multiple interacting agents, where each agent is a coarse-grained computational system in its own right. The hypothesis/goal of multi-agent systems is creating a system that interconnects separately developed agents, thus enabling the ensemble to function beyond the capabilities of any singular agent in the set-up. To arrive at a multi-agent solution, concepts such as those found in object-oriented computing, distributed computing, expert systems, and so forth, are necessary but do not suffice because distributed computing modules are usually passive and dumb. Also, their communications are usually low-level while multi-agent systems require high-level messages. Lastly, and importantly, multi-agent systems applications require a cooperation-knowledge level while these systems (object-oriented computing, expert systems, etc.) typically operate at the symbol and knowledge levels (Newell, 1982).

The approach of multi-agent systems seems to be a suitable framework for developing IC systems since many of the properties of IC systems or requirements on these systems such as being autonomous in that they are able to exercise control over their actions and act without user intervention, being adaptive (learning) in that they are able to change their behavior based on their previous experience, and being proactive (goal-oriented) in that they are able to take actions that involve resource identification, query formulation and refinement, retrieval, and information organization for their users, coincide with those required on multi-agent systems and on agent-based systems in general (see, for e.g., Bradshaw (1997), Franklin and Graesser (1997), and Stuart (2000) for a thorough discussion of agent-based systems and their properties). The IC system proposed in this chapter for dealing with the problem of academic advising adopts the multi-agent paradigm.

Machine Learning

Human expertise, needed for solving problems, should be transferred and transformed from some source of knowledge to a program. This transfer is usually accomplished by a series of lengthy and intensive interviews between a knowledge engineer, who is normally a computer specialist, and a domain expert who is able to articulate his expertise to some degree.

Unfortunately, the productivity of the interviewing process is typically so poor for many reasons (Jackson, 1999): First of all, specialist fields have their own jargon, and it is often difficult for experts to communicate their knowledge in everyday language. Secondly, the facts and principles underlying many domains of interest cannot be characterized precisely in terms of a mathematical theory or a deterministic model whose properties are well understood. Thirdly, experts need to know more than the mere facts and principles of a domain in order to solve problems. For example, they usually know which kinds of information are relevant to which kinds of judgment, how reliable different information sources are, and how to make hard problems easier by splitting them into sub-problems which can be solved more or less independently. Eliciting this kind of knowledge is much more difficult than eliciting particular facts or general principles. Fourthly, human expertise, even in a relatively narrow domain, is often set in a broader context that involves a good deal of commonsense knowledge about the everyday world and it is difficult to delineate the amount and nature of general knowledge needed to deal with an arbitrary case.

The rather low output of the knowledge acquisition phase has led researchers to look upon it as 'the bottleneck problem' of expert systems applications (Feigenbaum, 1977). This dissatisfaction with the interview method has encouraged some researchers to try to automate the process of knowledge acquisition by looking at the sub-field of AI known as machine learning for a solution to the bottleneck problem. The idea is that a computing system could perhaps learn to solve problems in much the same way that humans do, that is to say, by example. A program is needed which learns the concepts of a domain under varying degrees of supervision from a human teacher. In one approach, the teacher presents the program with a set of examples of a concept, and the program's task is to identify what collection of attributes and values defines the concept.

The field of machine learning has enjoyed a period of continuous growth and progress in recent years. Precise definitions of learning are hard to find, but most researchers would agree that it is a characteristic of adaptive systems which are capable of improving their performance on a problem as a function of previous experience, for example, in solving similar problems (Simon, 1983). Thus, learning is both a capability and an activity. Any learning program must have the ability to represent and reason about problem solving experience, as well as the ability to apply such representations and inferences to the solution of the current problem.

Learning programs are often classified in terms of the underlying strategy employed (see, e.g.,Carbonell, Michalski, anf Mitchell (1983). Roughly speaking, the strategy used depends upon the amount of inference that the program has to perform on the information available to it.

At one extreme, programs which learn by the direct implanting of new knowledge (for example by being reprogrammed, or being supplied with new data), are performing no inference at all. This is usually referred to as rote learning: a reasonable human analog would be the learning of multiplication tables. Programs using this approach to achieving problem-specific expertise in a computer are also called hand-built classifiers. Hand-built classifiers correspond to teaching by giving a person a domain theory without an extensive set of examples; one could call this learning by being told. Hand-built classifiers are non–learning systems (except insofar as they are later altered by hand). They simply do what they are told; they do not learn at the knowledge level (Dietterich, 1986).

At the other extreme, there is unsupervised learning: a generic term which covers tasks such as theory formation, which more closely resemble human efforts at scientific discovery.

Supervised learning is a kind of learning which can be regarded as having a strategy which is halfway between the two extremes mentioned above. In supervised learning, a program is typically presented with examples which help it to identify the relevant concept. These examples have known properties, which are normally represented as attribute-value pairs. The learning involved is supervised, because the examples provide the program with clues as to what it is looking for, as well as providing a space of attributes for its consideration.

The most common form of supervised learning is called inductive learning. An inductive learning program is one which is capable of learning from examples by a process of generalization. This kind of learning is sometimes also called empirical learning (Rumelhart, Hinton, & Williams, 1986; Quinlan, 1993). Empirical learning corresponds to giving a person lots of examples without any explanation of why the examples are members of a particular class. Empirical learning systems inductively generalize specific examples. Thus, they require little theoretical knowledge about the problem domain; instead they require a large library of examples.

Artificial neural networks (ANNs) are a particular method for empirical learning. ANNs have proven to be equal, or superior, to other empirical learning systems over a wide range of domains, when evaluated in terms of their generalization ability (Atlas et al.,1990; Shavlik, Mooney, & Towell, 1991).

Although the almost complete ignorance of problem-specific theory by empirical learning systems may mean that they do not address important aspects of induction, it is interesting to see in the following study, how domain-specific knowledge about academic advising of students can be employed by a domain free neural network learning algorithm. A back-propagation neural network is used to automate the process of knowledge acquisition, that is, acquire the expertise of the human academic adviser.

Web Mining

Data Mining is a multidisciplinary field which supports knowledge workers who try to extract information in our "data rich, information poor" environment. Its name stems from the idea of mining knowledge from large amounts of data. The tools it provides assist us in the discovery of relevant information through a wide range of data analysis techniques. Any method used to extract patterns from a given data source is considered to be a data mining technique. When the data resides on the Web, it is analyzed by means of Web mining techniques and the process is that of Web mining.

Given the vast and ever growing amount of information available in the Web and the fact that search engines do not seem to help much, how does the average user quickly find what he or she is looking for?

As mentioned earlier, IC systems seem to be the appropriate solution. The approach is to personalize the Web space—create a system which responds to user queries by potentially aggregating information from several sources in a manner that is dependent on the user's identity.

Existing commercial systems seek to do some minimal personalization based on declarative information directly provided by the user, such as their zip code, or keywords describing their interests, or specific URLs, or even particular pieces of information they are interested in (e.g., price for a particular stock). More elaborated solutions are eagerly awaited from applying new information customization techniques, that is, developing specific IC systems specialized on the Web—Web mining systems.

Current Web mining research aims at creating systems that (semi) automatically tailor the content delivered to the user from a Web site. This is usually done by mining the Web—both the contents, as well as the user's interaction (Cooley, Mobasher, & Srivastava, 1997). Web mining, when looked upon in data mining terms, can be said to have three operations of interest: clustering (finding natural groupings of users, pages, etc.), associations (which URLs tend to be requested together), and sequential analysis (the order in which URLs tend to be accessed). As in most real-world problems, the clusters and associations in Web mining do not have crisp boundaries and often overlap considerably. In addition, bad exemplars (outliers) and incomplete data can easily occur in the data set, due to a wide variety of reasons inherent to Web browsing and logging. Thus, Web mining and personalization requires modeling of an unknown number of overlapping sets in the presence of significant noise and outliers (i.e., bad exemplars). Moreover, the data sets in Web mining are extremely large. The Web contains a mix of many different data types, and so in a sense subsumes text data mining, database data mining, image mining, and so on. The Web contains additional data types not available in large scale before, including hyperlinks and massive amounts of (indirect) user usage information. Spanning across all these data types there is the dimension of time, since data on the Web changes over time. Finally, there is data that is generated dynamically, in response to user input and programmatic scripts.

To mine data from the Web is therefore different from mining data from other sources of information. Interesting results are expected from novel mixings of these different data types to achieve novel goals. Also, any discussion of data mining from the Web requires a discussion of issues of scale (Hearst, 1997). In addition, scalable robust techniques to model noisy data sets containing an unknown number of overlapping categories should be developed (Krishnapuram, Joshi, Nasraoui, & Yi, 2001).

For the problem of academic advising in hand, MASACAD has to mine a huge amount of educational data available in different formats. The Web represents the main source of information. A solution to this problem will therefore mine the Web. The Web mining technique adopted, bases on the multi-agent paradigm combined with machine learning and ideas from user modeling.

The Problem of Academic Advising

We will illustrate our ideas using MASACAD, an example consisting of an e-learning application. In this application, the focus is on the academic advising for students.

Academic Advising

The general goal of academic advising is to assist students in developing educational plans which are consistent with academic, career, and life goals and to provide students with information and skills needed to pursue those goals. More specifically, advisors will assist students in the following ways:

- Guide students through the university's educational requirements.
- Assist in scheduling the most appropriate courses.
- Introduce them to pertinent resources.
- Promote leadership and campus involvement.
- Assist in career development.
- Assist students with the timely completion of their degree.
- Help students find ways to make their educational experience personally relevant.

Why a Software Assistant is Needed for Academic Advising?

In order to help the student, improve the advising process and make it easier, and overcome the many problems that may occur, an intelligent assistant in the form of a computer program will be of great interest. Such an intelligent assistant will automate the advising process in the university. It will also simplify the task of faculty, staff, students, and professional advisors and make it possible to save time and effort and prevent mistakes. These benefits are added to the many other advantages of any assistant software that is used to solve problems that ordinarily require human expertise.

Restriction of the General Goal of Academic Advising

The goal of academic advising, as stated above, is too general because many experts are involved and because a huge amount of expertise is needed. Hence, realizing an intelligent software assistant that is able to deal with all the details shown above will be too difficult, if not impossible. In the following implementation we will therefore restrict academic advising and understand it as just being intended to provide the student with an opportunity to plan programs of study, select appropriate required and elective classes, and schedule classes in a way that provides the greatest potential for academic success.

The task is still interesting and of moderate size since when planning a program of study and selecting classes, there are quite a lot of things to consider such as prerequisites, course availability, effective course sequencing, work load, and instructor-student match-ups. Later, when the major problems are understood, improvements and extensions can be attempted, and attempts can be made to tackle the advising problem in a more general framework.

Resources Needed for Academic Advising

There are a lot of diverse resources that are required to deal with the problem of academic advising (see Table1).

First of all, one needs the student profile that includes the courses already attended, the corresponding grades, the "interests of the student" concerning the courses to be attended, and perhaps a lot of other information. The part of the profile consisting of the courses already attended, the corresponding grades, and so forth, is maintained by the university administration in appropriate databases to which the access is restricted to some administrators. The part of the profile consisting of the "interests of the student" concerning the courses to be attended exists actually only in the head of the student and should therefore be asked for from the student before advising is performed. However, attempts may be made to let the system learn the interests, for example, by monitoring the student and/or looking at his profile.

The second resource needed for solving the problem of academic advising are the courses that are offered in the semester for which advising is needed. This information is also maintained by the university administration in appropriate Web sites and is accessible for everyone.

Table 1. Information resources for the problem of academic advising

Student Profile			Courses Offered	Expertise
Interests of the Student	**Courses Already Attended**	**Other Information**		

• Entered by the student
• Attempts can be made to learn them by monitoring the user and/or looking to his profile
• Frequently changed
	• All information concerning courses already attended by the student
	• Stored in a database
	• Access is restricted to the administration
	• Frequently changed
		Other useful information about the student	• All information available about courses offered in the semester for which advising is needed
			• Available online and accessible for everyone
			• Frequently changed
				• Documented knowledge:
				  ○ All details and regulations concerning courses, programs, and curriculums
				  ○ Available in many forms: Web, booklets, etc.
				  ○ Accessible for everyone
				  ○ Rarely changed
				• Knowledge of a human expert:
				  ○ Heuristics, strategies, meta-knowledge, etc.
				  ○ More complex than documented knowledge
				• Expertise is gained through a learning process

The third resource needed for solving the problem of academic advising is expertise. Expertise is the extensive, task-specific knowledge acquired from training, reading, and experience. It is the knowledge that allows experts to make better and faster decisions than non-experts when solving complex problems. It consists of facts, and theories, as well as rules and procedures about a problem area.

For the problem of academic advising, this type of expertise may be referred to as the university regulations concerning academic advising. They consist of all the details concerning courses, programs, and curriculums such as names/codes of courses, in which term (fall, spring, etc.) courses are offered, prerequisites for courses, descriptions of courses, teaching and assessment methods, statuses (compulsory, elective, etc.) of courses, number of credit hours of courses, definitions and implications of curriculum terminology (e.g., cross-listing, interdisciplinary, etc.), established programs, established tracks, curriculum total credit hours and their distribution (e.g., compulsory vs. elective), titles of academic degrees offered by the university, and so forth. This kind of information is provided by the university and is accessible for everyone. It is published in Web pages, booklets, and in many other different forms such as printouts and announcements. There are many sources of knowledge, however, the primary source will be a human expert. A human expert should possess more complex knowledge than can be found in documented sources. This kind of knowledge includes rules (heuristics) of what to do in a given problem situation, global strategies for solving specific problems, and meta-knowledge.

Since, as mentioned earlier, knowledge acquisition is the major "bottleneck" in developing expert systems, we will approach a solution to gaining the expertise needed for academic advising by adopting a machine learning paradigm.

Why a Multi-Agent System?

First of all, academic advising is intended to be a good domain and problem to test the adequacy of the multi-agent paradigm for dealing with information customization. It provides a complex and dynamic environment and constitutes a wonderful experimental test-bed for investigating the issue. Conversely, dealing effectively with the problem of academic advising will require a multi-agent system. The multi-agent paradigm seems to be appropriate and even superior to other approaches such as a traditional distributed database approach enhanced with an intelligent user interface for the reasons elaborated in the following.

The resources needed for academic advising are physically distributed and dynamic:

*   **Their content may change:** It is for example frequent that, at the beginning of a semester, some of the offered courses are canceled, and some other ones are

added. The profile of the student also changes frequently, for example when the grades of the exams taken are entered. Also the interests of the student concerning the courses to be attended may change. As an example, students usually want to enroll themselves in courses that are attended by some of their friends. Changes to the university regulations, in contrast, especially those concerning the advising process like the curriculums for the different majors, are comparatively less frequent.

- **Their form (structure) may change:** They may be available via a Web page, an intelligent agent, a data base, a legacy system, and so forth.

- **Their location may change:** Existing ones may be moved and new ones may be incorporated.

Hence, dedicating a separate intelligent agent to each individual resource for coping with all of its peculiarities will have many advantages such as:

- **Reduction of the scope of changes:** There is no need to change the whole system when changes concern only a specific resource. In this case, only the concerned agent is changed.

- **Easy incorporation of new resources:** Only one new agent is needed for each new resource.

- **Easy extension and improvement of the system:** We may think, for example, of a self adjusting system, that is, the system itself searches for appropriate resources and each time a resource is identified, it is wrapped with an appropriate agent.

Details of the Multi-Agent-Based Solution

MASACAD, the multi-agent system described in the following, offers a service to a student wmho needs academic advising, that is, he wants to know which courses he should enroll himself in for the upcoming semester. The service is currently available only for computer science students. In the current version, no attempt is made to learn the student profile, that is, the part the profile consisting of the interests of the student regarding the courses to be attended. The interests are therefore asked for from the student before advising him. The focus in the current version is on the individual agents of the system, on how they cooperate to solve the problem, and on how one of them, namely, the "Learning Agent," learns to perform the advising process by adopting a supervised learning solution using neural networks (see "Advising Procedure").

As a solution to the problems of network communication, we use Bee-gent (bonding and encapsulation enhancement agent) (Kawamura, Hasegawa, Ohsuga, & Honiden, 2000), a communication framework based on the multi-agent model. The Bee-gent framework comprises two types of agents. "Agent wrappers" are used to agentify (i.e., providing an agent interface) existing applications, while "mediation agents" support inter-application co-ordination by handling all communications. The mediation agents move from the site of one application to another where they interact with the agent wrappers. The agent wrappers themselves manage the states of the applications they are wrapped around, invoking them when necessary. MASACAD consists of three "agent wrappers" (learning agent, data base agent, WWW Agent) and one "mediation agent" (Searcher).

System Architecture of MASACAD

MASACAD consists of a mediation agent that provides the information retrieving service (Searcher) and of a "User System," a "Grading System," and a "Course Announcement System" that are technically applications, each of them existing within an agent wrapper, that is, they represent different agents of the advising system (see Figure 2).

The student (user) uses a graphical user interface (GUI) to utilize the service of the advising system. When the student enters his identifier and password, the agent wrapper for the "User System" application creates a mediation agent (Searcher), which migrates to the agent wrappers of the "Grading System" application and of the "Course Announcement System" application to retrieve the needed informa-

Figure 2. Process flow through MASACAD

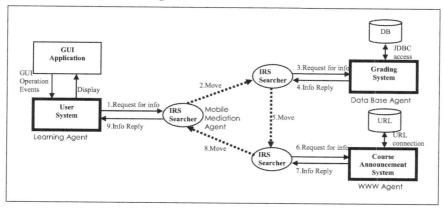

tion ("courses successfully taken by the student with the corresponding grades" and "courses offered in the semester for which advising is needed"). After that, the student has to enter his interests by choosing courses among those that are offered in the semester for which advising is needed by checking some boxes showing the course names. When the student finishes entering his interests, he has to just click on the "Get Advise" button to obtain a list of courses sorted in descending order of importance in which he is advised to enroll himself in.

In the following, each of the individual components of the system is be described in detail.

Grading System

The application "Grading System" is a data base application for answering queries about the students and the courses they have already taken. The agent wrapper for the application "Grading System" is responsible for invoking the database by using JDBC (Java DataBase Connectivity), transforming requests for information about the students and courses into queries to the database system, collecting the results of the queries, and finally replying these results to the mediation agent. Table 2 summarizes the steps performed by the agent wrapper of the application "Grading System."

Course Announcement System

The application "Course Announcement System" is a Web application for answering queries about the courses that are expected to be offered in the semester for which advising is needed. The agent wrapper for the application "Course Announcement System" takes on the invocation of the Web application. It is responsible for initiating communication with the Web application, transforming requests for information about the courses into queries to the Web application, collecting the results of the queries, and finally replying these results to the mediation agent. Table 3

Table 2. Agent wrapper for "Grading System"

–	Receive request from mediation agent
–	Perform database access setup
–	Perform information retrieval
–	Inform the mediation agent of the result

Table 3. Agent wrapper for "Course Announcement System"

- Receive request from mediation agent
- Initiate communication with the URL
- Prepare data to be sent to the Web server (this data consists of the request for information communicated by the mediation agent represented in the appropriate way as expected by the Web application)
- Send data to the Web server (the CGI (Common Gateway Interface) program on the server site reads this information, performs the appropriate actions, and then sends information back to the agent wrapper via the same URL)
- Read data from the URL
- Extract information from this data; that is, extract course identifiers of offered courses
- Inform the mediation agent of the result

Table 4. Mediation agent

- Receive request for information retrieval from agent wrapper for "User System"
- Move to agent wrapper for "Grading System"
- Judge the migration result:
    - o   If failure: end
    - o   If success:
        - ▪   Request for retrieval of (course, grade) pairs for the given student ID
        - ▪   Receive the reply
        - ▪   Move to agent wrapper for "Course Announcement System"
        - ▪   Judge the migration result:
        - •   If failure: end
        - •   If success:
            - o   Request for retrieval of IDs of offered courses for the given semester, college, and subject
            - o   Receive the reply
            - o   Move to agent wrapper for "User System"
            - o   Judge the migration result:
                - ▪   If failure: end
                - ▪   If success:
                    - o   Report retrieved results to agent wrapper for "User System"
                    - o   End

summarizes the steps performed by the agent wrapper of the application "Course Announcement System."

Mediation Agent

The mediation agent realizes services by interacting with the agent wrappers on the basis of conversations (sending and receiving XML (eXtensible Markup Language) messages). When the mediation agent migrates, it carries its own program, data and current state. Frequency of communication is reduced compared to a purely message-based system and network loads are decreased largely because communication links can be disconnected after the launch of the mediation agent. Processing efficiency is improved because the mediation agent communicates with the applications locally. The behavior of the mediation agent is described in Table 4.

User System

The agent wrapper for the "User System" application creates a mediation agent (Searcher), which migrates to the agent wrappers of the applications "Grading System" and "Course Announcement System" to retrieve the needed information.

Table 5. Agent wrapper for "User System"

– When GUI event occurs (student enters ID, password, and e-mail address the first time, or asks again for advice by clicking the button "Get Advice Again") or when periodic monitoring of changes in student profile and offered courses is due:
o   Create mediation agent
o   Request mediation agent to perform information retrieval
o   Receive results from mediation agent
o   If information retrieval was initiated by a GUI event then:
▪   Output information concerning the offered courses to the GUI (the "GUI Application" represents this information appropriately (boxes that can be checked by the student))
▪   When GUI event occurs (student clicks on "Get Advice" button):
•   Prepare input (input vector stored in a text file) for "Advising Procedure"
•   Invoke "Advising Procedure"
•   Process results (the results are found in a text file) and output them to GUI
o   Else (periodic monitoring): compare retrieved information with old version and alert the user via e-mail in the case that something has changed

After that, the "GUI Application" is contacted to give the opportunity to the student to express his interests. The "Advising Procedure" (see next subsection) is then started and results are sent back to the "GUI Application." The agent wrapper for the "User System" application also monitors changes in the offered courses and in the student profile and alerts the user by sending an e-mail. Table 5 summarizes the steps performed by the agent wrapper of the application "User System."

The Advising Procedure

The "Advising Procedure" is focused on advising computer science students. Computer science students, in order to complete their degree, must accomplish during their study a total of 132 credit hours by choosing, at each term, courses among the 85 courses that are specified by the curriculum. Some of these courses are compulsory, others are elective. The choice should of course occur according to the university regulations and in a way that provides the greatest potential for academic success as seen by a human academic advisor.

Taking into account the adequacy of the machine learning approach for gaining human expertise added to the availability of experience with advising students makes the adoption of a paradigm of supervised learning from examples obvious. Back-propagation is the best-known example of a supervised neural network training algorithm (Patterson, 1996) and is therefore used to implement the "Advising Procedure." The known information (input variables) consists of the profile of the student and of the offered courses grouped in a suitable way. The unknown information (output variables) consists of the advice expected by the student. In order for the network to be able to infer the unknown information, prior training is needed. Training will integrate the expertise in academic advising into the network.

Settings of the Neural Network Solution

For the problem of academic advising, information about 250 Computer Science students in different stages of study was collected, which means that 250 examples were available for the learning procedures. The 250 examples were used to form three sets: a training set containing 150 examples, a selection set consisting of 50 examples, and a test set consisting of 50 examples. In an attempt to reduce the number of parameters that should be tuned, we decided to use two hidden layers. To implement the network, a slightly modified version of the package developed by Mark Watson (2005) was used.

Each one of the 250 examples consists of a pair of input-output vectors. The input vector summarizes all the information needed for advising a particular student. It consists of 85 components each of them containing a number for one of the 85 courses in the curriculum. The number consists of the grade earned if the student has already passed the given course. Otherwise, the number encodes the availability of the course in the semester for which advising is needed and the interest of the student in the course. The output vector encodes the final decision concerning the courses in which the student actually enrolled himself based on the advice of the academic advisor. This happens by assigning priority values to each of the 85 courses in the curriculum.

Learning Phase

The aim of the learning phase was to determine the most suitable values for the learning rate, the size of the network, and the number of training cycles that are needed for the convergence of the network.

Learning rate: To determine the most suitable learning rate, experiments with ten network configurations 85-X-X-85 with X in {3, 5, 7, 9, 20, 30, 50, 85, 100, 120} were performed (85-X-X-85 represents a network with 85 input neurons, X neurons in each of the two hidden layers, and 85 output neurons). For each of these networks, experiments with the five learning rates: 0.01, 0.25, 0.50, 0.75, and 1.0 were conducted. In each of these 50 experiments, the network was allowed to learn for a period of 1,000,000 cycles. After each epoch of 50,000 cycles, the average selection error for the 50 pairs from the selection set was calculated. From the 50 experiments, it was clear that the learning rate 0.01 is the most suitable one for this application because it produces the smallest selection error in most of the cases and more importantly, it causes the selection error to decrease continuously which forebodes the convergence of the network.

Network size: Figure 3 shows the average selection error for the 50 pairs from the selection set plotted as a function of the number of training cycles for the ten different network configurations 85-X-X-85 with X in {3, 5, 7, 9, 20, 30, 50, 85, 100, 120}. In all ten cases, the network was allowed to learn for a period of 1,000,000 cycles and the learning rate was set to 0.01. The network configurations 85-X-X-85 with X in {50, 85, 100, 120} seem to work best in combination with the learning rate 0.01. To determine which one of them is more suitable, a longer learning period is needed. The results for a learning period of 10,000,000 cycles are illustrated in Figure 4. The configurations 85-100-100-85 and 85-120-120-85 cause the selection error to decrease continuously and reach a very satisfactory level. Both networks have similar performances. However, following the standard scientific precept that, all else being equal, a simple model is always preferable to a complex one, we can also select a smaller network in preference to a larger one with a negligible improvement in selection error. The network configuration 85-100-100-85 is therefore retained as the best network configuration (in terms of selection error).

Number of training cycles: After a given number of training cycles, when the selection error and consequently the performance reaches a satisfactory level and when the improvement becomes negligible, learning can be stopped and the network producing the smallest selection error can be retained as a solution for the problem of academic advising. In our case, this happens with the learning rate 0.01 and the network configuration 85-100-100-85 after a training period of 8,000,000 cycles.

Testing Phase

The final model was tested with the test set data. For 42 of the 50 test cases (84%) the network's actual output was exactly the same as the target output, that is, the network suggested the same courses in the same order as specified by the test examples. In the remaining eight test cases, the target courses were always present at the beginning of the course list produced by the network. However, the network proposed some additional courses. The courses proposed additionally occur always at the end of the course list. This, in addition to the fact that the system is an advisory one, makes these errors tolerable. In 4 of the 8 cases, the additional courses were correct choices. In the other four cases, some of the additional courses were wrong choices because the student has not yet taken their prerequisite courses.

Figure 3. Determination of the best network size (learning period = 1000000 cycles).

Figure 4. Determination of the best network size (learning period = 10000000 cycles).

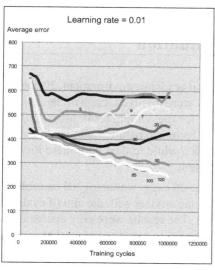

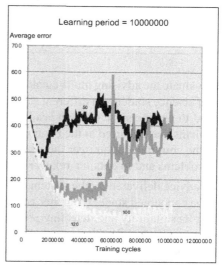

Benefits and Limitations of the Neural Network Solution

The research reported showed the applicability of the neural network approach to academic advising. The rewards of a successful "marriage" of neural networks and expert systems are too enticing. The back-propagation network performed favorably and seems interesting and viable enough to be used to automate the process of knowledge acquisition, usually looked upon as 'the bottleneck problem' of expert systems applications, and help in extracting human expertise, needed for solving the problem of academic advising. In this vein, a possible way to incorporate neural networks into expert systems was described. This would smooth the way for a real and significant "fusion" of neural networks and expert systems. With a network topology of 85-100-100-85 and systematically selected network parameters (learning rate of 0.01, 8,000,000 training cycles), the multiple-layered, fully connected back-propagation network was able to deliver a considerable performance.

Despite the promising results demonstrated in various applications, back-propagation network development still requires extensive experimentation, parameters selection, and human judgment. Developing a good neural network is not a trivial task as the technique currently stands. Some interesting research questions about adopting neural networks remain to be answered. For example, can we develop a systematic and simple methodology and blueprint for neural network modeling and analysis? Can we automate the selection of topology and parameters? Can we let the network ''learn'' incrementally without major network re-training when new information is discovered (e.g., curriculum changes)? Incremental learning would require the exploration of other neural network models, such as fuzzy ARTMAP (Carpenter, Grossberg, Markuzon, Reynolds, & Rosen, 1992) and ARAM (Tan, 1995).

Real System Evaluation

To evaluate the advising multi-agent system in real academic environment, 20 computer science students in different stages of study were involved. Each of them was asked to use the system to get academic advice for the coming term. Most of the problems that occurred at the beginning were of technical nature, mainly concerning the communication over the network. It took a while to deal with these kinds of problems and to obtain a relatively stable system.

The advice delivered by the system in each of the 20 cases was analyzed carefully by the concerned student together with an academic adviser with the aim of evaluating its suitability and detecting possible errors. The results were very encouraging. In no one of the 20 cases the advice was found to contain errors; that is, to contain courses that, if chosen, will violate the university regulations such as those concerning course prerequisites. Also, all of the results (suggested courses) were judged by the concerned students and academic advisers to be suitable and in most of the cases even very appropriate to be taken by the students. Actually, 15 of the 20 students took during the term for which advising was needed exactly the courses suggested by the advising system. In one of the remaining five cases, the student, because of her poor health, was later (at the beginning of the term) forced to drop three courses and to take only 2 of the 5 suggested ones. In another case, the student did not take any course during the term because of leave of absence for the whole term. In the other three cases, each of the students exchanged a suggested course (the same course in all three cases) with another one. Later, it became clear that the three students were in a clique and that one of them did not care for the instructor of the course, so they all moved to the other course.

Benefits and Limitations of MASACAD

MASACAD, in addition to providing a solution for the problem of academic advising, was also used to demonstrate, on an example, the suitability of the multi-agent paradigm for dealing with information customization and personalization. Information customization and personalization provides users with relevant content based on their needs and interests and this is exactly what MASACAD does. It provides the user (student) with an interactive, personal Web experience and customizes the information to the user's desires and needs. The preferences (profile) of the user determine the behavior of the system. Using the multi-agent approach combined with other techniques, we were able to devise an elegant solution to a problem that depends on distributed information existing in differing formats. Conversely, as mentioned earlier, the distributed and dynamic nature of today's information resources makes the adoption of the multi-agent approach necessary.

However, there are some other important characteristics of information customization systems that were not demonstrated on this example. In general, in an information customization system, there should be some strategy for discovering the location of potential useful information, for example, among the whole Web, among a reasonable part of the Web, among a set of databases, or among any other heterogeneous set of resources. Also, it should be possible to automate the creation of the mediation agent and the agent wrappers, that is, the creation of the whole multi-agent system. The multi-agent system to be created depends on the resources to be invoked and on their locations. The automation task may therefore be very difficult: the resources can be numerous and may have very different formats (they may be unstructured Web pages, databases, or agents) and this complicates the creation of the agent wrappers (how to wrap an unknown application), as well as the creation of the mediation agent (which route to take to navigate to the different agent wrappers, how to communicate with the different agent wrappers).

Future Improvements and Extensions of MASACAD

As mentioned earlier, the MASACAD system in its current version is available only for computer science students. The next step for this work is, therefore, to focus on extending the system to cope with all other degrees in the university. This will imply that for each of these degrees, data about advising students should be collected in order to construct the training, selection, and testing sets. Also, for each degree, a neural network should be developed which requires extensive experimentation, parameters selection, and performance judgment.

However, before extending the system to cope with other degrees, the system should be tested on a larger scale to detect possible errors, be convinced of its usefulness, and better assess its power. This will be done by trying to involve all Computer Science students (more than 300) in evaluating the system. Before allowing a student to register to any course, the student should get advice from the system and discuss its appropriateness with his human academic adviser.

Another improvement, necessary to think about, is how can we let the neural networks ''learn'' incrementally without major network re-training when new information that is suspected to affect the process of academic advising is discovered (e.g., curriculum changes)? This will make the system more flexible and avoid the repeated new development of neural networks each time a change occurs.

Another problem that should be considered is how can the system be made flexible against changes in the location of course announcements and student profiles (where do they reside?) and against changes in the type of application that enables access to this information (is it a Web site, a data base, an intelligent agent, etc.?). To solve this problem, one can think of automating the multi-agent system, that is, creating the mediation agent and the agent wrappers automatically. This will, of course, require knowing which sites should be wrapped by agent wrappers (i.e., knowing the location of resources), and how this wrapping should be done (based on the type of the site/application).

Related Work on the Topic of Academic Advising

In recent years, the administration of academic advising has undergone radical transformation, as technological developments have altered the processes by which information is collected, stored, and accessed the systems by which communication is enabled, and the structures by which transactions are conducted. Technological innovations have created an abundance of opportunities for new practices and enhanced services "frequently characterized as 'real-time,' 'student-centered,' and ' any time, any place'" (Moneta, 1997, p. 7). The technological environments on many campuses are evolving rapidly and comprise numerous elements: information dissemination, transactional interaction, communications applications, and educational technologies. McDonald (n.d.) contains an annotated bibliography compiled by George Steele and Melinda McDonald for research related to technology and advising.

The problem of course assignment has been studied in the literature from different angles. Advising tools are usually intended to complement the student-advisor relationship. The Course-Planning Consultant (CPC), for example, is a computerized Web-based prerequisite checker developed for students in the General Engineering undergraduate curriculum at the University of Illinois at Urbana-Champaign. It was reported that the program has been field-proven to have helped prevent costly mistakes when planning future courses (Course Planning Consultant, n.d.).

There are also few learning environments where similar problems, such as learning objects assignment, were addressed using the multi-agent system approach. In Sheremetov and Arenas (2002), for example, personalized learning trajectories are constructed by agents in the learning space based on users' profiles.

It is surely difficult to compare the performance of MASACAD with these systems because they do not perform exactly the same task. However, the technical novelty of MASACAD seems to lie in its ability to perform academic advising while taking into account not only visible static information but also hidden expertise. MASACAD also demonstrates the capability of exploiting the digital infrastructure, enabled by the online mode of teaching and learning, to extract and infer useful knowledge. This is done in an elegant way through a multi-agent system inspired from human teams and organizations involved in the problem-solving activities.

IC Systems and Their Challenges

Mostafa Javed (2002) summarizes the challenges for IC systems in collecting contextual information that relates to users' interests and information needs and in the interest representation itself (its complexity and issues related to it such as security and privacy). In Menczer, Monge, & Street (2002), Jenamani, Mohapatra, & Ghose (2002), Bauer and Leake (2002), Ho Ha (2002), and Paik and Benatallah (2002), various approaches to tackling the challenges associated with IC systems are described. Although these approaches differ in actual technique and implementation, they share some common attributes. Clearly, unobtrusive means of collecting interest information is generally favored. Researchers leveraged implicit interest indicators such as users' navigation paths through the content and users' interaction patterns. They also avoided using representation techniques that require extensive batch or a priority knowledge engineering. Representations were generally inspired by machine-learning approaches employing "learn while performing" or unsupervised learning principles. In the present work, the system asks the student to provide his interest, represents it numerically, and incorporates it into an input vector before feeding it into the neural network.

Another important point in relationship with IC systems concerns their evaluation. Evaluation of IC systems and real world knowledge acquisition systems in general, as Shadbot, O'Hara, and Crown (1999) discuss, is both tricky and complex. A lot of evaluations are performed with user log data simulating real user activity or with standard benchmark collections. Although these evaluations are useful, especially for technique comparison, they must be backed up by real world studies so we can see how the benchmark tests generalize to the real world setting. A comparison of IC systems is also difficult since there are no widely used standards for reporting results. Where machine learning techniques are employed, standard tests such as precision and recall provide useful metrics for comparing learning algorithms. However, the best test of an IC system's ability to help a user is a user trial. Unfortunately, user trials in the literature do not follow a consistent methodology. These problems are also seen in the more general agent domain where it has yet to be conclusively demonstrated if people really benefit from such information systems (Nwana, 1996). In the present work, we evaluate the IC system for academic advising both by standard tests (performance of the learning algorithm) and by user trials (performance of the whole system).

As wireless and location-aware information systems are becoming more ubiquitous, new and exciting avenues are opening up for delivering customized information. These new devices, however, are bringing with them new challenges.

Conclusion

Academic advising is an important area in any university, which seldom gets adequate resources. Hence, any system that can support this operation will be worthwhile. The idea of realizing such a system is very interesting and highly related to the current research and development trends. In this chapter, MASACAD, a well defined architecture for a multi-agent system for addressing the problem of academic advising was proposed. It uses intelligent agents and neural networks for learning and recommendation. The prototype implementation and preliminary testing show that the multi-agent paradigm, combined with ideas from machine learning, user modeling, and Web mining, would be a good approach for the problem of information customization. It was very interesting to see an e-learning system that is able to learn and react according to the characteristics of the client (in this case the student). The results are encouraging and future work will be focused on improving the system and studying how such simple examples, built with insight, should lead to the identification of key difficulties, useful abstractions, and a general method for solving the problem and revelation of the issues.

MASACAD was just an example that demonstrates how the careful combination of various AI techniques could help approaching information customization and hence combating information overload.

Today many systems are already making their very first steps in customization. In online search engines, for example, customizing search is being looked into and it is sensible to expect search to change in the next few years. To resolve information overload to some extent, and enable users to collect just the information they require using customized search engines which run all over the internet looking for the correct information, it seems to be important to distribute the search and to move as much of it as possible to the user's own machine, allowing more customization. The user's own machine can become more like a friend when answering the user's questions. This would agree with the general consensus which is that giving direct answers to questions by extracting data from online sources rather than giving links to Web pages is what is needed to look into. Customizing search seems, therefore, to be an important issue and will surely have a strong impact on search engine optimization efforts and how these will adapt to the possible future of search.

Again, the right combination of AI technologies may be the clue. Hamdi (2007b), for example, in an attempt to circumvent some of the current problems of search engines and contribute to resolving the problem of information overload over the Web, proposes improving the quality of Web search by combining meta-search and self-organizing semantic maps. The goal is to conceptualize an information retrieval approach which uses traditional search engines as information filters and the semantic map as a browsing aid to support ordering, linking, and browsing information gathered by the filters.

References

Ali, S., & Smith, K. (2006). On learning algorithm selection for classification. *Applied Soft Computing, 6*(2), 119-138.

Atlas, L., Cole, R., Muthusamy, Y., Lippman, A., Connor, J., Park, D., El-Sharkawi, M., & Marks, R.J. (1990). A performance comparison of trained multi-layer perceptrons and trained classification trees. In *Proceedings of IEEE 78* (pp. 1614-1619).

Bauer, T., & Leake, D. (2002). Using document access sequences to recommend customized information. *IEEE Intelligent Systems, 17*(6), 27-33.

Bradshaw, J.M. (1997). An introduction to software agents. In J.M. Bradshaw (Ed.) *Software agents* (pp. 3-46). Menlo Park, CA: AAAI Press.

Carbonell, J.G., Michalski, R., & Mitchell, T. (1983). An overview of machine learning. In R.S. Michalski, J.G. Carbonell, & T.M. Mitchell (Eds.), *Machine learning* (Chapter 1). Palo Alto, CA: Tioga.

Carpenter, G., Grossberg, S., Markuzon, N., Reynolds, J., & Rosen, D. (1992). Fuzzy ART-MAP: A neural network architecture for incremental supervised learning of analog multidimensional maps. *IEEE Transactions on Neural Networks, 3*, 698-713.

Cooley, R., Mobasher, B., & Srivastava, J. (1997, November). Web mining: Information and pattern discovery on the World Wide Web. In *Proceedings of the 9th IEEE International Conference on Tools with Artificial Intelligence (ICTAI'97)* (pp. 558-567). Newport Beach, CA.

Course Planning Consultant (CPC). (n.d.). *Background and guest user information.* Retrieved from http://www.ge.uiuc.edu/ugrad/advising/cpc.html

Dietterich, T.G. (1986). Learning at the knowledge level. *Machine Learning, 1*, 287-316.

Feigenbaum, E. (1977). The art of artificial intelligence: Themes and case international. *Journal of Intelligent Information Technologies, 2*(1), 1-19

Franklin, S., & Graesser, A. (1997). Is it an Agent, or just a program?: A taxonomy for autonomous agents. In *Proceedings of 3rd International Workshop on Agent Theories, Architectures, and Languages, published as Intelligent Agents III* (pp. 21-35). Berlin: Springer-Verlag.

Hamdi, M. S. (2005). Extracting and customizing information using multiagents. In A. Scime (Ed.), *Web mining: Applications and techniques* (pp. 228-252). Hershey, PA: Idea Group Publishing.

Hamdi, M.S. (2006a). MASACAD: A multi-agent system for academic advising. *International Journal of Intelligent Information Technologies, 2*(1), 1-19

Hamdi, M.S. (2006b). MASACAD: A multiagent-based approach to information customization. *IEEE Intelligent Systems, 21*(1), 60-67.

Hamdi, M.S. (2006c). Information overload and information customization. *IEEE Potentials, 25*(5), 9-12.

Hamdi, M.S. (2007a). MASACAD: A multi-agent approach to information customization for the purpose of academic advising of students. *Elsevier Applied Soft Computing Journal, 7*(2007), 746-771.

Hamdi, M.S. (2007b). Improving the quality of Web search. In C. Calero, M. A. Moraga, & M. Piattini (Eds.), *Handbook of research on Web information systems quality.* Hershey, PA: Idea Group Publishing.

Hearst, M. (1997, August 16). Distinguishing between web data mining and information access. *Presentation for the Panel on Web Data Mining, KDD 97,* Newport Beach, CA. Retrieved from http://www.sims.berkeley.edu/~hearst/talks/data-mining-panel/index.htm

Ho Ha, S. (2002). Helping online customers decide through Web personalization. *IEEE Intelligent Systems, 17*(6), 34-43.

Jackson, P. (1999). *Introduction to expert systems* (3rd ed.). Harlow, UK: Addison-Wesley.

Jenamani, M., Mohapatra, P.K.J., & Ghose, S. (2002). Online customized index synthesis in commercial Web sites. *IEEE Intelligent Systems, 17*(6), 20-26.

Kawamura, T., Hasegawa, T., Ohsuga, A., & Honiden, S. (2000). Bee-gent: Bonding and encapsulation enhancement agent framework for development of distributed systems. *Systems and Computers in Japan, 31*(13), 42-56.

Kobsa, A. (1990). User modeling in dialog systems: Potentials and hazards. *AI & Society: The Journal of Human and Machine Intelligence, 4*(3), 214-231.

Krishnapuram, R., Joshi, A., Nasraoui, O., & Yi, L. (2001). Low complexity fuzzy relational clustering algorithms for Web mining. *IEEE Trans. Fuzzy Systems, 9*(4), 596-607.

Menczer, F., Monge, A.E., & Street, W.N. (2002). Adaptive assistants for customized e-shopping. *IEEE Intelligent Systems, 17*(6), 12-19.

Mitchell, T.M. (1997). *Machine learning.* New York: McGraw-Hill.

Moneta, L. (1997). The integration of technology with the management of student services. *New Directions for Student Services: Using Technology to Promote Student Learning, 78,* 5-16.

Moore, M. (1996). *Distance education: A systems view.* Wadsworth Publishing Company. Retrieved from http://www.cde.psu.edu/de/what_is_de.html#definition

Mostafa, J. (2002). Guest editor's introduction: Information customization. *IEEE Intelligent Systems, 17*(6), 8-11.

Newell, A. (1982). The knowledge level. *Artificial Intelligence, 18,* 87-127.

Nwana, H.S. (1996). Software agents: An overview. *The Knowledge Engineering Review, 11*(3), 205-244.

Paik, H., & Benatallah, B. (2002). Building adaptive e-catalog communities based on user interaction patterns. *IEEE Intelligent Systems, 17*(6), 44-52.

Patterson, D. (1996). *Artificial neural networks.* Singapore: Prentice Hall.

Quinlan, J.R. (1993). *C4.5: Programs for empirical learning.* San Francisco: Morgan Kaufmann.

Rich, E. (1979). User modeling via stereotypes. *Cognitive Sciences, 3,* 329-354.

Rumelhart, D.E., Hinton, G.E., & Williams, R.J. (1986). Learning internal representations by error propagation. In D.E. Rumelhart & J.L. McClelland (Eds.), *Parallel distributed processing, Volume 1* (pp. 318-362). Cambridge, MA: MIT Press.

Sebastiani, F. (2002). Machine learning in automated text categorization. *ACM Computing Surveys (CSUR), 34*(1), 1-47.

Shadbot, N., O'Hara, K., & Crown, L. (1999). The experimental evaluation of knowledge acquisition techniques and methods: History, problems and new directions. *International Journal of Human-Computer Studies, 51*, 729-755.

Shavlik, J., Mooney, R., & Towell, G., (1991). Symbolic and neural net learning algorithms: An empirical comparison. *Machine Learning, 6*, 111-143.

Sheremetov, L., & Arenas, A. (2002). EVA: An interactive Web-based collaborative learning environment. *Computers & Education, 39*(2), 161-182.

Simon, H.A. (1983). Why should machines learn? In R.S. Michalski, J.G. Carbonell, & T.M. Mitchell (Eds.), *Machine learning* (Chapter 2). Palo Alto, CA: Tioga.

Steele, G., & McDonald, M. (n.d.). Technology and advising. Retrieved from http://www.nacada.ksu.edu/Clearinghouse/Research_Related/advtechbib.htm

Stuart, E.M. (2000, August). *Interface agents: A review of the field.* Technical Report, University of Southampton.

Tan, A. H. (1995). Adaptive resonance associative map. *Neural Networks, 8*(3), 437-446.

Watson, M. (2005). *Practical artificial intelligence programming in Java.* Retrieved from http://www.markwatson.com/opencontent/

Section II

Agents and Online Auctions

Chapter V

An Agent-Oriented Perspective on E-Bidding Systems

Ivan Jureta, University of Namur, Belgium

Manuel Kolp, Université catholique de Louvain, Belgium

Stéphane Faulkner, University of Namur, Belgium

Abstract

Today, a high volume of goods and services is being traded using online auction systems. The growth in size and complexity of architectures to support online auctions requires the use of distributed and cooperative software techniques. In this context, the agent software development paradigm seems appropriate both for their modeling, development and implementation. This chapter proposes an agent-oriented patterns analysis of best practices for online auction. The patterns are intended to help both IT managers and software engineers during the requirement specification of an online auction system while integrating benefits of agent software engineering.

Introduction

The emergence and growing popularity of electronic commerce in general and online auctions in particular, has raised the challenge to explore scalable global electronic market information systems, involving both human and automated traders (Rachlevsky-Reich, Ben-Shaul, Tung Cho, Lo, & Poggio, 1999).

Online auctions are a particular type of Internet-based electronic markets, that is, worldwide-open markets in which participants buy and sell goods and services in exchange for money. Most online auctions rely on classical auction economics (Beam & Segev, 1998; Bikhchandani, de Vries, Schummer, & Vohra, 2001S). In the economics literature, "an auction is an economic mechanism for determining the price of an item. It requires a pre-announced methodology, one or more bidders who want the item, and an item for sale" (Beam & Segev, 1998). The item is usually sold to the highest bidder. An online auction can be defined as an auction which is organized using an information system and is accessible to auction participants exclusively through a Web site on the Internet.

Recently, online auctions have become a popular way to trade goods and services. During 2002, the leading online marketplace, eBay.com, provided a trading platform for 638 million items of all kinds. The value of all goods that were actually traded amounted to nearly $15 billion, which represented, at the time, a third of all online sales in the U.S. This trend results from specific advantages of online auctions over traditional ones, as well as the fact that people are becoming increasingly comfortable with online shopping, which is reflected in strong growth of online sales, on both auction-based (e.g., eBay.com) and other e-commerce platform types (e.g., fixed-price marketplaces, such as Amazon.com).

Today, with the increasing number of online auctions being organized, there is a need for distributed, large-scale and dynamic information system (IS) architectures to support online auction marketplaces (Rachlevsky-Reich, Ben-Shaul, Tung Chau, Lo, & Poggio, 1999). From the information system development perspective, multi-agent systems (MASs) are a powerful new software engineering paradigm for designing and developing complex information systems (Yu, 1997). The use of agents as intentional, autonomous, and social entities which act according to their self-interest (Yu, 2001) provides advantages in both the modelling of an online auction system, and in its implementation using an agent-oriented IS.

In this chapter, we propose agent-oriented analysis patterns for an online auction information system (OAIS). These patterns are intended to help both IT managers and software engineers during the analysis of OAIS. We develop the social dimension of patterns on the basis of the analysis of leading existing online auction information systems.

Our motivation stems from the fact that auction mechanisms for exchanging goods and services will become more and more popular with both consumers and companies.

Providing agent-oriented patterns for such systems can reduce their development cost and time, while integrating benefits of agent-orientation in software development. Patterns of current best practices in the online auction domain facilitate the development of new auction systems, by clearly showing the functionalities that are particularly valued by auction participants; these should be included in any auction system if it wishes to attract both consumers and corporate users.

MAS are composed of autonomous agents that interact and coordinate to achieve their intentions. This makes them particularly adapted to modeling complex information systems composed of both human and software actors (Do, 2003).

Today, a high volume of goods and services is being traded using online auction information systems. The growth in size and complexity of the software infrastructure used to support auctions requires the use of distributed large-scale IS. In this context, the agent software development paradigm seems adequate both for their modeling and development.

Auctions are increasingly popular in business-to-business transactions. Patterns of both critical aspects and best practices of online auction IS can provide significant aid in the development process of such systems. In addition, auctions can be used as underlying economic models for resource management in peer-to-peer and grid computing, making it possible to deploy online auction patterns in other domains that are not immediately obvious.

The rest of this chapter is organized as follows. Section 2 gives an overview of the core concepts and of their relevance in the context of online auctions. Section 3 describes our analysis method and identifies existing online auction information systems on which we base our analysis. Section 4 describes the patterns of a basic online auction information system (OAIS). Section 5 describes best practices in the domain of OAIS. Section 6 concludes the text and discusses the limitations of our approach.

Online Auctions, Agents, and Agent Patterns

Online auctions are highly dynamic processes which involve numerous participants. Their structure changes rapidly to reflect the entry and exit of bidders as well as the impact of their behavior on the price of the item being auctioned. MAS allow the creation of dynamic and evolving IS structures which can change at runtime to benefit from the capabilities of new system entities and replace obsolete ones (Do, 2003).

Our work revolves around three main concepts: online auctions, agents, and patterns. We discuss each one below. We also discuss reasons why agent-orientation is appropriate for modeling, design, and implementation of online auction IS.

Current State of Online Auctions

There is currently multi-billion dollar annual activity in the online auction market with a growing variety of sophisticated trading mechanisms (Pinker, Seidmann, & Vakrat, 2001). There are numerous reasons for the popularity of online auction marketplaces (Lucking-Reiley, 2000; Pinker, Seidmann, & Vakrat, 2001; Re, Braga, & Masiero 2001). We classify them into following categories: *Market efficiency, accessibility, managing complexity, information gathering.*

There have been several studies presenting online auction business models (Beam & Segev, 1998; Lucking-Reiley, 2000). These studies propose different classification criteria for online auctions, such as the auction mechanism (English, Vickrey, Dutch, etc.), the type of participants (businesses and/or consumers), the number of participants, and so forth. We retain here the classification proposed by (Pinker, Seidmann, & Vakrat , 2001) which is primarily based on the number of participants. This classification is shown in Figure 1.

In bilateral negotiations, the two parties negotiate the sale of an item. Negotiation involves the price of the item, but may also involve its qualitative characteristics. In Web-based reverse procurement auctions, many sellers compete to win a single buyer (e.g., a government accepts bids for a construction project from several companies). In Web-based exchanges, many buyers face multiple sellers (e.g., the stock market). In Web-based sales auctions, a single seller offers an item for sale to many bidders (e.g., eBay.com).

In Web-based sales auctions on the Internet, the most common auction mechanism is the "English" auction, with "Vickrey," "Dutch," and "first-price sealed bid" auctions. We briefly describe their mechanisms.

Figure 1. Classification of online auction types, according to Pinker, Seidmann, and Vakrat (2001)

	ONE BUYER	MANY BUYERS
ONE SELLER	Bilateral negotiations	Web-based sales auctions
MANY SELLERS	Web-based reverse procurement auctions	Web-based exchanges

English auction. Each bidder sees the highest current bid, can place a bid and update it many times. The winner of the auction is the highest bidder who pays the price bid, that is, the final auction bid that this bidder placed. An example is eBay.com. English auctions are by far the most popular auction type and their success lies most probably in the familiarity of English auctions as well as in the entertainment they provide to participants (in the form of bidder competition).

First-price sealed bid auction. Each bidder makes a single secret bid; the winner is the highest bidder, and the price paid is the highest bid. An example is The Chicago Wine Company (tcwc.com).

Vickrey auction. Each bidder makes a single secret bid; the winner is the highest bidder. However, the price paid is the amount of the second highest bid. Some online auction systems propose it as an option (e.g., iauction.com).

Dutch auction. The seller steadily lowers the price of the item over time. The bidders can see the current price and must decide if they wish to purchase at that price or wait until it drops further. The winner is the first bidder to pay the current price. An example is klik-klok.com.

In the context of the classification proposed in Figure 1, our analysis focuses on *Web-based sales auctions*. The analysis is applicable on any type of auction as far as the participant type is concerned: both the seller and buyers may be either customers and/or businesses. Our analysis is independent of the auction mechanism, as long as it is a mechanism involving a single seller and many buyers.

Benefits of Agent-Orientation

An agent can be defined as an intentional, autonomous, and social entity, which acts according to its self-interest (Yu, 2001). In the IS development perspective, an agent is an autonomous software entity that is responsive to its environment, proactive (in that it exhibits goal-oriented behavior), and social (in that it can interact with other agents to complete goals) (Kauffman & Walden, 2001). Multi-agent systems involve the interaction of multiple agents, both software and human, so that they may achieve common or individual goals through cooperative or competitive behavior.

The use of agent-orientation in the modeling, design, and implementation of online auction information systems provides at least the following benefits:

- When modeling an online auction IS, we can represent (using e.g., the $i*$ modeling framework (Yu, 1995) the intentional dimension of agents participating in the auction process, as well as their interdependencies. Consequently, the use of agents as the core modeling concept, makes it possible to understand more profoundly the environment in which the IS will be used. We can then explore alternative IS structures incorporating different functionalities during the requirements engineering phase of the IS development. We can evaluate alternative IS structures in terms of their contribution to user's needs (such as e.g., ease of use, speed, etc.) and to the system's other non-functional requirements (such as e.g., security, reusability, development cost, development time, etc.) in order to select the most adequate IS structure.

- Online auction IS are large-scale, complex, and distributed systems. The use of MAS as a powerful new software engineering paradigm for designing and developing complex IS has been advocated in (Faulkner, Kolp, & Do, 2004). Social organization-based MAS (Kolp, Giorgini, & Myloupoulos, 2006) match the system architecture with its operational environment (Do, Kolp, & Pirotte, 2003). They provide a strong basis for the development of robust and highly customizable software able to cope with the changing environment, while being sufficiently secure to protect personal data and other belongings of system agents. Agent architectures are more flexible, modular and robust than, for example, object-oriented ones. They tend to be open and dynamic as their components can be added, modified or removed at any time (Yu, 1997).

Online Auction Patterns

Patterns are reusable solutions to recurring information system design problems, and provide a vocabulary for communicating these solutions to others (Weiss, 2003). They aid in the reuse of IS analysis and design experience, as each pattern describes a reusable and flexible solution for a specific problem type (Do, 2003).

Patterns for online auction IS have already been proposed by (Resnick & Zeckhauser, 2002) However, these patterns are specified using the UML. Consequently, they do not show agents as intentional, autonomous, and social entities. In addition, the pattern language provided by (Resnick & Zeckhauser, 2002) does not integrate best practices that can be identified on currently operating auction IS on the Internet. Kumar and Feldman (1998) only provide a global architecture of a basic online auction system in the context of object-oriented software development. GEM (Rachlevsky-Reich et al., 1999) provides system architecture for developing large distributed electronic markets but it only addresses the system's basic functionalities required to organize trading among agents. It provides patterns without treating intentional aspects, and uses agents at implementation level.

Analysis Method

Our analysis is based on three leading online auction IS on the Internet: eBay.com, Amazon.com Auctions, and Yahoo.com Auctions. We examined the Web sites of these systems, and used literature that provides either strategic analysis (Pinker et al., 2001), and/or economic analysis (Lucking-Reiley, 2000; Resnick & Zeckhauser, 2002) of aspects of auctions being conducted on these systems.

We do not provide a comparative analysis of the three. However, it is necessary to note that eBay is by far the leading online auction marketplace, and provides most advanced functionalities that support both the auction process and the exchange of items and valuables that follows the auction. eBay is also the only one for which online auctions constitute its core business, making it particularly sensible to the needs of its users (Amazon is specialized in fixed-price retailing, and Yahoo is an all-purpose Web portal). We have found that both Yahoo.com Auctions and Amazon.com Auctions are late entrants to the online auction market, and that they copy the eBay business model. Consequently, we focus the analysis of the IS structure and the identification of best practices on eBay, while comparing our findings with its two main competitors.

We model the social dimension of each pattern using the *i** modeling framework (Yu, 1995). *i** is an agent-oriented modeling framework used to support the early phase of requirements engineering (Yu, 1997), during which we wish to represent and understand the wider context in which the IS will be used. The framework focuses on dependencies that exist among actors, and provides two types of models to represent them: a strategic dependency (SD) model used for describing processes as networks of strategic dependencies among actors, and the strategic rationale (SR) model used to describe each actor's reasoning in the process, as well as to explore alternative process structures.

Main modeling constructs of the *i** framework are actors, roles, goals, softgoals, resources, and tasks. Both the SD and SR models can represent dependencies among actors or roles. A dependency is a relationship in which an Actor or Role A_1 depends on some other Actor or Role A_2, for the provision of a dependum. We call A_1 the depender, and A_2 the dependee in the relationship. Each dependency can be seen as a matching of a want from the depender side to an ability on the dependee side (Liu & Yu, 1995). The following dependency types exist:

- **Goal dependency:** A goal is a condition or state of affairs in the environment that the actors would like to achieve. In a goal dependency, the depender depends on the dependee to achieve a goal. The dependee has the freedom to choose the way in which the goal will be achieved.

- **Softgoal dependency:** A Softgoal is similar to a Goal, but differs in that there are no clear-cut criteria for knowing whether the Softgoal has been achieved or not. It is then up to the stakeholders to judge whether a particular IS structure sufficiently satisfies the Softgoal. In a Softgoal dependency, the depender depends on the dependee to act in such way as to contribute to the softgoal.

- **Task dependency:** A Task specifies a particular way of doing something. In a Task dependency, the depender specifies the course of action to be taken by the dependee.

- **Resource dependency:** A Resource is a physical or informational entity which may serve some purpose. In a Resource dependency, the depender requires the dependee to provide some Resource.

In *i**, software agents are represented as actors. Actors can play roles. A role is an abstract characterization of the common behaviour of an actor in some specific context (e.g., a consumer, a salesman, a buyer, a seller, etc.).

Basic Agent-Oriented Patterns Analysis

We focus on an online auction process that is appropriate for the cited auction types (English, Vickrey, Dutch, and First-price sealed bid auction) involving a single seller and multiple buyers. We first provide the social dimension of separate patterns required to run an OAIS. We then integrate these patterns in order to show how they constitute an OAIS that provides basic auction functionality.

Figure 2. Actors and roles in the online auction information system

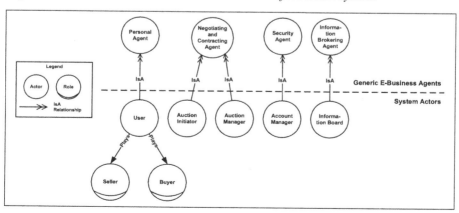

In our analysis, we identified system actors shown in Figure 2. The figure shows that these actors are specializations of common generic e-business agents from the business agent typology proposed in (Papazoglou, 2001). This is useful since much work has been put into their specification, development and testing of these generic agent types (Guttman, Moukas, & Maes, 1998; Papazoglou, 2001).

Personal agents work directly with the human user to help support the creation and management of the user's profile. *User agents* can play the roles of *buyers* and *sellers* with regards to selling and/or buying in auctions. *Negotiating and contracting agents* negotiate terms of business transactions, in terms of, for example, transaction rules, payment methods, and so forth. *Security agents* manage security aspects of the system such as, for example, user registration, access authorization, and so forths. *Information brokering agents* manage, summarize, and manipulate information. They search for information on behalf of *user agents*.

We have identified a set of generic features that compose the online auction process. We provide analysis patterns for these features by allocating responsibilities to agents according to their capabilities briefly described above.

User authentication. In order to use the system, *users* first need to register on the system, by providing personal data. This data is necessary for identification when they return to participate in auctions. They can then access and use the system by logging on. Figure 3 shows the authentication pattern as a strategic dependency model, involving the *user* and the *account manager*.

Auction Setup. A *user* will set up an auction when he/she wishes to sell an item. In such case, the *user* plays the role of the *seller* in the auction. The *seller* must

Figure 3. Social dimension of the user authentication pattern

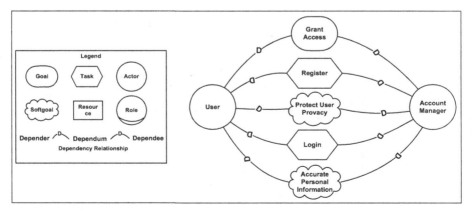

Figure 4. Dynamic dimension of the user authentication pattern

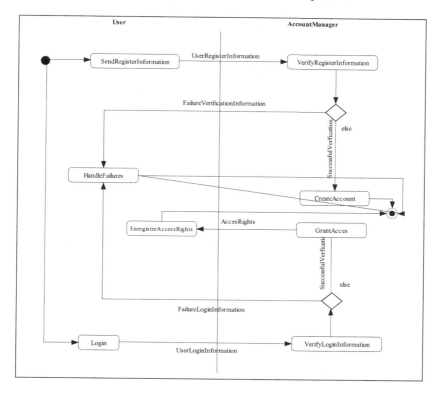

provide a description of the item using a procedure specified by the *auction initiator* (e.g., by filling out a series of Web forms on the auction Web site). Ideally, the *seller* would *provide exact item details*, which would contribute to the quality of service of the system, with regards to the *buyers*. The *seller* depends on the *auction initiator* to provide a procedure for selecting among alternative auction rules (e.g., English auction, Dutch auction, etc.), and to specify the schedule of the auction. The *seller* depends on the *auction initiator* to advertise the item that the *seller* has put on auction, so that the potential *buyers* can be informed about the auction event.

The auction setup pattern is independent of the auction type. However, specific constraints do apply for specific auction types. For example, if the *user* selects the English auction rules, he must specify the minimum bid increment. The same information is irrelevant for, for example, a Dutch auction. The specification of such constraints is outside the scope of this text, and should be discussed with specialists of the auction domain.

Figure 5. Social dimension of the auction setup pattern

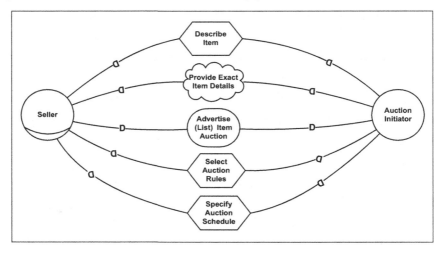

Figure 6. Dynamic dimension of the auction setup pattern

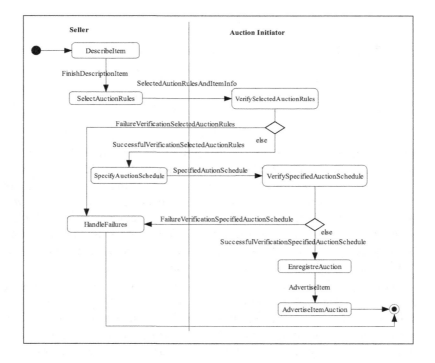

Figure 7. Social dimension of the auction search pattern

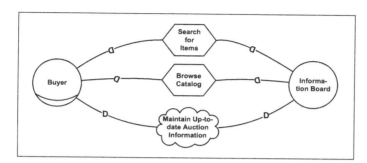

Figure 8. Dynamic dimension of the auction search pattern

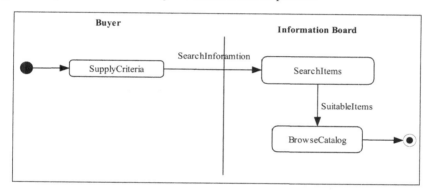

Auction (item) search: A *user* looks for auctioned items by using either a search interface, or by browsing the catalogue which provides a hierarchical organization of items. Search and browsing features are provided by the *information board*. The *user* depends on the *information board* to maintain an up-to-date database of current auctions.

Auction bidding: *Buyers* can *place bids*, and *retract bids*. The way in which these tasks are accomplished is defined in the IS (e.g., through a specific Web/wap/i-mode interface). *Buyers* depend on the *auction manager* to *verify bids* that they place, in terms of bid coherence with the auction rules (e.g., Is the minimum bid increment respected?). The *auction manager* provides notifications to all *buyers* participating in the auction whenever a new high bid is placed. The *auction manager* depends on the users to *respect system policies*, in terms of incorrect behaviour such as "multiple bidding." Finally, both *buyers* and the *seller* in the auction depend on the *auction*

Figure 9. Social dimension of the auction bidding pattern

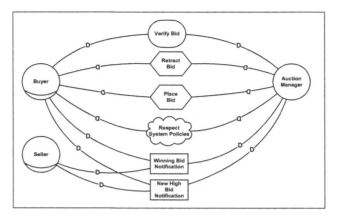

Figure 10. Dynamic dimension of the auction bidding pattern

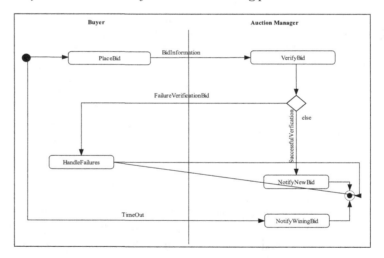

manager to supply the *winning bid notification* so that the *seller* and the winning *buyer* can then proceed to the trade settlement. In addition, they both depend on the *auction manager* to supply the *new high bid notification*.

Trade settlement: Trade settlement consists of the exchange of valuables between the *seller* and the winning *buyer*. The *buyer* depends on the *seller* to send the item,

Figure 11. Social dimension of the agent coordination pattern

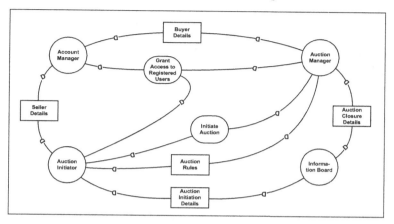

and the *seller* depends on the *buyer* to provide the payment. It should be noted that this aspect of the online auction, however significant, is generally not managed by any part of the online auction IS (Resnick & Zeckhauser, 2002). The only aspect of the trade settlement that could be treated through interaction of OAIS (online auction information system) agents is the exchange of contact information between the *seller* and the winning *buyer*. It is then up to the two human parties to manage the actual exchange.

Coordination: The online auction IS is a multi-agent system and coordination is required among agents participating in the system. Coordination among non-*user* agents is established through dependencies among these agents, as shown in Figure 11. The coordination between the *user* agents and each other agent type is already established in each of the patterns.

The pattern in Figure 11 shows the dependencies required for coordination of system agents. The *auction initiator* depends on the *account manager* for the provision of the *seller details*, in order to integrate them into the *auction initiation details*. Both the *auction initiator* and the *auction manager* depend on the *account manager* to *grant access to registered users*, so that these *users* can participate in the auction. The *auction manager* requires *buyer details* in order to distinguish among buyers and to associate bids to respective buyer identities. *Buyer details* should be provided by the *account manager*. For the *auction manager* to run the auction, the *auction initiator* is required to actually *initiate auction*. In addition, the *auction manager* depends on the *auction initiator* for the provision of *auction rules* of the auction that has been initiated. Finally, the *information board* keeps track of auction initiation and closure, in order to be able to inform *users* of auctions being initiated and closed.

Best Practices Patterns Analysis

Today's online auction IS offers additional features to those that automate the traditional auction. In addition to enhancing the user experience, these additional features are essential to the commercial success of an online auction IS. We provide patterns for several additional features that we consider being best practices in the domain of online auctions.

We will see that some of the features can be introduced in the system in several ways, requiring comparison and evaluation. To select the most adequate alternative, we represent relevant system qualities (e.g., security, privacy, usability, etc.) as softgoals and use contribution links to show how these softgoals are affected by each alternative, as in the Non-Functional Requirements framework (Chung, Nixon, Yu, & Mylopoulos, 2000).

Proxy bidding. Online auctions can last for several days, making it impossible for human buyers to follow the auction in its integrity, as is the case in traditional ones. Proxy bidding allows buyers to specify their maximum willingness to pay. A procedure is then used to automatically increase their bid until the specified maximum is reached, or the auction is closed (Kurbel & Loutchko, 2001). This enables human buyers to be represented in the auction, without requiring their physical presence in order to interact with their *buyer* agent. It is important to note that proxy bidding is applicable only when English Auction rules are enforced in the auction.

Proxy bidding can be introduced in the basic online auction IS in several ways in terms of responsibility assignment. Two alternatives are shown in Figure 12. Each alternative is represented as a simple strategic rationale model. A series of softgoals have been selected as criteria for alternative comparison—*privacy, security, reliability, speed*, and *workload*. These are non-functional requirements (Chung, Nixon, Yu, & Mylopoulos, 2000) for the information system and were selected according to issues often raised in e-commerce IS design (Mylopoulos, Kolp, & Castro, 2001; Weiss, 2003), online auction IS design (Kumar & Feldman, 1998), and so forth.

The first alternative seems more adequate. In this alternative, the responsibility of managing proxy bidding is allocated to the *buyer* agent. Several reasons support this choice:

- When the *buyer* manages proxy bidding, price preferences are not communicated to outside agents. Consequently, *privacy* is higher than in the second alternative which requires the transfer of price preferences to the *auction manager*.

- *Workload* of the system is lower, since automatic bidding is distributed among multiple *buyer* agents participating in the auction. We consider that system

Figure 12. Two alternative responsibility assignments expressed in two strategic rationale models of the proxy bidding feature. Positive (favorable) (+) and negative (not favorable) (-) contributions of each alternative structure are shown. They aid in alternative selection.

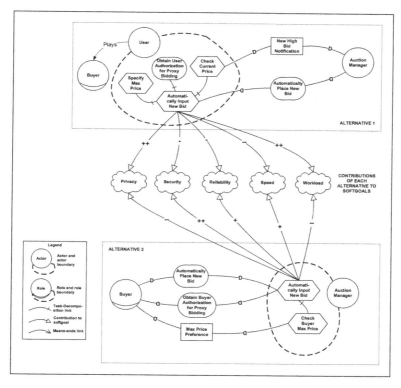

workload is much higher when all proxy bidding activity in one auction is centralized at the *auction manager*.

- We consider that *security* of data transfers between the *buyer* and *auction manager* is not of high priority in an English online auction, since the bid made by the *buyer* is made publicly available by the *auction manager*.

Reliability concerns the probability of error in terms of, for example, a new proxy bid not being taken into account by the *auction manager*. This probability is higher when proxy bidding is distributed among multiple *buyers*. Finally, it is probable that speed of bid input is higher when proxy bidding is centralized, since there are no data transfers between the *auction manager* and *buyer* agents.

Based on this discussion, we select the first alternative on Figure 12. Consequently, proxy bidding is introduced in the is as a service that a *user* agent playing *buyer* role can provide to the human user, and requires the human user to specify the maximum price that he/she is willing to pay. In addition, the *buyer* agent needs to obtain an authorization from the user in order to initiate proxy bidding.

Reputation management: In classical exchanges where buyers and sellers actually meet, trust[1] results from repeated buyer-seller interactions, from the possibility to inspect items before the purchase, and so forth. In online auctions, sellers and buyers do not meet, and little personal information is publicly available during the auction. In addition, product information is limited to information provided wilfully by the seller. In such a context, a mechanism for managing trust should be provided in order to reduce uncertainty in transactions among auction participants.

According to Ramchurn, Huynh and Jennings (2004), "trust is a belief an agent has that the other party will do what it says it will (being honest and reliable) or reciprocate (being reciprocative for the common good of both), given an opportunity to defect to get higher payoffs." Trust can be favored in an OAIS through a reputation mechanism, which should satisfy specific requirements (Ramchurn et al., 2004): it should be costly to change identities in the community; new entrants should not be penalised by initially having a low reputation rating; participants with low ratings should be able to rebuild reputation; it should be costly for participants to fake reputation; participants with high reputation should have more influence on reputation ratings they attribute to other participants; participants should be able to provide more qualitative evaluations than simply numerical ratings; and finally, participants should be able to keep a memory of reputation ratings and give more

Figure 13. Social dimension of the reputation management pattern

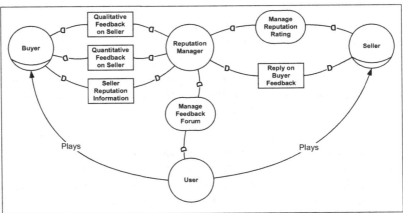

importance to the latest ones. Such reputation mechanism can reduce the hesitancy of new buyers and sellers when using the online auction IS for the first time, as it implicitly reduces the anonymity and uncertainty among trading partners.

It is difficult to construct a reputation system that satisfies all of these requirements. Seller reputation can be established through feedback of buyers on the behavior of sellers during the trade settlement which follows the closure of the auction (Resnick & Zeckhauser, 2002). As a result of buyer feedback in repetitive sales, a seller receives a rating which is indicative of the trust that the trading community has in him/her.

In order to enable the management of trust in the OAIS, we introduce an additional agent: *reputation manager*, which is a specialization of the *information brokering agent* (Papazoglou, 2001). Informally, its responsibility is to collect, organize, and summarize reputation data. The *reputation manager* depends on the winning *buyer* of each auction to provide feedback on the *seller* after the trade settlement. *Reputation manager* uses *qualitative* (textual) and *quantitative* (numerical) *feedback on seller* to establish reputation ratings of *users* that have played the role of *sellers* in auctions. As information on reputation is valuable to any *user* of the OAIS, any *user* depends on the *reputation manager* to *manage feedback forum*, in which the feedback and rating information is contained and organized. Each *buyer* depends on the *reputation manager* to provide summarized *seller reputation information*, so that the *buyer* can have an indication on the trust he/she can put into the relationship with the *seller*. The *seller* can post replies on feedback provided by *buyers*. Finally, the *seller* depends on the *reputation manager* to *manage reputation rating*.

This pattern satisfies all but one of the requirements specified above: it does not make it costly for participants to change identities. For example, eBay deals with this problem by requiring each seller to provide a valid credit card number. We do not introduce such possibility into the pattern as it is not a standardized solution (eBay applies it only for its US users and none of its competitors applies it anywhere in the world).

Dispute resolution: The trade settlement that follows the closure of the auction may not be successful for many reasons (e.g., late deliveries, late payment, no payment at all, etc.). It then results in dispute that can require mediation by a third party in order to be resolved. The third party (here, a *negotiation assistant*) can be either a software agent that manages an automated dispute resolution process, or a human mediator.

The *negotiation assistant* collects *buyer* and *seller arguments*, and makes them available to both parties. On the basis of these *arguments* and its *solution knowledge base*, the agent *selects solution*—both the *buyer* and the *seller* depend on the agent to *suggest solution* to their dispute.

Payment: Payment can be accomplished by numerous ways in the context of an online auction. They can be either managed (in part) through the online auction IS

Figure 14. Strategic rationale model of the dispute resolution pattern with focus on negotiation assistant agent rationale

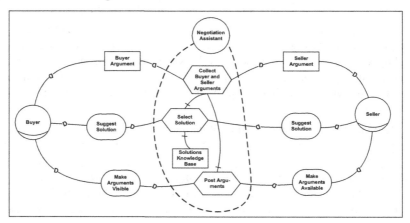

(e.g., credit card-based transactions), or outside the scope of the IS (e.g., cash, checks, etc.). The payment choice of auction participants is not repetitive and differs according to the payment cost, convenience, and protection. Consequently, it is important to take these criteria into account when structuring an online auction IS.

In the payment pattern, the *payment agent* (specialization of the *negotiating and contracting agent* (Papazoglou, 2001)) mediates the payment interaction between the *Seller* and the *Buyer*. This agent depends on the *account manager* for data on *users*, which is then used in providing *payment details* to the *payment system*. In addition to user identification, *payment details* should also contain transaction-related data. The *payment agent* depends on the *payment system* to *realize payment* and to provide *money transfer confirmation*, which is used to *confirm money transfer* to the *seller*. The *payment system* is outside the boundary of the online auction information system (OAIS). Upon closure of the auction, the *seller* depends on the *payment agent* to *invoice buyer*. The *buyer* depends on the *payment system* to provide *invoice* and in return, the *buyer* is expected to *authorize transfer*.

The pattern structure in Figure 15 is adapted to PayPal and all common credit card-based payment systems. Any of these payment systems intervenes in the pattern as the *payment system*, which is specialized in money transfers.

Personalization: Personalization generally refers to making an information system more responsive to unique and individual needs of each user. In online auctions, human users require a personalized interface that facilitates tracking of auctions,

Figure 15. Social dimension of the payment pattern

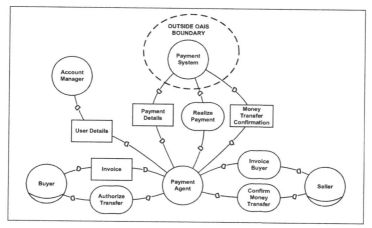

placing bids, and listing items for sale. As users differ in their level of expertise, needs, and preferences, we need to tailor information to the user by, for example, making recommendations on auctions in which the user might wish to participate.

Personalization requires specific capabilities from the *user* agent. This agent should be able to observe and record actions of the human user, in order to adapt the user interface of the application and suggest behavior to the human user. Suggestions should be made by analysis of both the behavior of the user, as well as the behavior of other users that exhibit similar behavior and have similar preferences. Figure 16 shows the partial strategic rationale model of the *user* agent, with focus on the way it provides the personalization feature of the OAIS, for two alternative recommender systems.

In practice, very different kinds of recommender systems are used in e-commerce systems in general. In online auctions, eBay allows the user to provide indications on the item he/she is interested in buying, by describing it by a set of keywords and a price limit. This is particularly adapted to online auction environments as the quantity of products being sold is extremely high and product descriptions are inconsistent, even for identical products (this is due to the freedom left to sellers to describe items the way they want). eBay then performs automatic searches for the user (during a limited period of time: 30, 60, or 90 days) and informs him/her by e-mail when the item with such description becomes available. Strategic Rationale model of this system is provided as the second alternative on Figure 16.

Figure 16. Two alternative rationales for providing personalization through recommendations are shown.

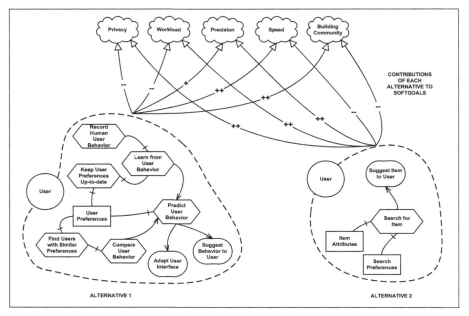

The first alternative is commonly used on traditional e-commerce systems (such as Amazon.com). It requires somewhat sophisticated methods for tracking user behavior, interpreting it, and extrapolating future behavior. In addition, compared to Alternative 2, it leads to higher workload of the IS, and consequently to higher operating costs of the system (more processing power is needed to run data mining algorithms). It does provide significant benefits, notably in terms of community building, as users may be provided with indications on preferences of others (e.g., such system would suggest behavior in terms of "Buyers who bought this item, also bought:"), and may be able to contact these other buyers.

Alternative 1 is used in traditional e-commerce IS. Alternative 2 is used currently on eBay.

The second alternative is more cost effective (in terms of workload) and probably more precise, as it provides suggestions on the basis of explicit item attributes provided willfully by the user. In addition, it provides better privacy protection, since it does not record the behavior of the user. The choice between the two could be guided by, for example, operating cost considerations and target audience (Alternative 1 is more interesting for C2C auctions in which niche segments are targeted, since it helps in building the community among buyers; Alternative 2 is more interesting for large-scale cost-conscious auction IS, which do not have a particular target audience).

Fraud detection: Fraud is common in online auctions. In 2002, more than 33,000 online auction fraud complaints were filled. Fraud issues are strongly related to trust and reputation, and should be accounted for in an online auction system, in terms of specific parts of the system that are specialized in fraud detection activities. These may be human and/or automated agents, provided that the latter dispose of high performance automated methods for fraud detection.

The fraud detection pattern (Figure 17) is based on two main agents: *the fraud complaint centre* and the *fraud detector*. The *fraud complaint center* gathers all the *fraud complaints* posted by both *sellers* and/or *buyers*. The Internet Fraud Complaint Center (IFCC) typically plays this role. Besides, *users* also expect active fraud detection. They depend on a *fraud detector* to *detect fraud* in a secure and reliable way. The *fraud detector* requires specific *user* information and therefore depends on the *reputation manager* for *seller reputation information*, the *account manager* for *user information*, and on the *auction manager* for *auction information*.

The fraud detection methods are based on statistical methods and association analysis. This is particularly helpful to detect *shilling*, one of the most common fraud practice

Figure 17. Social dimension of the fraud detection pattern

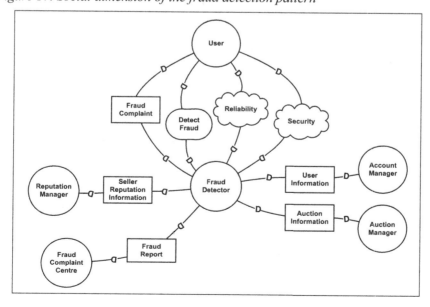

in online auction. The seller tries to hike up the prices in auction by placing buy bids under distinct aliases or through associates. Though eBay does not publicize its fraud detection methods, it is known that eBay has a large fraud division. eBay also provides a fraud protection service which allows buyers to receive merchandise before the seller is paid and allow seller to protect themselves from credit card and other payment fraud.

Conclusion

Online auctions have become increasingly popular in e-business transactions. Companies require such systems to be developed on tight budgets and in a short time in order to deploy auctions in managing relationships with their suppliers and clients. Patterns of best practices of online auctions can provide significant aid in the development process of such systems.

This chapter explores such patterns by analyzing some advanced online auctions functionalities through the lens of the agent paradigm. Compared to the literature, our approach is innovative in several aspects: we consider that multi-agent systems are adapted particularly to modeling and implementing online auction systems; we provided the *i** agent-oriented modeling perspective of each of the patterns we considered and for some of them the process-oriented perspective. We focused on specifying best practices in current online auction systems.

There are limitations to our work. We have not provided dimensions other than the *i** (social and intentional) and process-oriented ones for the patterns. This is well beyond the scope of this chapter, as it requires much more time and space. As future work, the patterns will be modeled using full UML-based notations as well as formally specified with the Z language.

References

Beam, C., & Segev, A. (1998). *Auctions on the Internet: A field study*. Working Paper 98-WP-1032, University of California, Berkeley, CA.

Bikhchandani, S., de Vries, S., Schummer, S., & Vohra, R.V. (2001). Linear programming and Vickrey auctions. In B. Dietrich & R. Vohra (Eds.), *Mathematics of the Internet: E-auction and markets*. New York: Springer-Verlag.

Chung, L., Nixon, B., Yu, E., & Mylopoulos, J. (2000). *Non-functional requirements in software engineering*. New York: Kluwer Academic.

Do, T., Kolp, M., & Pirotte, A. (2003). Social patterns for designing multiagent systems. In *Proceedings of the 15ᵗʰ International Conference on Software Engineering and Knowledge Engineering (SEKE 2003)*, San Francisco, USA.

Faulkner, S., Kolp, M., & Do, T. (2004). The SKwyRL perspective on agentoriented design patterns. In *Proceedings of the 6ᵗʰ International Conference on Enterprise Information Systems (ICEIS 2004)*, Porto, Portugal.

Guttman, R., Moukas, A., & Maes, P. (1998). Agent-mediated electronic commerce: A survey. *Knowledge Engineering Review, 13*(3), 45-69.

Kauffman, R., & Walden, E. (2001). Economics and electronic commerce: Survey and research directions. *International Journal of Electronic Commerce, 5*(4), 5-117.

Kolp, M., Giorgini, P., & Mylopoulos, J. (2006). Multi-agent architectures as organizational structures. *Autonomous Agents and Multi-Agent Systems, 13*(1), 3-25

Kumar, M., & Feldman, S. (1998). Internet auctions. In *Proceedings of the 3ʳᵈ USENIX Workshop on Electronic Commerce*, Boston.

Kurbel, K., & Loutchko, I. (2001). A framework for multi-agent electronic marketplaces: Analysis and classification of existing systems. In *Proceedings of International ICSC Congress on Information Science Innovations (ISI2001)*, Dubai, UAE.

Liu, L., & Yu, E. (2004). Designing information systems in social context: A goal and scenario modelling approach. *Information Systems, 29*, 187-203.

Lucking-Reiley, D. (2000). Auctions on the Internet: What's being auctioned, and how? *Journal of Industrial Economics, 48*(3), 227-252.

Mylopoulos, J., Kolp, M., & Castro, J. (2001). UML for agent-oriented software development: The tropos proposal. In *Proceedings of the Fourth International Conference on the Unified Modeling Language (UML 2001)*, Toronto, Canada.

Papazoglou, M.P. (2001). Agent-oriented technology in support of e-business. *Communications of the ACM, 44*(4), 71-77.

Pinker, E., Seidmann, A., & Vakrat, Y. (2001). *The design of online auctions: Business issues and current research*. Working Paper CIS-01-05, W. E. Simon Graduate School of Business Administration, University of Rochester.

Rachlevsky-Reich, B., Ben-Shaul, I., Tung Chau, N., Lo, A., & Poggio, T. (1999). GEM: A global electronic market system. *Information Systems, 24*(6), 495-518.

Ramchurn, S., Huynh, D., & Jennings, N. (2004). Trust in multi-agent systems. *Knowledge Engineering Review, 19*(1), 1-25.

Re, R., Braga, R., & Masiero, P. (2001). A pattern language for online auctions management. In *Proceedings of the 8ᵗʰ Conference on Pattern Languages of Programs (PLoP2001)*, Illinois, USA.

Resnick, P., & Zeckhauser, R. (2002). Trust among strangers in Internet transactions: Empirical analysis of eBay's reputation system. In M. Baye (Ed.), *Advances in applied microeconomics, 11* (pp. 77-106).

Weiss, M. (2003). Pattern-driven design of agent systems: Approach and case study. In *Proceedings of the 15ᵗʰ Conference on Advanced Information Systems Engineering (CAISE'03)*, Velden, Austria.

Yu, E. (1995). *Modelling strategic relationships for process reengineering.* PhD thesis, Deptartment of Computer Science, University of Toronto, Canada.

Yu, E. (1997). Why agent-oriented requirements engineering. In *Proceedings of 3rd International Workshop on Requirements Engineering: Foundations for Software Quality*, Barcelona, Spain.

Yu, E. (2001). Agent-oriented modelling: Software versus the world. In *Proceedings of the Agent-Oriented Software Engineering AOSE-2001 Workshop*. Berlin: Springer Verlag.

Endnote

[1]   The issue of trust between buyers and sellers in online auctions is an often treated topic in economics research (see, e.g., Pinker, Seidmann, & Vakrat, 2001).

Chapter VI

Implementing Seller Agent in Multiple Online Auctions

Patricia Anthony, Universiti Malaysia Sabah, Malaysia

Abstract

Online auctions are becoming extremely popular because of the convenience that it offers to the consumers. Much work has been done in designing bidding strategy that can be utilized by bidders who want to participate in online auctions. However, very little work has been done on the seller's strategy for online auctions. In any online auction, the final selling price of the item is unknown until the auction closes. This price is dependent on several factors such as the number of bidders participating in the auction, how much each bidder is willing to pay for the product, how many online auctions are selling the same item as well as the duration of each auction. Each item to be auctioned off has a reserved price set by the seller. Setting the reserved price too high for the item will result in the item not being sold and setting the price too low may result in profit reduction or even loss. Deciding on the reserved price of an item to be auctioned off is not a straightforward decision. This chapter reports on a preliminary implementation of a seller agent that recommends a reserved price for a given item to be auctioned off by the seller. The seller agent's objective is to suggest a reservation price that guarantees the sale of the item within a given period (as required by the seller) with a profit.

Introduction

Online auctions are one of the most popular and effective ways of trading goods over the Internet (Bapna, Goes, & Gupta 2001). Thousands of items are sold at online auctions everyday that ranges from books, toys, computer, antiques and even services. As an example, eBay the largest online auction house, has more than 220 million registered users today, and in the year 2006 alone, its consolidated net revenue was USD$6.0 billion (eBay, 2007). On any given day, there are more than 78 million items listed on eBay and approximately 6 million listings are added per day. It also has local sites that serve countries such as Australia, Austria, Belgium, China, Malaysia and many others. People spend more time on eBay than any other online site making it the most popular shopping destination on the Internet. This clearly shows that online auctions are attracting a lot of consumers and generating huge revenue to the net economy.

The practice of auctioning goods has been popular throughout the years because auctions are an extremely effective way of allocating resources to the individuals who value them most highly (Reynolds, 1996). Many of the geographical and temporal limitations of the traditional auctions are removed (Lucking-Reiley, 2000). Specifically, the consumers can be sitting in the comfort of their home while participating in an online auction that may be located many thousands of miles away. Moreover, online auctions generally last for days and weeks giving the bidders more flexibility about when to submit bids. Online auctions also allow sellers to sell their goods efficiently and with little action or effort required. Apart from that, sellers have fewer problems of getting a large group of bidders together within short notice because of the availability of the large number of online bidders distributed across the globe. This creates a larger market for the goods on sale. In summary, online auctions provide a selection of goods that Internet communities can buy or sell, allowing consumers a greater chance of getting their goods and the sellers a greater chance of selling their goods.

The type of auction dictates how the auction should be conducted. There are many types of auctions but the common ones are English, Dutch, first price sealed bid and second priced sealed bid auction. In the traditional English auction, participants bid openly against each other. The auctioneer starts with the lowest acceptable price and proceeds to solicit successively higher bids from customers until no one will increase the bid. The item is then sold to the highest bidder (Klemperer, 1999). In online auctions, each item being auctioned is associated with an auction duration.

The winner for this auction is only announced at the end of the auction and is the one with the highest bid. The highest bidder pays for the item according to the bid submitted.

The Dutch auction is the opposite of the English auction. The bidding starts at a high price and is progressively lowered until a buyer claims the item by calling "mine" or by pressing a buttons that stops an automatic clock (Klemperer, 1999). This is slightly different from the Dutch auctions that are used in online auction where sellers have many identical items to sell (eBay, 2005a). This variation of the Dutch auction is referred to as the multi-unit English ascending auction. The first price sealed bid auction is conducted by getting all the bidders to simultaneously submit bids without knowing what the others bid. The winner is the one with the highest bid and he pays the item according to the bid submitted. The second price sealed bid auction is very similar to the first price sealed bid auction. It is also known as Vickrey auction (Vickrey, 1961). The winner is the one with the highest bid but he pays the second highest bid.

Online auction is a method that is based upon competition, in which a buyer wants to pay as little as necessary and a seller wants to obtain as much money as possible. To date, much work has been done on designing bidding strategy that can be utilized by bidders who want to participate in online auctions with the goal of obtaining the item within a certain time period and at the lowest price possible. In the bidder's context, the purpose of participating in online auctions is to try and purchase a given item at a desired price. To ensure that this objective is fulfilled, the bidder has to possess a bidding strategy that will take into account the number of online auctions that are currently selling the item, the current price for the item in each individual auction, the number of bidders participating in each auction and the auction type used in each auction (different auction type requires different bidding strategy). Based on this information, the bidder strategy should suggest which auction to participate in and a series of bids that should be placed by the user in the selected auctions at different points in time. Some of the notable work in designing bidding strategy uses various techniques such as the possibility-based approach (Gimenez-Funes, Godo, & Rodriguez-Aguilar, 1998), the belief-based model (Preist, 2001), the optimal dynamic programming model (Byde, 2001), a probabilistic approach (Dumas, Governatori, Hofstede, & Russell, 2002) and a combination of genetic algorithm and a rule based approach (Anthony & Jennings, 2003).

On the other hand, very little work has been done in designing a seller strategy for online auctions. From the seller's perspective, the objective of participating in online auctions is to sell an item. The seller wishing to sell an item needs to register in an online auction, provide details about the item to be sold and suggest a reserved price for that item. The reserved price is defined as the minimum price that the seller is willing to accept for the item. In the instance where the item is auctioned off at a price lower than the reserved price, the seller can refuse to sell the item. In this case, the item can be put up for auction again (perhaps with a lower reserved price). The selling process may take sometime, since auctions usually last for weeks and even months. To make matters worse, auctioned items with a closing price less than the reserved price need to be re-auctioned again resulting in a longer selling time. This process of re-evaluating reserved price and re-auctioning unsold items is time consuming.

Selecting which auction to sell the item is another important issue. Consider this scenario: Seller XXX wants to sell item X with a reserved price of $100.00 and trades it in auction A. Seller YYY wants to sell item X with a reserved price $100.00 and trades it in auction B. Auction A's closing price is $150.00 whereas Auction B's closing price is $95.00. In the first case, seller XXX succeeded in selling the item with a profit margin of $50.00 whereas seller YYY is unable to sell item X since the closing price is lower than the item's reserved price. If seller YYY had traded his item in auction A, he would have succeeded in selling his item. In this case, the selection of auctions plays an important role in ensuring that an item can be sold at the desired price.

Apart from that, deciding on the reserved price of an item is also critical in ensuring that the item can be sold off. Determining a reserved price in an auction can be tricky since items that are sold in online auctions can be categorized into three types, namely new, used and reconditioned. A new item will definitely be more expensive than a used item or a reconditioned item. The price of the used item is dependent upon condition of the item. The determination of the reserved price of an item is also affected by the desperateness of the seller. If the seller's intention is to get rid of the item, a lower pricing strategy may be acceptable, but if the seller's intention is to obtain a profit, then a higher pricing strategy is inevitable. The number of competitors is another determinant to the pricing mechanism for the sellers. The price would be higher if there are a few identical items being auctioned. However, if there are a lot of identical items on sale, the seller may be forced to sell the item at a lower price.

The reserved price of the item can also be determined by the number of bidders that are interested in the item. If there is a huge demand for the item, the seller can mark up the item's reserved price. However, if the number of bidders requiring the item is small, then the item should be priced at a reasonably low value to ensure that the item can be sold off. As mentioned earlier, the main thing for the seller is to gain as much profit as possible. In auction, this can be translated to deciding the best reserved price for the item.

In this particular scenario, the main problem is to determine the value of the reserved price that the seller should impose on the item to ensure that the item is sold at a given time with the possibility of earning a profit. This decision is not a straightforward one because the auction environment is very complex, dynamic and unpredictable making it very difficult to come up with a single optimal value for the seller (Byde, Preist, & Jennings, 2002). To address this shortcoming, we believe that it is necessary to develop an autonomous agent that is capable of making its own decision based on the available information. In more detail, the agent should monitor and collect information from the ongoing and completed auctions, make decisions on the reserved price of the item being sold on behalf of the customer and endeavors to guarantee that the item will be sold at the stipulated time with the best price.

To this end, this chapter reports on our work in developing a seller agent that makes pricing decisions on behalf of the seller. The seller agent's decision takes into account several constraints such as the given time in which the item should be sold, the competitors' information, and whether the seller is looking for a profit. The suggested reserved price is computed by combining these three constraints. Each constraint will suggest a price in isolation and these prices are then given a weighted combination according to their importance as requested by the seller.

The chapter advances the state of the art in the following way. First, we develop a high level decision making framework for an agent to determine the item's reserved price based on the user preferences. Secondly, the pricing strategy that we are proposing takes into account the dynamic nature of online auctions by updating the auctions information and makes a future prediction for the ongoing auctions. This information is used in the decision making model of the seller agent.

The remainder of the chapter is structured in the following manner: In the next section, we describe our electronic marketplace scenario in which our algorithms are evaluated followed by the description of the fundamentals of the bidding algorithm, and our initial experimental results. The last two sections discuss related work and conclusions, and further work.

The Electronic Marketplace (RoboSAR)

The simulated electronic marketplace consists of a number of English auctions that run concurrently. These auctions have a finite start time and duration generated randomly from a uniform probability distribution. Each auction also has a reservation price for the item being sold. The start and end times vary from one auction to another. At the start of each auction, a group of random bidders are generated to simulate other auction participants. These participants operate in a single auction and have the intention of buying the target item and possessing certain behavior. They maintain information about the item they wish to purchase, their private valuation of the item (the maximum amount that they are willing to pay for the desired item), the starting bid value and their bid increment. These values are generated randomly from a standard probability distribution. In the auction, they initiate bidding at their starting bid value; when making a counter offer, they add their bid increment to the current offer (provided the total is less than their private valuation), and they stop bidding when they acquire the item or when their private valuation is reached.

The English auction starts with a predefined starting value: a small value. Offers and counter offers are accepted from bidders that are picked randomly from the pool of bidders in that particular auction. These processes are repeated until either the private valuation or the end time for that auction is reached. The winner is the bidder with the highest bid value at the end of the auction. An item will remain unsold if the highest price offered is less than the item's reservation price and it will be re-auctioned again. The marketplace is flexible and can be configured to run any number of auctions and operate for any length of discrete time. We assume that all auctions in the marketplace are auctioning similar items that the sellers are interested in selling.

The marketplace is a virtual simulation in that it is supposed to represent all the auctions that are selling the desired item anywhere on the Internet. It is obviously a simplification, since by grouping them in this way we can focus on the agent's selling strategy (our main aim) and we do not have to worry about the (very important and difficult) problems of finding all the auctions that sell the desired item, semantic interoperability due to heterogeneous information models and ontologies, latency due to network traffic variability, or interfacing our software to proprietary commercial auction houses.

Designing the Seller's Strategy

Before we describe the proposed seller's strategy, there are several assumptions that we have made. Firstly, it is assumed that the item to be sold is used or reconditioned. We do not consider new items since the price of a new item can be easily obtained from a fixed online store. Secondly, we assume that the outcome of an auction can be one of two possibilities: if the highest bid at the end of the auction exceeds the reserved price for that item, then a transaction will take place. However, if the highest bid does not exceed the item's reserved price, then there is no transaction, as no winner will be declared for that auction. Thirdly, we assume that bidders have their own reservation price and this value reflects their true valuation of the item. Finally, we assume that our seller agent has access to important information in RoboSAR such as the list of auctions that are ongoing and completed, the closing price for each auction and whether the item is sold or not.

To ensure that the seller is able to sell the item at a given time and at a profit, it needs to possess a strategy that takes into account several constraints. These constraints (referred to as the selling constraints) are the determinants to the recommended reserved price for a given item to be sold by the seller. The constraints being considered here are the sell period (a time frame in which the seller wishes to dispose the item), the number of competitors and the desire for a profit. The seller is required to state his preferences by indicating the date by which he must sell the item as well as the amount of profit that he wishes to obtain (in percentage) and whether competitors need to be considered. The seller agent considers these constraints and combines it with the analysis of the available information obtained from the electronic marketplace to generate the recommended reservation price based on the preferences indicated by the seller.

In the marketplace, we categorize the online auctions into three groups, namely the successful auctions (completed auctions that succeed in disposing the item being sold), the failed auctions (completed auctions but unable to sell the item) and the ongoing auctions (auctions that have started but are not completed yet). The relationship among these three criteria is shown in Figure 3. Analysis of the available information can be conducted at any point in time and takes into account the three groups of auctions. First, we will present our notation.

Successful Auctions

Let α be the number of auctions that have completed successful and let β be the closing price for the each of the auctions that has completed successfully. Let ASP_v be the **A**verage **P**rice for the **S**uccessful auctions, and is defined as the division of the summation of the ending prices by the number of successful auctions in the marketplace.

Figure 1. Successful, failed, and ongoing auctions

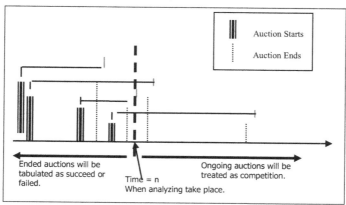

$$ASP_v = \frac{\sum \beta_i}{\alpha} \tag{1}$$

Let ϕ_i be the duration for each of the auctions that has completed successfully. Let ASD_v be the Average number of Days for Successful auctions. This is calculated by summing up the durations of all the successful auctions and dividing it by the number of successful auctions.

$$ASD_v = \frac{\sum \phi_i}{\alpha} \tag{2}$$

Failed Auctions

Let σ be the number of failed auctions and let δ_i be the highest bid value for the individual auctions that did not complete successfully. Let AFP_v be the Average Price for the Failed auctions. It is defined as the summation of all of the maximum prices for the failed auctions divided by the total number of failed auctions.

$$AFP_v = \frac{\sum \delta_i}{\sigma} \tag{3}$$

Let χ_i be the duration for the individual failed auction. Let AFD_v be the Average number of Days for Failed auctions. This is defined as the summation of the duration of all the failed auctions divided by the total number of failed auctions.

$$AFD_v = \frac{\sum \chi_i}{\sigma} \tag{4}$$

Ongoing Auctions

Ongoing auctions cannot be excluded from the analysis, hence to compensate for this, we calculate the estimated price for the successful auctions and the estimated price for the failed auctions. Let ESP_v be the Estimated Price for the auction that is expected to complete Successfully. This is defined as:

$$ESP_v = \lambda_i + (\frac{\eta_i}{ASD_V} \times ASP_v) \tag{5}$$

where λ_i is the current bid value of a particular auction and η_i is the number of days left for that particular auction to complete.

Let κ be the number of ongoing auctions. The ESP_v is calculated for every individual ongoing auction, therefore the $AESP_v$ is defined as the summation of the estimated prices for all the auctions that are expected to complete successfully.

$$AESP_v = \frac{\sum ESP_v}{\kappa} \tag{6}$$

Similarly the EFP_v is defined as the estimated price for a particular auction that is expected to fail.

$$EFP_v = \lambda_i + \left(\frac{\eta_i}{AFD_V} \times AFP_v \right) \tag{7}$$

And finally, the average estimated failed price for all the auctions that are unsuccessful is defined as:

$$AEFP_v = \frac{\sum EFP_v}{\kappa} \tag{8}$$

The Sell Period Function

The sell period function generates a single price that is based on the sell period requested by the seller. This price can be easily generated by looking at the past transaction history as well as the ongoing auction. Let f_{sp} be the function that will suggest the price based on the sell period and is defined as:

$$f_{sp} = \frac{ASP_v * duration\_required}{ASD_v} \tag{9}$$

The Competitors Function

The number of competitors that are selling the same item in the same marketplace needs to be considered as well, since this directly affects the pricing of the items. A small number of competitors will suggest a higher pricing and more competitors implies a lower price. Assume that n is the number of competitors in a given auction. Let f_{co} be the function to determine a single price based on the competitors information. f_{co} is then calculated as:

$$f_{co}(n) = p(n) \tag{10}$$

where p is the average price for a given number of competitors. This average price is calculated by taking the average of all the prices for the same number of competitors in all the auctions including the ongoing auctions.

The Profit Function

The profit function f_{pr} generates a single price based on how much profit is required by the seller. Computing the price for this function is done in two stages. Firstly, the actual recommended price, p_{in} is computed, then this price is inflated according to the percentage of profit that the seller wishes to obtain. p_{in} is computed in the following manner:

$$p_{in} = \frac{\sum \beta_i + \sum ESP_v}{\alpha + \kappa} \tag{11}$$

f_{pr} is then computed as follows:

$$f_{pr} = (1.00 + PP) * p_{in} \tag{12}$$

Generating the Final Reservation Price

At any given time, the agent may consider any of the selling constraints individually, or it may combine them depending on the seller's preferences. In this work, if the agent combines multiple selling constraints, it allocates a weight to denote their relative importance. Thus, let ω_j be the weight on constraint j where $\forall j \in Selling\_Constraint$, $0 \le w_j \le 1$, and $\sum w_j = 1$. The final reservation price is then calculated as:

$$p_v = \sum w_j f_j \tag{13}$$

Experimental Evaluation

To evaluate the performance of the seller agent, we performed an empirical evaluation. We ran the experiments in an environment where there are a total number of 20 auctions running and each auction has between 2 and 10 participants. The participants use the optimal (dominant) strategies to their respective one-shot auctions. The marketplace was run for 20 time steps and at $t = 10$, we recorded all the successful, failed and ongoing auctions and these are shown in Table 1, 2 and 3. It can

Table 1. Successful auctions

No.	Duration	End Price
1	8	68
2	7	74
3	8	81
4	7	75
5	8	74
6	7	80
7	7	68

Table 2. Failed auctions

No.	Duration	Highest Bid
1	7	84
2	7	84
3	7	87
4	9	89
5	9	85

Table 3. Ongoing auctions

No.	Time Left	Current Bid
1	5	31
2	3	56
3	3	43
4	3	36
5	5	25
6	3	44
7	4	39
8	1	69

be observed that the closing price for the successful auctions is much lower than the failed auctions' highest bids. This is because the seller has put up a high reservation price for the item being sold. As a result, the highest bid at the end of the auctions are still lower than the item's reservation price. Hence, the item is not sold.

The calculations of ASP_v, ASD_v, AFP_v, AFD_v, and ESP_v, are shown below.

$$ASP_v = \frac{520}{7} = 74.29$$

$$ASD_v = \frac{52}{7} = 7.43$$

$$ASF_v = \frac{339}{5} = 67.80$$

$$AFD_v = \frac{39}{5} = 7.80$$

The next step is to calculate the ESP_v and EFP_v for each of the ongoing items and this is shown in Table 4.

The $AESP_v$ and the $AEFP_v$ are calculated as follows:

$$AESP_v = \frac{614}{8} = 76.75$$

Table 4. The calculated ESP_v and EFP_v

No.	Time Left	Current Bid	ESP_v	EFP_v
1	5	35	79.00	84.00
2	3	56	85.00	88.00
3	3	50	74.00	77.00
4	3	49	66.00	69.00
5	5	32	77.00	82.00
6	3	49	74.00	77.00
7	4	35	80.00	84.00
8	1	66	79.00	80.00

$$AEFP_v = \frac{641}{8} = 80.13$$

It can be observed from the results obtained that the estimated failed price ($AEFP_v$) is a lot higher than the estimated success price ($AESP_v$). Thus, seller should try to select a reservation price between 66 and 79 for the item to ensure a sale. This is because putting up a reservation price of 80 or more would most likely result in the item not being auctioned off.

To compute the actual reservation price that will be recommended by the seller agent, we consider the three selling constraints. Here we assume that the seller wants to sell Item A within 7 days, and that he is interested in a 2% profit and that information about competitors is very important to him. The seller also values the profit more than the competitors or the selling period. The calculation is as follow:

$$f_{sp} = \frac{74.29 * 7}{7.43} = 70.00$$

$$f_{co}(4) = 72.73$$

Assume here, that there is a table that will generate the average value for prices that are dependent on the total number of competitors.

$$p_{in} = \frac{520 + 614}{7 + 8} = 69.33$$

$$f_{pr} = (1.00 + 0.02) * 69.33 = 70.72$$

And finally, the recommended reservation price for the item being auctioned is:

$$p_v = 0.20(70.00) + 0.50(72.73) + 0.30(70.72)$$

$$p_v = 71.18$$

In this particular example, the seller highly values the competition, followed by the profit, and the selling time is considered as the least important. The recommended reservation price obtained falls in the range of the estimated selling price in which if the auction ends successfully, the seller will obtain a 3% profit (from the recommended price) which is higher than the seller's preference of 2%. If the seller chose only the competitor constraint, then a higher profit can be obtained.

We ran another set of experiments to validate the reliability of the recommended reservation price. To perform this experiment, we set the marketplace to run for 20 time steps, and chose an auction randomly (from those that are running for a duration of 7 time steps) for the seller agent to participate. The reservation price for the item to be auctioned off is set to 71, which is the recommended reservation price. For each auction run, we checked whether the particular auction that the seller has participated in resulted in a sale or not. If the auction is successful, the closing price is recorded. Unsuccessful auctions are those auctions with a closing price lower than the reservation price. This experiment was repeated for 20 runs and the results are summarized in Table 5.

It can be seen from the table that the agent was able to sell the item 75% of the time. The seller agent also obtained an average of 12% profit for the sale of the item. This profit is more than the required profit that was initially specified by the seller. However, the profit obtained is dependent on which particular auction is selected and the types of bidders that are participating in that auction. The result obtained confirmed that the seller has the edge over the other competitors if the reservation price is known in advanced. The number of unsuccessful auctions could also be minimized if the seller can predict ahead of time which auctions have the potential to complete successfully.

Related Work

There have been several attempts to design sophisticated and efficient bidding strategies for agents participating in online auctions. However, very little work is ongoing for seller's strategy. The work on developing seller agent was drawn from previous work conducted by other researchers in the development of bidder agents. Anthony and Jennings (2003) developed a heuristic decision-making framework that an autonomous agent can exploit to tackle the problem of bidding across multiple auctions with varying protocols. In this particular environment, three auctions protocols are considered: English, Dutch and Vickrey. All auctions have a known start time and English and Vickrey auctions have a known end time. The bidding agent is given a deadline by when it must obtain the desired item, it is told the consumer's private valuation and it must not buy more than one instance of the desired item.

Dumas et al. (2000; 2000) address the issue of developing autonomous agents capable of participating on behalf of the user in several potentially simultaneous auctions, with the goal of achieving the best price for a single item. The agents participate in several auction houses that run first-price sealed bids, Vickrey and

Table 5. Seller agent's auction results

Run No.	Closing Price	Profit
1	unsuccessful	
2	74	3
3	unsuccessful	
4	80	9
5	85	14
6	82	11
7	82	11
8	77	6
9	81	10
10	unsuccessful	
11	86	15
12	90	19
13	74	3
14	79	8
15	unsuccessful	
16	unsuccessful	
17	74	3
18	80	9
19	75	4
20	74	3

English auctions. Each auction is assumed to be for a single unit of item and has a fixed deadline. It is also assumed that the outcomes of the auctions are available immediately after their deadlines. The proposed architecture is a multi-agent system in which a manager agent cooperates with several expert agents. The manager agent has information about the user's constraints and preferences and it cooperates with multiple expert agents. Each expert agent specializes in a specific kind of auction for a type of item within a given auction house. Based on the feedback of the expert agents combined with a probability function, the manager agent will generate a bidding plan and this plan may be revised from time to time depending on the current situations at hand.

The Decision Procedures for Multiple Auctions is a decision theoretic framework that an autonomous agent can use to bid effectively across multiple simultaneous auctions (Byde, Preist, & Jennings, 2002). This decision-theoretic framework combines probability theory with utility theory to give a general theory that can distinguish good actions from bad ones (Russell & Norvig, 1995). It is assumed that the users are interested in purchasing multiple items and have private valuations for each item. The auctions have varying start time and end times and they embody different protocols. The auctions considered are English, Dutch, first-price sealed bid and Vickrey. The main concern here is that a rational agent should choose to bid in a given auction if the expected return from the future is greater than the expected return from the future if the agent does not bid.

Bagchi et al. (2000) provided an algorithmic approach to the study of online auctioning. They designed an algorithmic strategy that fairly maximizes the revenue earned by selling a number of identical items to bidders who submit bids online. However, this work is slightly different from ours in that we are interested in coming up with an ideal reserved price for a given item rather than to multiple items. The Optimal Strategy for Sellers considers an online auction setting where the seller attempts to sell an item (Guo, 2002). Bids arrive over time and the seller has to make an instant decision whether to accept the bid and close the auction or reject it and move on to the next bid, with the hope of higher gains. This strategy uses techniques from convex analysis to provide an explicit closed-form optimal solution for the seller. This work focuses on one particular form of auction that is the allocation of communication network bandwidth by a network manager. Here, the bidders arrive at a different time and state the price they are willing to pay for the bandwidth. The network manager has to make an instant decision whether to accept the bid or not to accept the bid. This setting is different from the auction set up discussed in this work.

Jank, Shmueli and Wang (2006) derived a model for forecasting the final price of ongoing online auctions. They used modern functional data analysis methods that take into account the price velocity, and the price acceleration. It was noted that there are three typical features of online data auction data that are unequally spaced bids, the limited time horizon and the dynamics of bidding change drastically over time. In this research, they were able to achieve a high forecasting accuracy and were able to accommodate for the dynamic price changing of auctions. There is a possibility that this model can be used to replace the simple predicting technique discussed in this chapter.

Conclusion and Future Work

This chapter presented a selling strategy that can be used by a seller agent to recommend the reservation price for a given item with the objective of disposing the item at a given period of time as well as obtaining a profit from the sale of the item. The experimental evaluation showed that the proposed selling strategy can guarantee that the item is auctioned off with a profit. This framework is flexible enough to allow any additional constraints to be added to the existing ones. The strategy will be refined further to improve the performance of the the seller agent. Some of the techniques that will be explored include genetic algorithm, fuzzy logic and machine learning. This will enable the seller agent to be more adaptive and receptive to the existing environment and to address the complexity and dynamic of the online auction environments.

In this chapter, we have chosen to assume that there is a lookup table that is readily available. However, in reality, we have to come up with a more realistic function for competitors that will suggest values depending on the number of competitors and the type of the item being auctioned. The placement of the item in different auctions requires further investigation, since placing two identical items in two different auctions does not necessarily produce the same result as discussed in the introduction section. Another area that requires further investigation is the ability to accurately predict the outcome of each auction. In our work, we did not try to predict the outcome of the auction but we proposed a way to calculate the range of pricing that makes use of the average successful auction and average failed auction. The marketplace will be expanded by including other auction protocols (such as Dutch and sealed bid auctions), apart from English auctions to further test the efficiency of our strategy in many different conditions.

References

Anthony, P., & Jennings, N. (2003). Developing a bidding agent for multiple heterogeneous auctions. *ACM Transactions on Internet Technology, 3*(3), 185-217.

Bagchi, A, Chaudhary, A., Garg, R., Goodrich, M., & Kumar, V. (2000). *Seller-focused algorithms for online auctioning.* (LNCS 2125, pp. 135-146).

Byde, A. (2001). Programming model for algorithm design in simultaneous auctions. In *Proceedings of the 2nd International workshop on Electronic Commerce* (pp. 152-163), New York, USA.

Byde, A., Preist, C., & Jennings, F. (2002). Decision procedures for multiple auctions. In *Proceedings of The First International Joint Conference on Autonomous Agents and MultiAgent Systems, Part II* (pp. 613-620).

Dumas, M., Aldred, L., Governatori, G., Hofstede, A., & Russell, N. (2000). A probabilistic approach to automated bidding in alternative auctions. In *Proceedings of The Eleventh International Conference on the World Wide Web* (pp. 99-108).

Dumas, M., Governatori, G., Hofstede, A., & Russell, N. (2000). An architecture for assembling agents that participate in alternative heterogeneous auctions. In *Proceedings of the Workshop on Research Issues in Data Engineering* (pp. 75-83).

eBay. (2007). eBay Inc. announces fourth quarter 2006 and full year 2006 financial results. Retrieved from http://files.shareholder.com/downloads/ebay/BayInc-EarningsRelea-seQ42006.pdf

Gimenez-Funes, E., Godo, L., & Rodriguez Aguilar, J. (1998). Possibilistic-based design of bidding strategies in electronic auctions. In *Proceedings of the Thirteenth Biennial European Conference on Artificial Intelligence* (pp. 575-579). Chichester, UK.

Guo, X. (2002). An optimal strategy for sellers in an online auction. *ACM Transactions of Internet Technology, 2*(1), 1-13.

Jank W, Shmueli, G., & Wang, S. (2006). Dynamic, real-time forecasing of online auction via functional models. In *Proceedings of the Twelfth ACM SIGKDD International Conference On Knowledge Discovery and Data Mining (KDD 2006)* (pp. 580-585). Philadephia.

Klemperer, P. (1999). Auction theory: A guide to literature. *Journal of Economic Surveys 13(3)*, 227-286.

Lucking-Reiley, D. (2000). Auctions on the Internet: What's being auctioned, and how? *Journal of Industrial Economics, 48*(3), 227-252.

Preist, C., Bartolini, C., & Phillips, I. (2001). Algorithm design for agents which participate in multiple simultaneous auctions. *Agent Mediated E-Commerce* (pp. 139-154). Berlin: Springer-Verlag.

Reynolds, K. (1996). Auctions going, going, gone! A survey of auction types. Retrieved from http://www.agorics.com/Library/autions.html

Russell, S., & Norvig, P. (1995). *Artificial intelligence: A modern approach.* NJ: Prentice Hall International Editions.

Vickrey, W. (1961). Counterspeculation, auctions and competitive sealed bid tenders. *Journals of Finance, 16,* 8-3.

Chapter VII

The Importance of Interface Agent Characteristics from the End-User Perspective

Alexander Serenko, Lakehead University, Canada

Abstract

This chapter reports on an empirical investigation of user perceptions of the importance of several characteristics of interface agents. Interface agents are software entities that are incorporated into various computer applications including electronic mail systems. As evidenced by the growing body of empirical studies and the increasing number of interface agent-based applications on the software market, there is a strong need for the development of this technology. According to a meta-review of agent-related literature by Dehn and van Mulken (2000), there are several characteristics of interface agents that require special attention from agent developers. However, prior to this study, the importance of these characteristics from the end-user perspective remained unclear. In order to identify the significance of these characteristics, a group of the actual users of an e-mail interface agent was surveyed. The results indicate that information accuracy and the degree of the usefulness of an agent are the most salient factors, followed by user comfortability with an agent, the extent of user enjoyment, and visual attractiveness of an agent. The implications of the findings for both theory and practice are discussed.

Introduction

To create an artificial being has been a dream of men since the birth of science.

Professor Hobby (William Hurt),

Artificial Intelligence by Spielberg 2002 (Spielberg, 2002)

For thousands of years, people have thought of someone doing basic tasks for them. That could be a robot, a cyborg, or a well-trained pet. Not until the beginning of the twenty-first century had it become possible. Now, with the recent development of telecommunications networks and computer technologies, a new type of software application plays the role of virtual assistants that may potentially alleviate some of the problems associated with the employment of software systems. This class of applications is often referred to as intelligent agents, software agents, avatars, or interface agents. As demonstrated by the growing body of academic literature and by the increasing number of agent-based software applications on the market, there is increased interest in the creation of such software entities. In this chapter, these software systems are labeled as interface agents.

Interface agents emerged from the recent developments in the field of intelligent agents. The idea of software agents was first introduced by John McCarthy (1956; 1958) and later coined by the MIT Lincoln Laboratory computer scientist Oliver Selfridge. In the eighties, this concept was explored by agent visionaries such as Marvin Minsky and Alan Kay and further utilized in the recent classic works of Pattie Maes, Nicolas Negroponte, Jeffrey Bradshaw, Hyacinth Nwana, and Divine Ndumu. The past decade has witnessed the rapid development of prototypes and working models of intelligent agents, many of which are already incorporated in end-user commercial applications. A number of recent studies demonstrate the fruitfulness and viability of using agent-based technologies in various areas, for example, in automatic negotiation (Castro-Schez, Jennings, Luo, & Shadbolt, 2004; Fatima, Wooldridge, & Jennings, 2005), natural-language customer support services (J. Lester, Branting, & Mott, 2004), education (Takacs, 2005), and user notification systems (Horvitz, Kadie, Paek, & Hovel, 2003). Some academics have shifted their research from human-agent interaction to human-agent cooperation (Rickel & Johnson, 2000; Rickel et al., 2002) and man-machine symbiosis (Lesh, Rich, & Sidner, 1999; Klein, Woods, Bradshaw, Hoffman, & Feltovich, 2004; Lesh, Marks,

Rich, & Sidner, 2004) when the human user and the software agent collaborate towards achieving shared goals.

In terms of this chapter, an interface agent is defined as an autonomous (i.e., independent), continuous (i.e., long-lived), reactive (i.e., it monitors an external environment and reacts to any changes), and collaborative (i.e., it cooperates with other software processes or agents) software entity that exhibits strong visual or audio presence in the computer interface and that communicates with a user directly (i.e., by bypassing intermediaries) (Lieberman & Selker, 2003; Detlor, 2004; Serenko & Detlor, 2004; Serenko, Ruhi, & Cocosila, 2007). "Interface agents draw their strength from the naturalness of the living-organism metaphor in terms of both cognitive accessibility and communication style" (Laurel, 1997, p. 68). Typically, interface agents are personalizable and implemented in the form of human-like or cartoon-like animated characters, electronic figures, graphical user interfaces, textual boxes, or any other visual components (Godoy, Schiaffino, & Amandi, 2004; Schiaffinoa & Amandi, 2004; Serenko, 2007).

Having the available agent technology is insufficient; it should also be accepted and utilized appropriately by its target users. For the past ten years, there have been various attempts to understand what people like or dislike in interface agents, and why they adopt or reject them. The goal of this stream of research is to develop a valid, complete list of characteristics that interface agents should possess that would warrant the end-user acceptance of this technology.

By performing a meta-analysis of the human-computer interaction literature, Dehn and van Mulken (2000) presented a comprehensive, yet exhaustive, list of characteristics of interface agents that may potentially influence the human-interface agent interaction process. Most of these characteristics are drawn from various independent investigations conducted in laboratory settings. At the same time, no study reports how real-life users value the characteristics of an interface agent-based technology. In order to bridge that void, the present investigation attempts to solicit and analyze the opinions of interface agent users on several key characteristics of the technology. It is assumed that this information may potentially improve the quality of the technology and the way it is delivered to the customer. For example, if agent manufacturers could know what interface agent characteristics are more or less important for users, they would be able to concentrate their short-term efforts to improve positive user perception of these characteristics. This, in turn, might increase user satisfaction with agent-based technology and accelerate the rate of innovation diffusion.

As such, Dehn and van Mulken (2000) classified the various characteristics of interface agents, for example, user subjective experience of the system, user behavior while interacting with the system, and the outcome of the interaction. Each category includes several factors. However, it is not viable to investigate the importance of these characteristics applied to all types of interface agents in a single project.

Since interface agents may be incorporated in the form Web guides, shopping or electronic commerce companions (McBreen & Jack, 2001; Lieberman & Wagner, 2003), virtual tutors in interactive learning environments (J. C. Lester et al., 1997; Johnson, Rickel, & Lester, 2000; Person et al., 2000; Gulz, 2004), storytellers (Cavazza, Charles, & Mead, 2002), presenters, virtual actors (Hornby & Pollack, 2001; Miranda, Kögler, Hernandez, & Netto, 2001), application assistants (Serenko, Bontis & Detlor, 2007) or entertainers (Gebhard, Kipp, Klesen, & Rist, 2003), a separate study is required for each kind of interface agents. It is believed that interface agents embedded in different types of software environments may require certain system-specific features and facets. For example, users who work with an interface agent that facilitates online shopping may look for effectiveness and efficiency. In contrast, people who employ an interface agent as entertainers may emphasize the aspect of enjoyment over that of effectiveness or efficiency.

With respect to the present study, interface agents for electronic mail were chosen for two reasons. First, e-mail is an important telecommunications medium that is heavily utilized by both individuals and organizations. However, today's e-mail systems provide inadequate support for constantly changing user needs, fail to convey ambiguous content and human emotions, overload people with continually growing flows of unstructured information, and exhibit an inefficient direct manipulation interface. For example, Dow et al. (2006) report that the level of user satisfaction with e-mail is lower than that with online shopping or land-line phone services. As a result, many individuals feel frustrated utilizing e-mail. The use of interface agents is a potential solution to the currently challenging task of e-mail management. Second, the software market presents several versions of interface agents that have been delivered to end-users. Currently, most other types of interface agents have been realized in the form of pilot studies, working prototypes, or beta-versions. This identifies the opportunity to reach the actual users of this technology and poll them directly. It is for these reasons interface agents for e-mail were selected.

A review of the general characteristics of interface agents presented by Dehn and van Mulken (2000) allowed identifying several factors that were believed to be applicable to the e-mail environment. Table 1 offers a list of these characteristics. However, little is known about how important these characteristics are for the actual users of e-mail interface agents. As noted by Dehn and van Mulken (2000), the results of the empirical studies that identified these characteristics appear to be mixed and inconsistent.

To bridge this void and to rank the importance of the characteristics above, this study polled the actual users of e-mail interface agents. It was believed that the end-users, who have utilized this technology for a long period of time, may present valid and reliable information that will be of interest to agent researchers and developers. The following research question was proposed:

Table 1. Characteristics of Interface Agents

N	Characteristics
	With respect to interface agents for e-mail, it is important for users to:
1	believe that an interface agent's appearance should correspond to its level of intelligence
2	believe that the information provided by an interface agent is accurate
3	like the appearance of an interface agent
4	feel comfortable with an interface agent
5	perceive an interface agent useful
6	perceive an interface agent enjoyable
7	perceive all interactions with an interface agent as natural
8	avoid being distracted by an interface agent while engaged in important tasks

How important are the characteristics of e-mail interface agents identified in Table 1 from the end-user perspective?

Methodology and Results

In order to answer the study's research question, a survey of current and past users of an interface agent-based application for e-mail was conducted. Despite the extensive work underway in the incorporation of interface agents in e-mail applications, most previous studies and projects have been realized in forms of conceptual discussions, preliminary empirical investigations, and pilot systems

(Lashkari, Metral, & Maes, 1994; Maes, 1994; Florea & Moldovanu, 1996; Gruen, Sidner, Boettner, & Rich, 1999; Bergman, Griss, & Staelin, 2002; Griss et al., 2002 ; Voss, 2004; Dabbish, Kraut, Fussell, & Kiesler, 2005) rather than in end-user products. **E-mail notification applications** are one of the first commercial systems that utilize interface agent technologies in the electronic mail environment. This type of interface agents was chosen to conduct a user survey. Out of all commercially available interface agent systems for e-mail, Blind Bat Software was randomly chosen by the researcher, the executives of the company were approached, and agreement reached. The list of customers who might potentially serve as the study's participants was sent to the researcher. Figure 1 presents a screenshot of the software product.

In order to poll e-mail agent users on their perceptions of the importance of the characteristics of interface agents, a survey instrument was designed. The questionnaire provided basic instructions, a definition of an interface agent for e-mail, and several

Figure 1. E-mail Announcer developed by Blind Bat Software (http://www. blindbat.com)

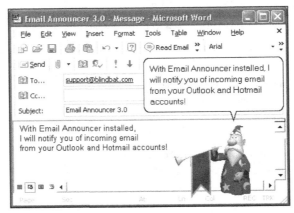

screenshots of the agent developed by Blind Bat. Users were asked to indicate their opinion on perceptions of the importance of agent characteristics outlined in Table 1. Particularly, the question stated: "Based on your experience with interface agents for e-mail, how important is it for you?" After this, eight statements were provided measured on a seven-point Likert-type scale ranging from totally unimportant to very important. In addition, demographic information was solicited. The data for this investigation were collected as part of a larger project conducted by Serenko (2005).

By utilizing the Total Design Method (Dillman, 1999), the four-phase survey process was developed. As such, all respondents were e-mailed an initial request to participate in the study, and three follow-up reminders. Fifty-nine usable responses were obtained. An acceptable response rate was achieved. Note that the actual response rate may not be revealed as per the non-disclosure agreement with Blind Bat Software.

Eighty percent of the surveyed users were male and 20% female. Over 65% of all users were between 31 and 50 years old, and the 46-50 age category was the most frequent user group. Over 1/2 of the respondents were occupied in the information technology sector, most of them were well-educated, financially well-off, and demonstrated a high degree of personal innovativeness in the domain of IT. According to Rogers (2003), this group of people corresponds to innovators, who constitute 2.5% of all people that adopt a particular product or service.

Recall that respondents were asked to rate their perceptions of the importance of eight characteristics of interface agents on a seven-point Likert-type scale. The

Figure 2. User perceptions of the importance of interface agent characteristics

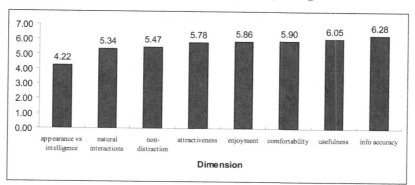

Table 2. User perceptions of the importance of interface agent characteristics

Based on your experience with interface agents for e-mail, how important is it for you to:	Mean	Std dev
believe that the information provided by an interface agent is accurate?	6.28	1.04
perceive an interface agent useful?	6.05	1.13
feel comfortable with an interface agent?	5.90	1.10
perceive an interface agent enjoyable?	5.86	1.13
like the appearance of an interface agent?	5.78	1.17
avoid being distracted by an interface agent while engaged in important tasks?	5.47	1.74
perceive all interactions with an interface agent as natural?	5.34	1.36
believe that an interface agent's appearance should correspond to its level of intelligence?	4.22	1.86

purpose was to understand what characteristics were more or less imperative from the end-user's point of view. Figure 2 visualizes the results, and Table 2 presents the list of questions sorted by the mean.

To analyze whether there were differences in these eight means, the ANOVA test was conducted. The goal of this statistical method is to determine the existence of differences among several population means (Aczel, 1996, p. 358). This technique is an extension of the two-sample t test. The results demonstrated that there was a high degree of confidence that at least some of the means differed from one another (F = 12.846, d.f. between = 7, d.f., within = 456, significance level = 0.000). To measure the practical value of the detected differences, the effect size was calculated as the ratio of sum of squares between to sum of squares total. The effect size was very strong ($\eta^2 = 0.16$).

Table 3. The Tukey Test

(I) CHARACTERISTIC	(J) CHARACTERISTIC	Mean Difference (I-J)	Sig.
1 appearance corresponds to the level of intelligence	2	-2.05(*)	.000
	3	-1.55(*)	.000
	4	-1.67(*)	.000
	5	-1.83(*)	.000
	6	-1.64(*)	.000
	7	-1.12(*)	.000
	8	-1.24(*)	.000
2 information accuracy	1	2.05(*)	.000
	3	.50	.486
	4	.38	.800
	5	.22	.986
	6	.41	.719
	7	.93(*)	.006
	8	.81(*)	.028
3 attractiveness	1	1.55(*)	.000
	2	-.50	.486
	4	-.12	1.000
	5	-.28	.956
	6	-.09	1.000
	7	.43	.674
	8	.31	.920
4 comfortability	1	1.67(*)	.000
	2	-.38	.800
	3	.12	1.000
	5	-.16	.999
	6	.03	1.000
	7	.55	.353
	8	.43	.674
5 usefulness	1	1.83(*)	.000
	2	-.22	.986
	3	.28	.956
	4	.16	.999
	6	.19	.995
	7	.71(*)	.092
	8	.59	.275

continued on following page

Table 3. continued

(I) CHARACTERISTIC	(J) CHARACTERISTIC	Mean Difference (I-J)	Sig.
6 enjoyment	1	1.64(*)	.000
	2	-.41	.719
	3	.09	1.000
	4	-.03	1.000
	5	-.19	.995
	7	.52	.440
	8	.40	.761
7 natural interactions	1	1.12(*)	.000
	2	-.93(*)	.006
	3	-.43	.674
	4	-.55	.353
	5	-.71(*)	.092
	6	-.52	.440
	8	-.12	1.000
8 little distraction	1	1.24(*)	.000
	2	-.81(*)	.028
	3	-.31	.920
	4	-.43	.674
	5	-.59	.275
	6	-.40	.761
	7	.12	1.000

After it was determined that differences existed among the means, the Tukey Honestly Significant Difference test was done by using SPSS. The Tukey post hoc test is a statistical method of pairwise comparisons of the population means. It allows comparing every possible pair of means using a selected single level of significance. The test yielded a matrix where asterisks (*) indicated significantly different group means at an alpha level of 0.1. Table 3 presents the results of mean comparisons.

Based on these results, several statistically significant differences in item means were observed. Overall, the means of the questions positioned on the left-hand-side and right-hand-side of Figure 2 strongly differed from one another. This demonstrated a strong degree of confidence that respondents were able to distinguish among the questions, and that the results presented in Figure 2 were statistically sound.

Discussion and Conclusion

Recall that the purpose of this study was to obtain strong empirical evidence on the importance of interface agent characteristics to bridge the gap in the human-agent interaction literature. The results of the survey showed that trust in an agent (i.e., information accuracy), as well as an agent's utility, (i.e., the persona effect) were the most important factors from the end-user's point of view. They were followed by the degree of conformability and enjoyment with an agent.

First, agent users believed that the accuracy of any information provided by an agent was the most critical factor. This finding is consistent with prior research that points out to the importance of trustworthiness in human-agent interaction (for example, see Hertzum, Andersen, Andersen, & Hansen, 2002; Bickmore & Cassell, 2005; Bickmore & Picard, 2005). Indeed, in order to delegate tasks to an agent, a person must believe that the agent will perform them accurately, and report back the true, rather than desirable, state.

Secondly, respondents indicated the significance of an agent's usefulness. This again, is consistent with prior empirical research and speculations on the importance of the persona effect in agents. The persona effect emerges when an interface agent adds the positive perceptions of usefulness, ease of use, or enjoyment with an existing system. The key outcome of the persona effect is the improvement of existing software applications by embedding interface agents. By emphasizing the importance of an agent's usefulness, subjects demonstrated that value-added services were the key factors influencing their adoption decisions.

Thirdly, perceptions of the importance of comfortability and enjoyment with an agent were also high. The extent to which a user feels comfortable employing an agent partially corresponds to the ease of use of the agent.

Fourthly, items pertaining to non-distraction and the naturalness of interactions received lower scores. Prior work suggests that a user should perceive all interactions with an agent to be natural, and the agent is not supposed to disrupt current user activities. However, this item received a lower score compared with information accuracy, usefulness, comfortability and enjoyment.

Lastly, in contrast to prior research, respondents stated that the appearance of an agent should not necessarily correspond to its level of intelligence. Two assumptions may explain this contradiction. First, highly innovative individuals might wish to utilize an agent which looks maximally intelligent regardless of its actual degree of intelligence. Second, if users were not satisfied with the agent's appearance, they might easily install another one given that there is a variety of cartoon or human-like agent characters available on the Web. Thus, end-users had control over the interface of an agent that reduced their perception of the importance of the agent's appearance.

Other studies that investigated the user experience with interface agents also demonstrate the importance of the accuracy of information and the usefulness of the agent as primary factors. Serenko (2007) reports that MS Office users acknowledge an interface agent's assistance when it helps them complete an important task by acting proactively and reliably. This contradicts attribution theory which states that people tend to give credit to themselves in cases of success. In fact, many users expect software to be generally unreliable, and they value when an agent delivers accurate, timely assistance. At the same time, they want to receive only accurate information from their software agents. Serenko (2006b), who documented a number of critical incidents with e-mail notification interface agents, argues that users tend to discontinue agent usage if it acts unreliably or offers incorrect information. This shows a need for generally reliable agent-based technologies. In line with this, Serenko (2006a) and Serenko et al. (2007) empirically tested two models of user adoption of interface agents for e-mail and concluded that the degree of an agent's usefulness is one of the most parsimonious factors affecting user adoption decisions.

These findings are important for both theory and practice. With respect to theory, the investigation discovered some discrepancies between the view of agent researchers and the opinion of real-life users. With regards to practice, it is suggested that agent designers begin emphasizing the more important characteristics of e-mail interface agents in their products. In the short-term, they need to concentrate their efforts on the development of interface agents that provide accurate and reliable information, and are perceived to be really useful by the end users. After the issues of information accuracy and usefulness are addressed, agent developers may attempt to improve several other characteristics of interface agents. They may improve the degree of user comfortability with the software, increase user enjoyment, and advance the visual appeal of an agent. In the long-term, agent manufacturers may want to decrease the degree of an agent's intrusiveness and facilitate the naturalness of human-agent interactions. However, it is unlikely that they will need to create an interface agent whose appearance would correspond to its level of intelligence. Instead, they should offer a variety of agent interfaces and leave it up to the end users to decide which one to utilize.

Overall, this investigation is one of the first documented attempts to explore the importance of interface agent characteristics by polling the actual users of this technology. The author hopes that other researchers will continue exploring this field that will lead to the creation of really useful interface agents.

References

Aczel, A. (1996). *Complete business statistics*. Chicago: Irwin.

Bergman, R., Griss, M., & Staelin, C. (2002). *A personal e-mail assistant* (Technical Report HPL-2002-236): Hewlett-Packard Company.

Bickmore, T., & Cassell, J. (2005). Social dialogue with embodied conversational agents. In J. van Kuppevelt, L. Dybkjaer, & N. Bernsen (Eds.), *Advances in natural, multimodal dialogue systems*. New York: Kluwer Academic.

Bickmore, T., & Picard, R. (2005). Establishing and maintaining long-term human-computer relationships. *ACM Transactions on Computer-Human Interaction, 12*(2), 293-327.

Castro-Schez, J., Jennings, N., Luo, X., & Shadbolt, N. (2004). Acquiring domain knowledge for negotiating agents: A case study. *International Journal of Human-Computer Studies, 61*(1), 3-31.

Cavazza, M., Charles, F., & Mead, S. (2002). Character-based interactive storytelling. *IEEE Intelligent Systems, 17*(4), 17-24.

Dabbish, L., Kraut, R., Fussell, S., & Kiesler, S. (2005). Understanding e-mail use: Predicting action on a message. In *Proceedings of the SIGCHI Conference on Human Factors and Computing Systems*, Portland, Oregon (pp. 691-700).

Dehn, D., & van Mulken, S. (2000). The impact of animated interface agents: A review of empirical research. *International Journal of Human-Computer Studies, 52*(1), 1-22.

Detlor, B. (2004). *Towards knowledge portals: From human issues to intelligent agents*. Dordrecht, The Netherlands: Kluwer Academic Publishers.

Dillman, D. (1999). *Mail and Internet surveys: The tailored design method* (2nd ed.). New York: John Wiley & Sons.

Dow, K., Serenko, A., Turel, O., & Wong, J. (2006). Antecedents and consequences of user satisfaction with e-mail systems. *International Journal of e-Collaboration, 2*(2), 46-64.

Fatima, S., Wooldridge, M., & Jennings, N. (2005). A comparative study of game theoretic and evolutionary models for software agents. *Artificial Intelligence Review, 23*(2), 187-205.

Florea, A., & Moldovanu, A. (1996). An intelligent e-mail agent. In *Proceedings of the 4th Romanian Conference on Open Systems*, Bucharest.

Gebhard, P., Kipp, M., Klesen, M., & Rist, T. (2003). Interfaces: Authoring scenes for adaptive, interactive performances. In *Proceedings of the Second International Joint Conference on Autonomous Agents and Multiagent Systems*, Melbourne, Australia (pp. 725-732).

Godoy, D., Schiaffino, S., & Amandi, A. (2004). Interface agents personalizing Web-based tasks. *Cognitive Systems Research, 5*(3), 207-222.

Griss, M., Letsinger, R., Cowan, D., Sayers, C., VanHilst, M., & Kessler, R. (2002). *CoolAgent: Intelligent digital assistants for mobile professionals: Phase 1 retrospective* (HP Laboratories report HPL-2002-55(R1)): Hewlett-Packard Company.

Gruen, D., Sidner, C., Boettner, C., & Rich, C. (1999). A collaborative assistant for e-mail. In *Proceedings of the Conference on Human Factors and Computing Systems*, Pittsburgh, Pennsylvania (pp. 196-197).

Gulz, A. (2004). Benefits of virtual characters in computer based learning environments: Claims and evidence. *International Journal of Artificial Intelligence in Education, 14*, 313-334.

Hertzum, M., Andersen, H., Andersen, V., & Hansen, C. (2002). Trust in information sources: Seeking information from people, documents, and virtual agents. *Interacting with Computers, 14*(5), 575-599.

Hornby, G., & Pollack, J. (2001). Evolving L-systems to generate virtual creatures. *Computers & Graphics, 25*(6), 1041-1048.

Horvitz, E., Kadie, C., Paek, T., & Hovel, D. (2003). Attentive user interfaces: Models of attention in computing and communication: from principles to applications. *Communications of the ACM, 46*(3), 52-59.

Johnson, W., Rickel, J., & Lester, J. (2000). Animated pedagogical agents: Face-to-face interaction in interactive learning environments. *International Journal of Artificial Intelligence in Education, 11*, 47-78.

Klein, G., Woods, D., Bradshaw, J., Hoffman, R., & Feltovich, P. (2004). Ten challenges for making automation a "team player" in joint human-agent activity. *IEEE Transactions on Intelligent Systems, 19*(6), 91-95.

Lashkari, Y., Metral, M., & Maes, P. (1994). Collaborative interface agents. In *Proceedings of the Twelfth National Conference on Artificial Intelligence*, Seattle, Washington (pp. 444-450).

Laurel, B. (1997). Interface agents: Metaphors with character. In J. M. Bradshaw (Ed.), *Software agents* (pp. 67-78). Menlo Park, Ca: The AAAI Press.

Lesh, N., Marks, J., Rich, C., & Sidner, C. (2004). *Man-computer symbiosis revisited: Achieving natural communication and collaboration with computers.* Cambridge, MA: Technical Report E87-C. The Institute of Electronics, Mitsubishi Electric Research Laboratories, Information and Communication Engineers Transactions on Electronics.

Lesh, N., Rich, C., & Sidner, C. (1999). Using plan recognition in human-computer collaboration. In *Proceedings of the Seventh International Conference on User Modelling*, Banff, Canada (pp. 23-32).

Lester, J., Branting, K., & Mott, B. (2004). Conversational agents. In M. Singh (Ed.), *Practical handbook of Internet computing* (pp. 10/11-10/17). Baton Rouge: Chapman & Hall/CRC Press.

Lester, J., Converse, S., Kahler, S., Barlow, S., Stone, B., & Bhoga, R. (1997). The persona effect: Affective impact of animated pedagogical agents. In *Proceedings of the Conference on Human Factors in Computing Systems,* Atlanta, Georgia (pp. 359-366).

Lieberman, H., & Selker, T. (2003). Agents for the user interface. In J. Bradshaw (Ed.), *Handbook of agent technology*. Boston: The MIT Press.

Lieberman, H., & Wagner, E. (2003). End-user debugging for electronic commerce. *Proceedings of the ACM Conference on Intelligent User Interfaces,* Miami Beach (pp. 257-259).

Maes, P. (1994). Agents that reduce work and information overload. *Communications of the ACM, 37*(7), 31-40.

McBreen, H., & Jack, M. (2001). Evaluating humanoid synthetic agents in e-retail applications. *IEEE Transactions on Systems, Man, and Cybernetics, 31*(5), 394-405.

McCarthy, J. (1956). Inversion of functions defined by turing machines. In C. Shannon & J. McCarthy (Eds.), *Automata studies* (pp. 177-181). Princeton, NJ: Princeton University Press.

McCarthy, J. (1958). Programs with common sense. In *Proceedings of the Teddington Conference on the Mechanization of Thought Processes,* London (pp. 77-84).

Miranda, F., Kögler, J., Hernandez, E., & Netto, M. (2001). An artificial life approach for the animation of cognitive characters. *Computers & Graphics, 25*(6), 955-964.

Person, N., Craig, C., Price, P., Hu, X., Gholson, B., & Greasser, A. (2000). Incorporating human-like conversational behaviors into AutoTutor. In *Proceedings of the Workshop on Achieving Human-like Behavior in the Interactive Animated Agents at the Agents 2000 Conference,* Barcelona, Catalonia, Spain (pp. 85-92).

Rickel, J., & Johnson, W. (2000). Task-oriented collaboration with embodied agents in virtual worlds. In J. Cassell, J. Sullivan, S. Prevost, & E. Churchill (Eds.), *Embodied conversational agents* (pp. 95-122). Boston: The MIT Press.

Rickel, J., Marsella, S., Gratch, J., Hill, R., Traum, D., & Swartout, W. (2002). Toward a new generation of virtual humans for interactive experiences. *IEEE Intelligent Systems, 17*(4), 32-38.

Rogers, E. (2003). *Diffusion of innovations* (5th ed.). New York: Free Press.

Schiaffinoa, S., & Amandi, A. (2004). User-interface agent interaction: Personalization issues. *International Journal of Human-Computer Studies, 60*(1), 129-148.

Serenko, A. (2005). *User adoption of interface agents for e-mail.* Unpublished Doctoral Dissertation, McMaster University, Hamilton, Canada.

Serenko, A. (2006a). A model of user adoption of interface agents for e-mail. In *Proceedings of the 34th Annual Conference of the Administrative Sciences Association of Canada (ASAC)*, Banff, Canada (pp. 1-22).

Serenko, A. (2006b). The use of interface agents for e-mail notification in critical incidents. *International Journal of Human-Computer Studies, 64*(11), 1084-1098.

Serenko, A. (2007). Are interface agents scapegoats? Attributions of responsibility in human-agent interaction. *Interacting with Computers, 19*(2), 293-303.

Serenko, A., Bontis, N., & Detlor, B. (2007). Understanding the user experience with interface agents in everyday work applications. *Behaviour & Information Technology.*

Serenko, A., & Detlor, B. (2004). Intelligent agents as innovations. *AI & Society, 18*(4), 364-381.

Serenko, A., Ruhi, U., & Cocosila, M. (2007). Unplanned effects of intelligent agents on Internet use: Social Informatics approach. *AI & Society, 21*(1-2), 141-166.

Spielberg, S. (Writer) (2002). *Artificial intelligence.* In J. Harlan, S. Spielberg, & K. Kennedy (Producer): DreamWorks.

Takacs, B. (2005). Special education and rehabilitation: Teaching and healing with interactive graphics. *IEEE Computer Graphics and Applications, 25*(5), 40-48.

Voss, I. (2004). The semantic of episodes in communication with the anthropomorphic interface agent MAX. In *Proceedings of the 9ᵗʰ International Conference on Intelligent User Interface*, Funchal, Madeira, Portugal (pp. 343-345).

Section III

Agents and Web Services

Chapter VIII

Multiagent Systems and Web Services in Enterprise Environments

Eduardo H. Ramírez, Tecnológico de Monterrey, México

Ramón F. Brena, Tecnológico de Monterrey, México

Abstract

*In this chapter, we discuss the general aspects related to the utilization of MultiA-
gent systems in Enterprise environments with special emphasis on the integration
architectures enabled by Web service technologies. Also, we present a decoupled
architectural approach that allows software agents to interoperate with enterprise
systems using Web services. The proposed solution leverages existing technologies
and standards in order to reduce the time-to-market and increase the adoption of
agent-based applications. Finally, we show some case studies of knowledge-oriented
Web services that have been designed following the discussed approach and outline
some current research and business concerns for the field.*

Introduction

Software agents (Jennings & Wooldridge, 1996) and Web services (W3C, 2003b) have become key research areas for a growing number of organizations and they are expected to bring a new generation of complex distributed software systems (Jennings, 2000). Even if Agent technology is finding its way little by little into the mainstream, Web services have been adopted much more widely and rapidly (Barry, 2003).

Several authors have pointed out some overlapping areas between Agents and Web services semantic capabilities (Hunhs, 2002; Preece & Decker, 2002). However, issues regarding how they may be competing or complementary technologies remain open (Petrie, 1996). Because of that, research involving Agents and Web services is mainly focused on building improved semantics (Hendler, 2001; Dickinson & Wooldridge, 2003), communication languages and interaction protocols (Labrou et al., 1999).

We assume that in order to impact real-world organizations, a greater emphasis should be made on interoperability between agent-based applications and enterprise information systems. Moreover, we believe that the adoption of agent technologies will grow by leveraging existing industry standards and technologies. Therefore, the problem we address is an instance of "the legacy software integration problem" (Genesereth & Ketchpel, 1994; Nwana & Ndumu, 1999).

In this chapter, we present a decoupled architectural approach and design principles, called "embedded web services architecture" (EWSA), that allows agent-based applications to be integrated into enterprise application environments (Peng et al., 1998) using Web services, thus allowing them to interoperate with robust conventional systems such as:

- Web-applications, portals and content management systems (CMS)
- Enterprise resource planning (ERP)
- Manufacturing execution systems (MES)
- Workflow engines and business process management systems (BPMS)

This integration allows agents to publish XML (W3C, 2000) Web services (W3C, 2003b) or standard HTML providing thus a convenient interface for other distributed components. The Web service architecture is widely understood as "a software system" designed to support interoperable machine-to-machine interaction over a network. It has an interface described in a machine-processable format (specifically WSDL (W3C, 2001)). Other systems interact with the Web service in a manner prescribed by its description using SOAP-messages (W3C, 2003a), typically conveyed using HTTP with an XML (W3C, 2000) serialization in conjunction with other Web-related standards (W3C, 2003b).

Regarding the external behavior of the agent-based application, our approach fits into the design paradigm identified as service oriented architecture (SOA). The SOA foundation ideas were introduced by Arsajani (2001); he defines SOA as: "the architectural style that supports loosely coupled services to enable business flexibility in an interoperable, technology-agnostic manner." SOA consists of a composite set of business-aligned services that support a flexible and dynamically re-configurable end-to-end business processes realization using interface-based service descriptions (Borges et al., 2004).

This chapter also discusses the kind of agent-based applications we have found to be suitable for this approach and the nature of Web services that agents can provide. The rest of the chapter is organized as follows. In the next section, we provide an overview of our solution approach. Specifically, we discuss the proposed embedded Web server architecture for integrating agent-based applications and enterprise applications and its implementation. Then, we discuss its evaluation and application to some example domains. Finally, the chapter concludes with some expected business results.

Solution Overview

Instead of making an agent-based application look "different" compared to other applications from the outside, which is indeed a "religious" point of view frequent in the agent research community, we intend to hide the *agentness* of a group of agents from the outside.

We contend that agents should solve problems for which they are well suited for, and should relate to other software components just as another software component. This is especially true when a set of technologies for gluing software components are maturing, such as Web services and service-oriented architectures. So, our approach relies much more on *hiding* the agents than on exposing them to the outside world.

Architecture

As shown in Figure 1, the underlying metaphor used to determine the design strategy is the aim to create a "black-box" in which agents can live and perform complex tasks. The main architectural principle consists of decoupling agent-based applications through the exposure of Web service interfaces. Enterprise applications should

Figure 1. Decoupled architecture top-level view

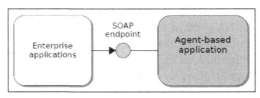

not be aware that a service is provided by agents if the system offers a standard SOAP endpoint as interface, appearing to the world as a conventional Web service or application.

An agent-based application that exposes Web interfaces requires the interoperability of Web components and agents and their respective containers, as they are built on different programming models, each following different sets of specifications. The relevant components and containers in a system combining agents and Web components would be:

- **Web container:** Also called the "Servlet container", it is the application that provides the execution environment for the Web components and implements the Java Servlet API in conformity with the JSR- 154 specification (Sun Microsystems, Inc., 2003). Web containers are usually built within Web servers and provide network services related with HTTP request processing.

- **Web component:** Servlets are the standard user defined Web components written in Java. JSR-154 defines them as "A Java technology-based Web component, managed by a container that generates dynamic content" (Sun Microsystems, Inc., 2003). They follow a synchronous processing model as they are designed to handle the content of the HTTP requests. The dynamic content delivered in the request may be HTML for Web pages or XML (W3C, 2000) for Web services.

- **Agent container:** The execution environment for the agents provided by the agent platform in conformity with FIPA (FIPA, 2002) specifications.

- **Web service agent:** A Java thread that periodically executes a set of behaviors containing the agent tasks. For the purposes of this work, we could say that an agent is a "Web service agent" if it receives and processes requests formulated by a human user or an application in collaboration with a Web component. The requests may be synchronous or asynchronous.

Figure 2. EWSA decoupled architecture

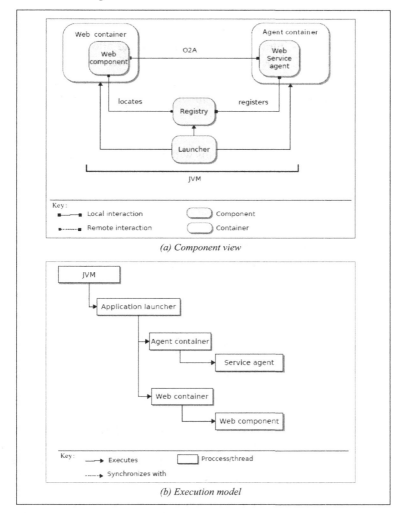

(a) Component view

(b) Execution model

Our proposed solution (Figure 2(a)) is designed around the idea of embedding a Web container into the agent-based application. This approach makes it easier to communicate with both containers because they are placed in the same memory space.

When the agent and Web containers are started on the same Java Virtual Machine operating system process, agents and Web components may communicate by sharing object references in a virtual object-to-agent (O2A) channel. The resulting execution model is shown in Figure 2(b).

As an intermediate result that will be shown later, the embedded Web server architecture (EWSA) provides intra-container integration and allows the agent-based application to process HTTP petitions in a simple and efficient way.

However, in order to leverage the achieved integration, it is necessary to provide some additional artifacts to simplify the interactions between the agents and the Web components, namely:

- An *agent registry*, where all the agents with Web services capabilities register in order to be located for Web component invocations
- A *platform launcher*, a boot system that initializes and configures the main containers

Moreover, from the structural view of the architecture as well as the behavioral or dynamic perspective, we notice that when the agents and Web components exist in the same space, synchronization becomes an issue. So, in the embedded architecture, the complexity of interactions is handled by two core framework components:

- A *call monitor* object that serves as a shared memory space between the agent and the Web component, and handles synchronization among them
- A *service behavior* object used by agents for exposing internal tasks as Web services

The call monitor is a simple implementation of the classic synchronization construct (Hoare, 1974), used to encapsulate the concurrent access to shared resources. In the EWSA framework, when a Web component requires an agent service, a call monitor object is created to handle the agent response, which may be synchronous or asynchronous.

When a synchronous Web service is invoked, a Web component attempts to access the agent results (the shared resource in this case) calling a monitor entry method, called "getResult" in our implementation, then the monitor makes the caller wait until the agent thread finishes its work and releases the monitor through the exit method *setResult*. In the case of asynchronous invocations to agent services, the call monitor releases the Web component process immediately. As the synchronization may involve a busy wait time, the monitor can optionally handle a maximum invocation timeout. Details of these interactions are shown in Figure 4(a).

On the other hand, as the agent request processing is asynchronous by nature, the service behavior allows agents to unqueue received message objects (each containing a monitor) and transparently translate them into internal service method invocations. In the case of synchronous requests, that is, when the Web component remains blocked until agent results are calculated, the service behavior object is responsible of delivering them to the call monitor object and thus releasing the lock. The service behavior object also implements a round robin service discipline within the agent, allowing it to serve many Web component requests simultaneously.

Implementation

Among FIPA platforms, JADE (Bellifemine et al., 1999) was selected because it is considered well suited for large scale deployments mainly due to its thread-per-agent programming model and the support of "virtual channels" that allow agents to interact with regular Java components (Rimassa, 2003).

In this particular implementation, the "Launcher" program, initializes and starts an instance of the JADE platform besides an embedded version of the Tomcat Web Server (Jakarta Project--The Apache Software Foundation, 2003). The aforementioned "Registry" is nothing but a data structure that holds references to the running Service Agents, implemented as a Singleton pattern (Gamma et al., 1995).

Access to the agent's source code is required as they need to be recompiled to include the Web service capability, which is encapsulated in a platform specific library. In JADE's particular case, agents are enhanced with a custom behavior class, which only requires the addition of one line of code.

Our architecture is applicable to FIPA platforms other than Jade; however, it would be necessary to port the framework components (registry and launcher) using its particular libraries and program interfaces and to add missing components provided by the platform like virtual channels between objects and agents.

Evaluation and Comparison

Our proposal is not the first solution that allows agents to interoperate with Web-based components. In fact, such an architecture was defined by developers (Berre &Fourdrinoy, 2002) of the Jade platform and later implemented on the WSAI Project (Whitestein Technologies, 2003) as a contribution to AgentCities initiative (Dale et al., 2002).

The WSAI solution assumes the existence of two agent containers—one stand-alone, which we may call the "main container" and another one contained within the Web container. Each container is executed in a separate JVM system process. WSAI introduces the concept of "Gateway Agent" as an agent living in the "Web

Figure 3. Gateway architecture

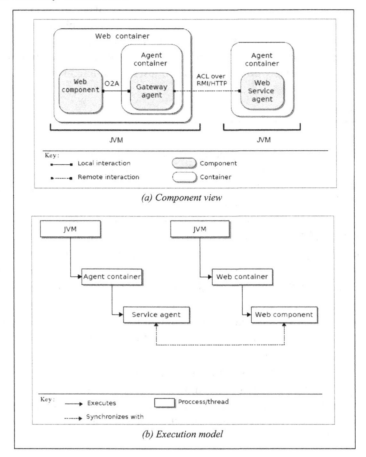

(a) Component view

(b) Execution model

container", responsible of translating HTTP requests into ACL messages. The general gateway architecture components are shown in Figure 3(a).

One of the major drawbacks of this approach resides in the existence of several processes that should synchronize using remote method invocations even if both of them are deployed on the same machine. The synchronization problem is addressed by instantiating the "Gateway Agents" and "Caller" objects on a request basis. "Callers" implement the Java synchronization and time out handling, as shown in Figure 4(a). Additional complexity comes from the fact that it is able to interoperate with any running FIPA compliant agent platform (even non Java-based ones) without access to its source code.

Figure 4. Interactions sequence diagrams

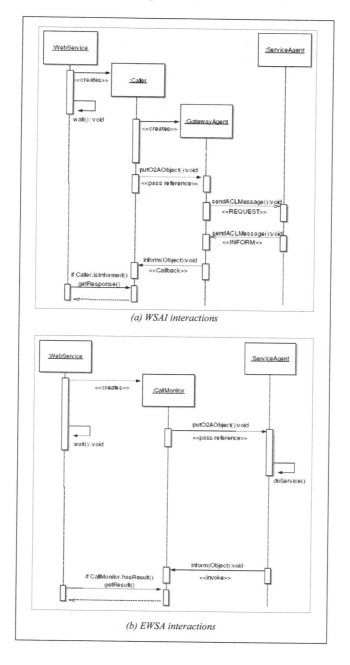

(a) WSAI interactions

(b) EWSA interactions

An alternative interesting proposal by Cowan and Griss (2002) is BlueJADE, a connector that allows the management of a JADE platform by a Java application server, and therefore its interaction with the enterprise applications deployed inside it. BlueJADE's main strengths are manifested at the container level. Although the containers are running separately, the connector eliminates the need for remote calls that enables the use of the object-agent channels. However, BlueJADE does not define any interaction model for the components inside the application and is highly dependant on the particular application server product running the applications.

We believe that in order to build enterprise-class agent-based applications, it is not critical to provide Web-interoperability to an indefinite number of FIPA platforms.

Figure 5. Mean service time for concurrent requests

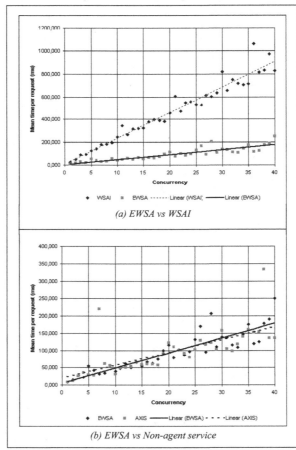

(a) EWSA vs WSAI

(b) EWSA vs Non-agent service

Therefore, we trade-off this flexibility in favor of good integration with the chosen agent platform, even though the architectural principles remain useful for them. As a result, our framework implementation is simple and provides good performance.

In the EWSA framework, interactions are reduced to a minimal subset which does not require any remote method invocation. The model shown in Figure 4(b) considers interactions similar to the ones in the gateway architecture until the HTTP request is delivered to the Gateway Agent.

In a benchmark comparison between WSAI and the EWSA decoupled architecture, an important performance and scalability gain was observed. A currency exchange Web service is provided in the WSAI platform. The service implementation is trivial as it only consists of a simple mathematical conversion performed by an agent. As shown in Figure 5(a), we may notice that not only EWSA's response times are better, but that they increase at a slower rate with respect to the number of concurrent requests which leads to better scalability. The performance gain in the embedded architecture can be explained as an effect of the elimination of network calls overhead between agents and Web components.

A complementary experiment was performed in order to measure the relative performance overhead of the agent-based architecture against a non-agent based solution implemented as a regular Axis Web service. Results shown on Figure 5(b) indicate that using the embedded architecture, the performance of the agent system follows a behavior pattern close to that of the pure Java solution. As a preliminary conclusion we may state that the embedded architecture solves the potential performance limitations for using agents in simple scenarios.

Additionally, by means of simple metrics we could show some of the desirable properties of the proposed architecture. As seen in Table 1, a functional implementation for embedding Web services into agent-based applications is several times smaller than the implementation of a gateway framework from the WSAI Project.

Table 1. Integration framework size comparison

Package	Total Classes	Abstract	Concrete
Embedded	6	1	5
Gateway	52	6	46

Table 2. Example implementation size comparison

Package	Total Classes	Abstract	Concrete
Embedded	2	0	2
Gateway	4	1	3

Although the number of classes is not an absolute metric of software complexity, from the interaction models we can deduce that the interactions present in the embedded model (Figure 4(b)) are nothing but a subset of the interactions required in a gateway approach (Figure 4(a)). Consequently, the internal complexity of the embedded Web services architecture (EWSA) is not significantly different from the gateway architecture. In the embedded architecture only one abstract class is provided as an extension point for service developers, which consequently simplifies the agent and Web service implementation as shown in Table 2.

This comparison is provided as a reference resulting from the programming models. Considering that even if a code generation tool could actually simplify the development process, the additional interactions remain with a significant performance penalization.

Applications

In general, we believe that the proposed integration model is useful to allow agent-based applications to provide knowledge-intensive services, such as:

- Search and automatic classification
- User profile inference
- Semantic-based content distribution
- Intelligent business activity monitoring

Web-enabled agent systems may serve in a variety of domains. As presented in the Just-in-Time information and Knowledge (JITIK) case study, they are well suited to support knowledge distribution in enterprise environments.

Just-in-Time Information and Knowledge

The proposed model has been successfully implemented for the JITIK (Just-in-Time information and Knowledge) environment that may be defined as a web-enabled agent-based intelligent system capable of delivering highly customized notifications to users in large distributed organizations (Brena et al., 2001). JITIK is aimed to support collaboration within organizations by delivering the right knowledge and information to the appropriate people just-in-time. JITIK is designed to interoperate with enterprise systems in order to retrieve and distribute contents in a flexible way.

Figure 6. JITIK and enterprise systems interaction

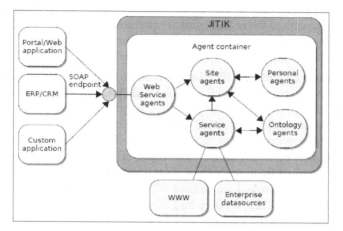

The JITIK agent model is shown in Figure 6. Personal agents work on behalf of the members of the organization. They filter and deliver useful content according to user preferences. Personal agents are provided with information by the site agent who acts as a broker between them and service agents. For the purposes of this work, the most relevant agents of JITIK are the so called service agents which collect and detect information and knowledge pieces that are supposed to be relevant for someone in the organization. Examples of service agents are the Web service agents that receive and process external requests, as well as monitor agents, which are continuously monitoring sources of information and knowledge (web pages, databases, etc.).

The ontology agent contains the knowledge about the interest areas of the members of the organization and about its structure (Brena and Ceballos, 2004). This knowledge is hierarchically described in the form of taxonomies, usually one for interest areas and one describing the structure of the organization. For example, in an academic institution, the interest areas could be the science domains in which the institution is specialized in, and the organizational chart of the institution gives the structure of the organization.

JITIK Web Services

JITIK is an example of an agent-based application able to provide knowledge intensive services, which may be grouped as follows:

- **Recommendation services:** A user's profile is represented by a set of points in the taxonomies, as each user could have many interests and could be located at different parts of the organizational structure. As JITIK keeps track of user interests and preferences, it is able to recommend content to users on demand. Recommended content may be used in Portals or Web applications.

- **Content search and classification:** One of the main difficulties for web users is obtaining relevant information. In normal conditions people waste a lot of time searching for documents on the web because the user must examine the documents in detail to determine if they are really relevant for the search purpose. In the context of JITIK, a service agent that searches the most relevant documents on the web can be constructed. The knowledge that guides the search is handled by the ontology agent where the keywords with which the search engine is invoked are defined. The documents obtained by the search are qualified by a fuzzy system and then the best ones are presented to the user.

- **Subscription services:** JITIK allows users to subscribe to changes in specific areas. Also, users may customize the media and frequency of JITIK notifications using simple web-based interfaces. Rules may be defined so that messages relative to certain topics are handled with higher priorities. A rule may state that several alerts may be sent to their cell-phone via SMS, and also define that interest-area messages be sent as a weekly summary via email. Organization managers may set high-level distribution rules.

- **Content distribution services:** Enterprise applications may deliver content to the system using its semantic-based content distribution services. When new content is received, it is classified and distributed to users who may be interested. Users receive the notifications of new content as specified by their own rules.

As shown above, the EWSA decoupled architecture allows an agent-based application like JITIK to provide enterprise communities with a number of knowledge oriented Web services, especially useful in large organizations where performance and scalability attributes become critical.

Implementation of a Recommendation Service

Standard collaborative applications could be enhanced by agent-based web services, for example, consider the simple scenario in which a user joins a workgroup using the collaborative application interface. After this event, the system will send recommendations about documents related to the group activity and interests on a daily basis. Some of the internal services interaction needed to fulfill this case are:

- Once the user joins the group, the collaborative application will invoke the agent-based service using a standard coarse-grained interface.

- Periodical updates to the document base will be programmed to be triggered upon certain conditions using the agent-platform scheduling service.

- Information gathered from data sources and repositories will be classified and filtered against the interests of the relevant groups using the semantic processing and classification services.

- Relevant information will be distributed to users using the agent-based notification services; the system may leverage the use of several distribution media (Email, SMS) to alert users of new documents and other application events according to its relevance.

The components and services interactions for the use-case are shown in detail in Figure 7. It should be noted that the use of generic services for scheduling, notification and classification allows the task specific code (read documents, send mail) to be encapsulated in the lower layers of the system, thus enhancing the abstraction level for the agent layer.

It should be noted that the information overflow that exists in today's corporate environments is driving attention to the quality of the recommendations provided by MultiAgent systems.

Figure 7. Recommendation service detailed view

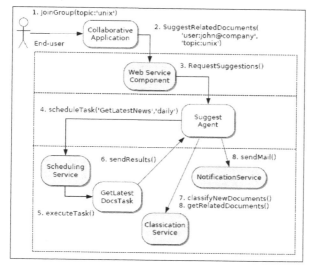

In this regard, some of the relevant related research focused on how to improve recommendation services involves the use of qualitative judgments through automated reasoning techniques such as defeasible logic programming (Chesñevar et. al, 2006).

Implementation of a Classification Service

Another use case that serves as an example to our integration approach is a news delivery and classification service. Interaction between agents and services causes the flow of events between services and agents, as shown in Figure 8. The sequence of interaction is as follows:

- Once the user of the content management system (CMS) publishes a new article, it triggers a notification to the JITIK service. The CMS application will invoke the content-distribution service using a standard coarse-grained interface.
- After that, the classification service will attempt to match a set of topics for the article, according the contents of the ontology of the organization.
- When the content is classified, the request is passed onto the agent-layer where agents determine the set of content receivers considering their interest profiles and personal preferences.

Figure 8. Classification service detailed view

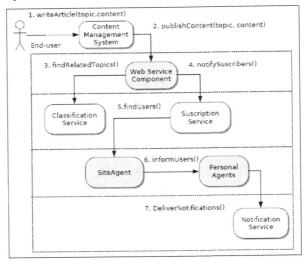

- Finally, relevant information will be delivered to users through the internal notification services; the system may leverage the use of several distribution media (Email, SMS) to alert users of new documents and other application events.

The described classification service leverages text-mining technologies in order to intelligently route a particular piece of information across the organization. Our classification agent implements a Bayesian classifier, similar to the described in Sebastiani (2005). However, there exist alternate approaches to the automatic text-categorization problem based on quantitative methods applied upon pre-classified training sets. Among the most popular of the latest we can name the Bayesian classifiers, Support Vector Machines (Joachims, 98) and Boosting (Schapire, 2000).

Related Work and Trends

The rapid growth and adoption of Web service technologies as open communication standards have imposed important interoperability challenges to the MultiAgent systems, however, the basic hurdles may be overcome with approaches like the ones we have described in this work, whether on Embedded or Gateway architectures.

Neverthless, the efforts to provide transparent interoperability between agents and Web services have not ceased. More recently, Shafiq (2006) have proposed an integration approach, with a greater emphasis on the service description and message translation between agents and Web services. From an architectural standpoint, their approach fits in what we have identified as "Gateway" approaches.

On the other hand, as the Web technologies become ubiquitous in enterprise environments and basic interoperability is achieved through open standarized interfaces, a new set of directions have started to shift the research interests of the community toward pragmatic issues with greater impact in business agility and user productivity. As main trends we can identify:

- Greater emphasis on distributed service coordination using Web services choreography specifications (Moyaux et al., 2006).
- Automatic service discovery and composition using Semantic Web ontology languages (Martin et al., 2006).
- Increased sophistication of personal agents through machine learning, argumentation and text analysis techniques for content recommendation and filtering (Chesñevar et al., 2006).

Conclusion

We have presented an architectural approach aimed to allow integration of multi-agent systems as Web services components. Besides its simplicity, the advantage of this approach is that it provides an efficient way of interoperating agent-based subsystems with web-centric loosely-coupled systems.

Also, based on the experience of the JITIK project, a multiagent system for information distribution in large organizations, we have provided several implementation case studies in which the presented design approach can be used to provide recommendation and classification services, as a part of the knowledge delivery process.

We think that this solution is a good compromise given the current status of technology, and it allows rapid integration of modular systems conforming to open standards. As expected business results, we hope the solution to be helpful to:

- Reduce the time to market of enterprise agent-based applications
- Deliver good performance for large volume of users, as shown experimentally
- Improve the code base maintainability, by promoting simplicity and modular design

It is to be noted that our solution assumes that the agent and web component source code is available. With respect to the architectures presented in the literature, this solution mostly trades-off flexibility in favor of robustness, simplicity and maintainability, which is a suitable policy, particularly for enterprise systems.

Finally, we think that Multiagent Systems' way to mainstream enterprise applications could be paved by practical integration technologies like the one we presented in this chapter.

References

Arsanjani, A. (2001). A domain-language approach to designing dynamic enterprise component-based architectures to support business services. In *Proceedings of the 39th International Conference and Exhibition on Technology of Object-Oriented Languages and Systems. TOOLS 39* (pp. 130-141).

Barry, D. (2003). *Web services and service-oriented architectures: The savvy manager's guide.* San Francisco: Morgan Kaufmann.

Bellifemine, F., Poggi, A., & Rimassa, G. (1999). JADE-A FIPA-compliant agent framework. In *Proceedings of PAAM'99*, London.

Borges, B., Holley, K., & Arsanjani, A. (2004). *Service-oriented architecture*. Retrieved from http://webservices.sys-con.com/read/46175.htm

Berre, D., & Fourdrinoy, O. (2002). *Using JADE with Java Server Pages*. Retrieved from http://sharon.cselt.it/projects/jade/doc/tutorials/jsp/JADE4JSP.html

Cowan, D., & Griss, M. (2002). *Making Software Agent Technology available to Enterprise Applications*. Retrieved from http://www.hpl.hp.com/techreports/2002/HPL-2002-211.pdf

Chesñevar, C., Maguitman, A., & Simari, G. (2006). Argument-based critics and recommenders: A qualitative perspective on user support systems. *Data Knowledge Engineering 59*(2), 293-319.

Dickinson, I., & Wooldridge, M. (2003). Towards practical reasoning agents for the semantic web. In *Proceedings of the Second International Joint Conference on Autonomous Agents and Multiagent Systems* (pp. 827-834). New York: ACM Press.

FIPA. (2002). *FIPA Abstract Architecture Specification*. Retrieved from http://www.fipa.org/specs/fipa00001/SC00001L.html

Gamma, E., Helm, R., Johnson, R., & Vlissides, J. (1995). *Design patterns: Elements of reusable object-oriented software*. Boston: Addison-Wesley.

Genesereth, M., & Ketchpel, S. (1994). Software agents. *Communication of the ACM, 37*(7), 48-55.

Good, N., Schafer, J., Konstan, J., et al. (1999). Combining collaborative filtering with personal agents for better recommendations. *AAAI/IAAI*, 439-446.

Hendler, J. (2001). Agents and the Semantic Web. *IEEE Intelligent Systems, 16*(2), 30-37.

Hoare, C. (1974). Monitors: An operating system structuring concept. *Communications of the ACM, 17*(10), 549-557.

Hunhs, M. (2002). Agents as Web services. *IEEE Internet Computing*, 6(4), 93-95.

Jakarta Project—The Apache Software Foundation. (2003). *The Tomcat Web Server v. 4.1*.

Jennings, N., & Wooldridge, M. (1996). Software agents. *IEE Review, 42*(1), 17-20.

Jennings, N. (2000). On agent-based software engineering. *Artificial Intelligence, 177*(2), 277-296.

Labrou, Y., Finin, T., & Peng, Y (1999). Agent communication languages: The current landscape. *IEEE Intelligent Systems, 14*(2), 45-52.

Martin, D., Burstein, M., McDermott, D., McGuinness, D., McIlraith, S., Paolucci, M., et al. (2006). Bringing Semantics to Web services with OWL-S. *World Wide Web Journal*.

Moyaux, T., Lithgow-Smith, B., Tamma, V., & Wooldridge, M. (2006). Towards service-oriented ontology-based coordination. In *Proceedings of the 2006 IEEE International Conference on Web services (ICWS 2006)*, Chicago.

Nwana, H., & Ndumu, D. (1999). A perspective on software agents research. *The Knowledge Engineering Review, 14*(2), 1-18.

Peng, Y., Finin, T., Labrou, Y , Chu, B., Long, J., Tolone, W. J., & Boughannam, A. (1998). A multi-agent system for enterprise integration. In *Proceedings of the 3rd International Conference on the Practical Applications of Agents and Multi-Agent Systems (PAAM98)* (pp. 155-169). London.

Petrie, C. (1996). Agent-based engineering, the Web and intelligence. *IEEE Expert, 11*(6), 24-29.

Preece, A., & Decker, S. (2002). Intelligent Web services. *IEEE Intelligent Systems, 17*(1), 15-17.

Rimassa, G. (2003). *Runtime support for distributed multi-agent systems.* Doctoral thesis, University of Parma.

Shafiq, M., Ding, Y., & Fensel, D. (2006). Bridging multi agent systems and Web services: Towards interoperability between Software Agents and Semantic Web services. In *Proceedings of the 10th IEEE international Enterprise Distributed Object Computing Conference (Edoc'06). Volume 00*, Washington, DC (pp. 85-96). IEEE Computer Society

Schapire, R., & Singer, Y. (2000). BOOSTEXTER: A boosting-based system for text categorization. *Machine Learning, 39*(2/3), 135-168.

Sebastiani, F. (2005). Text categorization. In L. Rivero, J. Doorn, & V. Ferraggine (Eds.), *The encyclopedia of database technologies and applications.* Hershey, PA: Idea Group Publishing.

Sun Microsystems, Inc. (2003). *JSR-000154 Java(TM) Servlet 2.4 Specification* (Final release).

W3C. (2000). *Extensible Markup Language (XML) 1.0 (2nd ed.).* Retrieved from http://www.w3.org/TR/2000/REC-xml-20001006

W3C. (2001). *Web services Description Language (WSDL)1.1.* Retrieved from http://www.w3.org/TR/2001/NOTE-wsdl-20010315

W3C. (2003a). *Simple Object Access Protocol (SOAP)1.2.* Retrieved from http://www.w3.org/TR/soap12-part1/

W3C. (2003b). *Web services Glossary*, Working Draft. Retrieved from http://www.w3.org/TR/2003/WD-ws-gloss-20030808/

Whitestein Technologies, A.G. (2003). Web services agent integration project.

Willmott, S., Dale, J. & Burg, B. (2002). Agentcities: A worldwide open aent network. *AgentLink Newsletter, 8,* 13-15.

Chapter IX

A Service Discovery Model for Mobile Agent-Based Distributed Data Mining

Xining Li, University of Guelph, Canada

Lei Song, University of Guelph, Canada

Abstract

Mining information from distributed data sources over the Internet is a growing research area. The introduction of mobile agent paradigm opens a new door for distributed data mining and knowledge discovery applications. One of the main challenges of mobile agent technology is how to locate hosts that provide services requested by mobile agents. Traditional service location protocols can be applied to mobile agent systems to explore the service discovery issue. However, because of their architecture deficiencies, they do not adequately solve all the problems that arise in a dynamic domain such as database location discovery. From this point of view, we need some enhanced service discovery techniques for the mobile agent community. This chapter proposes a new model for solving the database service location problem in the domain of mobile agents by implementing a service discovery module based on search engine techniques. As a typical interface provided by a mobile agent server, the service discovery module improves the decision ability of mobile agents with respect to information retrieval. This research is part of the

IMAGO system—an infrastructure for mobile agent-based data mining applications. This chapter focuses on the design of an independent search engine, IMAGOSearch, and discusses how to integrate service discovery into the IMAGO system, thus providing a global scope service location tool for intelligent mobile agents.

Introduction

Mobile agent systems bring forward the creative idea of moving user defined computations–agents towards network resources, and provide a whole new architecture for designing distributed systems. An agent is an autonomous process acting on behalf of a user. A mobile agent roams the Internet to access data and services, and carries out its assigned task remotely. Distributed data mining (DDM) is one of the important application areas of deploying intelligent mobile agent paradigm (Park & Kargupta, 2002; Klusch et al., 2003). Most existing DDM projects focus on approaches to apply various machine leaning algorithms to compute descriptive models of the physically distributed data sources. Although these approaches provide numerous algorithms, ranging from statistical model to symbolic/logic models, they typically consider homogeneous data sites and require the support of distributed databases. As the number and size of databases and data warehouses grow at phenomenal rates, one of the main challenges in DDM is the design and implementation of system infrastructure that scales up to large, dynamic and remote data sources. On the other hand, the number of services that will become available in distributed networks (in particular, on the Internet) is expected to grow enormously. Besides classical services such as those offered by printers, scanners, fax machines, and so on, more and more services will be available nowadays. Examples are information access via the Internet, E-commerce, music on demand, Web services and services that use computational infrastructure that has been deployed within the network. Moreover, the concept of service in mobile agent systems, which will be described in this chapter, has recently come into prominence.

Mobile agents must interact with their hosts in order to use their services or to negotiate services with other agents (Song & Li, 2004). Discovering services for mobile agents comes from two considerations. First, the agents possess local knowledge of the network and have a limited functionality, since only agents of limited size and complexity can efficiently migrate in a network and have little overhead. Hence specific services are required which aim at deploying mobile agents efficiently in the system and the network. Secondly, mobile agents are subject to strong security restrictions, which are enforced by the security manager. Thus, mobile agents should find services that help to complete security-critical tasks, other than execute code that might jeopardize remote servers. Following this trend, it becomes increasingly important to give agents the ability of finding and making use of services that are available in a network (Bettstetter & Renner, 2000).

Some of the mobile agent systems developed in the last few years are Aglets (Lange & Ishima, 1998), Voyager (Recursion Software Inc, 2005), Grasshopper (Baumer et al., 1999), Concordia (Mitsubishi Electric, 1998), and D'Agents (Gray et al., 2000). Research in the area of mobile agents looked at languages that are suitable for mobile agent programming, and languages for agent communication. Much effort was put into security issues, control issues, and design issues. Some state of the art mobile agent systems focus on different aspects of the above issues, for example, Aglets on security, D'Agents on multi-language support, Grasshopper on the implementation of the FIPA (FIPA, 2002) and MASIF (Milojicic et al., 1998) standard. However, few research groups have paid attention to offering an environment to combine the concept of service discovery and mobile agent paradigm. Most existing mobile agent systems require their programmer to specify agent migration itinerary explicitly. This makes mobile agents the weak ability to sense their execution environment and react autonomously to dynamic distributed systems. The objective of our research is to equip mobile agents with system tools such that those agents can search for data sites, move from hosts to hosts, gather information and access databases, carry out complex data mining algorithms, and generate global data model or pattern through the aggregation of the local results.

In this chapter, we propose a new service discovery model DSSEM (discovery service via search engine model) for mobile agents. DSSEM is based on a search engine, a global Web search tool with centralized index and fuzzy retrieval. This model especially aims at solving the database service location problem and is integrated with our IMAGO (intelligent mobile agent gliding on-line) system (Li, 2006). The IMAGO system is an infrastructure for mobile agent applications. It includes code for the IMAGO server—a Multi-threading Logic Virtual Machine, the IMAGO-Prolog—a Prolog-like programming language extended with a rich API for implementing mobile agent applications, and the IMAGO IDE—a Java-GUI-based program from which users can perform editing, compiling, and invoking an agent application. In our system, mobile agents are used to support applications, and service agents are used to wrap database services. Service providers manually register their services in a service discovery server. A mobile agent locates a specific service by submitting requests to the service discovery server with the description of required services. Web pages are used to advertise services. The design goal of DSSEM is to provide a flexible and efficient service discovery protocol in a mobile agent environment.

The rest of the chapter is organized as follows. The following section presents a brief background related to this chapter and discusses the problem of service discovery in mobile agent systems. The third section introduces DSSEM and compares it with several service discovery protocols (SDPs) currently under development. The comparison criteria include functionality, dependency on operating systems and platforms. The fourth section gives an overview of the design of service discovery module and integration with the IMAGO system. Finally, the last section provides some discussion and concluding remarks as well as future work.

Background and Motivation

The general idea of distributed services is that an application may be separated from the resources needed to fulfill a task. These resources are modeled as services, which are independent of the application. Services do not denote software services alone, but any entity that can be used by a person, a program or even another service (Hashman & Knudsen, 2001). Service discovery is a new research area that focuses not just on offering plug and play solutions but aims to simplify the use of mobile devices in a network allowing them to discover services and also be discovered (Ravi, 2001).

In general, the service usage model is role-based. An entity providing a service that can be utilized by other requesting entities acts as a provider. Conversely, the entity requesting the provision of a service is called a requester. To provide its service, a provider in turn can act as a requester making use of other services. To form a distributed system, requesters and providers live on physically separate hosting devices. Providers should, from time to time, advertise services by broadcasting to requesters or registering themselves on third party servers. From requests' point of view, it must be able to:

- Search and browse for services
- Choose the right service
- Utilize the service (Bettstetter & Renner, 2000)

Before a service can be discovered, it should make itself public. This process is called service advertisement. The work can be done when services are initialized, or every time they change their states via broadcasting to anyone who is listening. A service advertisement should consist of the service identifier, plus a simple string saying what the service is, or a set of strings for specifications and attributes. An example is given in Table 1.

There are several ways that a client looks up services it requires. If the client knows the direct address of services, it can make direct requests, or it can listen to broadcasting advertisements and select those it needs. The common method, however, is that the client forms a description of the desired service and asks a known discovery server if there is any service matching the request.

Table 1. A typical advertisement of service

Identifier: office-printer-4
Type : printer/postscript/HP20
Speed : 24ppm
Color : yes

A variety of service discovery protocols (SDPs) are currently under development by some companies and research groups. The most well-known schemes are Sun's Java based Jini™ (Sun, 1999), Salutation (Salutation Consortium, 1998), Microsoft's UPP (Universal Plug and Play, 2000), IETF's draft service location protocol (SLP) (Guttman et al., 1999) and OASIS UDDI (OASIS, 2005). Some of these SDPs are extended and applied by several mobile agent systems to solve the service discovery problem. For example, GTA/Agent (Rubinstein & Carlos, 1998) addresses the service location issue by extending SLP, a simple, lightweight protocol for automatic maintenance and advertisement of intranet services. Though SLP provides a flexible and scalable framework for enabling users to access service information about existence, location, and configuration, it only possesses a local function for service discovery and is not scalable up to global Internet domain because it uses DHCP and multicast instead of a central lookup mechanism. AETHER (Chen, 2000) makes an improvement to Jini by building a dynamic distributed intelligent agent framework. Jini provides a flexible and robust infrastructure for distributed components to find each other on the Internet. However, it relies on the use of standard Java-based interfaces implemented by both the clients and servers in their work. This requires existing systems to be modified for use with Jini, however, a significant amount of the production software currently available around the world is unlikely to be modified. After a study of different SDPs and mobile agent systems that are adopting these methods, we found that several problems cannot be easily solved by the existing protocols due to their limitations.

First of all, most existing works support an attribute-based discovery as well as a simple name lookup to locate a service. Usually, there is only a set of primitive attribute types in the service description, such as string and integer, to characterize a service. Thus, the service discovery process primarily involves activities such as type matching, string comparison, or integer comparison. Here, we define a service description as a sequence of flags or codes that can be multicast to service requesters or be registered on a third-party server for advertisement purposes. Generally speaking, a service description is composed of two parts: property and access. The property of a service description describes the type, characteristics, constraints, and so forth, of a service, which will be published in the service discovery server for advertising purpose. The access of a service is more complicated. It may contain

Table 2. An example of SLP service description

type = service: printer
scope = administrator, guest
name = hp6110
paper per min. = 10
Color-support = yes
usage = //hp6110: 1020/queue1

multiple access method tags as there could be multiple ways to invoke a service, for example, using the interface of services, downloading the client-proxy code, locating a database, RPC, RMI or URL location.

For example, Table 2 shows a service description in SLP, where the value of type tag, that is, "service:printer," indicates the property of the service. It also contains some other property tags to describe this resource in detail, such as paper per min. or color-support. In the searching phase, much of the power of SLP derives from its ability to allow exact selection of an appropriate service from among many other advertised services with the same tags. In other words, only the service or services that match the required keywords and attribute values specified by requesters will be found. These keywords and attribute values can be combined into boolean expressions via "AND" and "OR," or common comparison operators "<=," ">," or substring matching. Considering the above example again, the search request from a requester could be "< service:printer, guest, ((name = hp6110) (page per min.>8)) >."

A further step in SDPs development is using eXtensible Markup Language (XML) to describe services. In fact, Web service discovery protocol UDDI, its description language WSDL, as well as the communication protocol SOAP, are all based on XML. In addition, an XML description can be converted to a Java document object model (DOM) so that it can be merged into a service registry system. The example in Table 2 can be described in XML as follows:

```
<description ID="0198">
<type> service: printer </type>
<scope> administration, guest </scope>
<name> hp6110 </name> ......
<usage> //hp6110: 1020/queue1 </usage>

</description>
```

No matter what kind of description format is applied, the lack of rich representation for services has not been changed. The problem arising directly in our project is that these protocols are not adequate to advertise some special services, such as database services. In a DDM environment, data may be stored among physically distributed sites and may be artificially partitioned among different sites for better scalability. Therefore endowing mobile agents with the ability of accessing remote databases is the basis for DDM applications. Obviously, a database system already has a well-defined interface. A data-mining agent requires a way of finding the locations of specific databases and deciding where to move. In this situation, the only way we can accomplish is by registering the database's name and attributes for future discovery. However, for a database service, people care more about the content of the database than its name or structure. Considering an example of a bookstore, before placing an order to the bookstore, customers would like to know if the books they require are available in the store by checking the summary of all books with some keywords or a fuzzy search criterion. From this point of view, a simple string identifier or XML identifier cannot meet the requirement.

The second problem is ranking. After requesters have searched out all services that may be required, they still need to select the right one for utilization. Just imagine over the entire Internet, tens of thousands of providers could publish their services by their own will. We should be able to know which ones provide the most realistic and highest quality services that users want. Obviously, moving to the hosts one by one to find out the required information is not a wise choice. Therefore, generating a service rank is essential. However, none of the existing SDPs offer such a mechanism for ranking discovered services. They are satisfied with finding a service only, without considering whether the service would be able to serve the requester.

The most significant contribution of our research is that we enrich the service description by using Web pages' URL (later the search engine will index the content referenced by this URL) to replace the traditional string-set service description in mobile agent systems. Because of their specific characteristics, such as containing rich media information (text, sound, image, *etc.*), working with the standard HTTP protocol and being able to reference each other, Web pages may play a key role acting as the template of the service description. On the other hand, since the search engine is a mature technology and offers an automated indexing tool that can provide a highly efficient ranking mechanism for the collected information, it is also useful for acting as the directory server in our model. Of course, DSSEM also benefits from previous service discovery research in selected areas but is endowed with a new concept by combining some special features of mobile agents as well as integrating service discovery tool with agent servers.

Discovery Services via Search
Engine Model (DSSEM)

As the most important media type on the Internet today, hypertext Web pages are posted to advertise the information by industries and individuals. Though millions of them are published on the Internet, these Web pages still increase rapidly everyday for a variety of reasons. They are spidered and indexed by commercial search engines such as Google, Yahoo, AltaVista, and so forth. Users can easily find Web pages' locations by submitting the search request to those search engines.

In principle, if we install a lightweight search engine on the service discovery server that could retrieve Web pages posted by service providers and design a Web search interface for the incoming mobile agents, the problems described previously could be solved in an easy way. In this situation, service providers do not need to register the service description on the service discovery server. Instead, they register the URLs of their Web sites that advertise all the information concerning services. As a middleware on the service discovery server, the search engine will periodically retrieve the document indicated in URLs and all of their referencing documents, parse all the tags and words in the documents, and set up the relationship between the keywords and the host address of these service providers.

On the other hand, mobile agents can utilize the system interface by accessing the search engine's database and obtain a destination itinerary that includes a list of ranked host addresses of the service providers. Based on the above discussion, Figure 1 shows the service discovery process of DSSEM.

The current version of DSSEM concentrates on the database service discovery. The database service advertisement information can be easily converted to Web page representation. The specific characteristic of a Web page is that it contains rich media information and flexible layout, and can reference each other. As an example in

Figure 1. The service discovery process of DSSEM

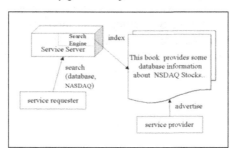

Figure 2. Web representation of database

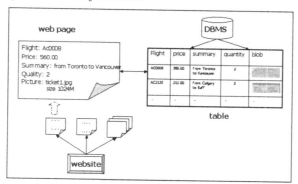

Figure 2, we can find that a two-dimensional database table can be converted into a one-dimensional Web page. Moreover, some binary data stored in the database such as image can be extracted from higher-dimensional space to a lower-dimensional space as the text representation in the Web page.

To use Web pages as a medium to advertise services for service providers, we should modify the template in the service description of SLP. The remarkable change is that some properties once represented by strings or XML language are now represented as the Web site's home URL. Table 3 illustrates a service description template of a bookstore example.

The proposed model is similar to SLP and Jini with respect to the service discovery process; however, it extends those protocols by setting up a centralized, seamless, scalable framework on the Internet. Unlike some multicasting services protocols, the centralized service discovery server makes DSSEM service discovery available on the Internet worldwide. The process of registration is similar to UDDI and the process of discovery is similar to the lookup service in Jini. Besides that, features of mobile agents bring DSSEM other incomparable advantages. First, code mobility

Table 3. An example of service description

| type = service: database |
| name = bookstore |
| URL = //www.cis.uoguelph.ca/ |
| location(URL)= www.uoguelph.ca |
| interface = dp_get_set(Handler, 'SQL statement', Result_handler) |

is almost impossible in most distributed systems. Therefore a client must download the resource drivers to invoke services. Although RPC or RMI mechanism can help to call services remotely, it might consume tremendous network bandwidth when dealing with services involving a huge amount of data, such as database services. DSSEM goes one step further. It makes agents migrate to the destination hosts and utilize services locally. Secondly, the security issue is seldom considered in current service discovery protocols. However, a mobile agent server requires a strict security concern for authorization and authentication when it accepts the incoming agents and provides them services for utilization.

Service Discovery in the IMAGO System

IMAGO is a mobile agent system in which agents are programs written in IMAGO Prolog that can move from one host on the Internet to another. Briefly speaking, an agent is characterized as an entity that is mature (autonomous and self-contained), mobile, and bears the mental model of the programmer (intelligent) (Li, 2001; Li & Autran, 2005). From an application point of view, the IMAGO system consists of two kinds of agent servers: stationary server and remote server. The stationary server of an application is the home server where the application is invoked. On the other hand, agents of an application are able to migrate to remote servers. Like a Web server, a remote server must have either a well-known name or a name searchable through the service discovery mechanism. Remote servers should provide services for network computing, resource sharing, or interfaces to other Internet servers, such as Web servers, database servers, and so forth.

In fact, an IMAGO server, no matter stationary or remote, is a multithreading logical virtual machine to host agents and provides a protected agent execution environment. The IMAGO system is portable in the sense that its servers run on virtually all Linux boxes with Gnu C compiler and Posix package. Tasks of an IMAGO server include accepting agents, creating a secure run time environment and supervising agent execution. It must also organize agent migration from or to other hosts, manage communications among agents, authenticate and control access for agent operations, recover agents and the information carried by them in case of network and computer failures and provide some basic services for the agents, such as database service and discovery service.

The architecture of the IMAGO server is shown in Figure 3. In this architecture, the system modules are configured to deal with different tasks. The core module of the IMAGO server is the scheduler. It maintains an agent list where each entry on the list matches different stages of the life cycle of an agent, such as creation, execution, memory management (expansion, contraction, or garbage collection),

Figure 3. The Infrastructure of IMAGO System

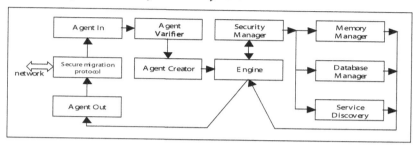

termination and migration. The agent list is sorted with respect to system-defined priorities. For example, the highest priority is given to agent migration, followed by agent creation and execution, memory manipulation, and finally database service and service discovery.

In the early phase of system design, database operation becomes the major service to applications in the IMAGO system. Thus, the problem of service discovery focuses on how to find such services effectively. Once a database server has been found, agents may migrate to that remote server and invoke database access locally through built-in primitives.

As an example, the following code shows a typical database access issued by an IMAGO agent:

```
dp_connect(URL, DatabaseName, UserName, Password, AccessMode),   //connection
dp_get_set(Handler, 'select .....', ResultHandler),   //data access
dp_disconnect(Handler).            //disconnection
```

Before a database service is advertised, the service provider should fill out a registration form and submit the form to an IMAGO service discovery server. The contents of the form include service type, database name, URL of the service provider host, access mode, HTTP URL of the service Web site, interface function, and the verification information. We choose URL as the host address since it is compatible with most commonly used Web browsers and independent of address families (such as IP, IPv6 and IPX).

To illustrate how DSSEM works, Figure 4 shows the steps involved in the service registration and discovery process in our IMAGO system. A service discovery server is called the service location host. In order to gather useful information, the search engine, called IMAGOSearch, should be independently installed on the service

Figure 4. The process of Web search module

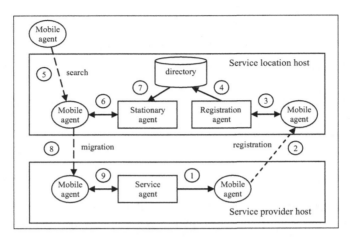

location host. This search engine maintains a special database system designed to index Internet addresses (URLs, Usenet, Ftp, image locations, *etc.*). Like traditional search engines, IMAGOSearch consists of three main components: *spider*, *indexer* and *searcher*. They are grouped into two modules, where one module includes spider and indexer, running in the background of a service location host, and the other module is the searcher, running in the foreground to provide discovery services. First, the spider gets the URLs from a URL list that contains initial Web site URLs registered by service providers. The spider then traverses along these URLs in the breadth-first manner and loads the referred hypertext documents into the service discovery server. The indexer extracts the salient words of these documents. Some related information such as text is also saved into the database for user retrieval. In addition, the indexer looks for URL anchors that reference other documents and adds them to the URL List. Besides considering the weight of each word in the documents (e.g., a word occurrence in the title should be assigned a higher weight than that occurs in the body), IMAGOSearch also pays attention to positions of each word and their relative distance during ranking. The ranking algorithm we use is called the shortest-substring ranking (Charles et al., 2000), which offers a simple way to weight each Web page based on a search criteria and total them up to form Web site ranking. The searcher behaves as a bridge between the IMAGO server and the search engine. It is responsible for accepting the search requests from mobile agents, querying the database, ranking search results and finally returning a destination itinerary.

The application programming interface for mobile agents is a built-in predicate, namely, *web_search(query, number, Result)*, where *query* is a compound term,

Figure 5. An example of service discovery and data mining process

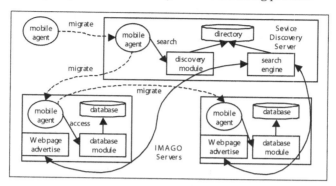

such as *locate("tsx," "stock transaction," "imago server")*, *number* is an integer indicating the maximum number of results expected, and *Result* is a variable to hold the returned values. When an agent issues a web_search(…) predicate, the agent is blocked and control is transferred to the service discovery module of the hosting IMAGO server. This module will communicate with the searcher, wait for search results, and resume the execution of the blocked agent. For example, suppose a food company wants to analyze the customer transaction records for quickly developing successful business strategies; its DDM agent may move to a known IMAGO service discovery server and then issue a query predicate requesting up to ten possible food industry database locations:

web_search(locate("food," "customer transaction," "imago data server"), 10, R)

Search result *R* will be delivered to the agent in the form of a list, where list entries are ranked in terms of priorities from high to low. Based on the given itinerary, the mobile agent may travel from host to host to carry out a DDM application. Figure 5 gives an example of service discovery and data mining process.

Discussion and Conclusion

In this chapter, we have discussed the design of a service discovery protocol, namely, DSSEM and its implementation in the IMAGO system. Table 6 (Bettstetter & Renner, 2000) summarizes the main features of selected protocols compared with DSSEM.

Table 6. Comparison of Different SDPs

Feature	SLP	Jini	Salutation	UPnP	DSSEM
Network transport	TCP/IP	Independent	Independent	TCP/IP	SITP
Programming language	Independent	Java	Independent	Independent	Independent
OS and platform	Dependent	Independent	Dependent	Dependent	Dependant
Code mobility	No	On demand	No	No	Yes
Srv attributes searchable	Yes	Yes	Yes	No	Yes
Leasing concept	Yes	Yes	No	Yes	Yes
Event notification	No	Remote event	Periodic and automatic	Publish events	No
Security	No	Java based	Authentication	No	Strict
Service Description and Scope	Service type and attribute matching	Interface Type and attribute matching	Functional units and Attributes within it	Description in XML	Webpage description and fuzzy matching

Table 7. Search Results for 'imago lab' keyword

draco.cis.uoguelph.ca	$R_w = 13.8$	100%
www.cis.uoguelph.ca	$R_w = 10.65$	77%
www.uoguelph.ca	$R_w = 4.6$	33%
www.cas.mcmaster.ca	$R_w = 4.23$	30.6%

From implementation point of view, the most critical issue about the performance of search engine is the quality of search results.

However, we cannot make a comparison with other major commercial search engines since they are operating at different levels. Thus, user evaluation is beyond the scope of this chapter. In order to show that our search engine does return useful information, Table 7 gives the experimental results for a query using the keywords "imago lab." The results show that all server URLs have come from reasonably high quality Web sites and, at last check, none were broken links. An R_w value is calculated according to word occurrence, weight and a factor value measuring the distance of keywords by a ranking algorithm (Charles at al., 2000). We define the result that has the highest R_w value as the highest priority and assign it a hundred percent rate, therefore the percentage of other results are rated relatively. Of course a true test of the quality of a search engine would involve extensive experiments, analysis and user evaluation, which is part of our future work.

Aside from the search quality, IMAGOSearch is designed to scale up cost effectively as the size of Web pages grow. Because IMAGOSearch only indexes Web servers registered by IMAGO Server users, we do not need to worry about indexed pages exceeding the maximum size of the database. One endeavour that we are undertaking is to reduce the table redundancy and use the storage efficiently. Our experiment shows that indexing 22,000 different documents consumes only 140Mb disk space. The search time is mostly dominated by the performance of CPU, disk I/O and the underlying database system. When a mobile agent wants to locate certain services, it must first move to the service discovery server, then make a local query and migrate to the destination hosts after obtaining the itinerary. This brings us to the problem that as a central unit, the service discovery server might become a bottleneck, especially when it is handling thousands of Web pages everyday and simultaneously hosting as many incoming mobile agents as possible. A possible solution is to duplicate service discovery servers. Replicas not only make the service discovery mechanism very efficient, but also increase the ability of fault tolerance.

The results of our work are encouraging and further studies in this field are being planned. First, the current implementation of search engine deals with only the AND logical relationship between search strings, it could be enhanced to parse some complex search criteria that combine keywords with Boolean expressions (AND, OR) and conditional expressions (<=, >=, substring match, *etc.*). Secondly, since a database contains multi-dimensional information, how to reflect dimensional relationship by a flat Web page is a big challenge. A possible way to address this issue is to use XML meta-data to describe the database dimension.

Acknowledgment

We would like to express our appreciation to the Natural Science and Engineering Council of Canada for supporting this research.

References

Baumer, C., Breugst, M., & Choy, S. (1999). Grasshopper: A universal agent platform based on OMG MASIF and FIPA standards. In *Proceedings of the First International Workshop on Mobile Agents for Telecommunication Applications (MATA'99)* (pp. 1-18).

Bettstetter, C., & Renner, C. (2000). A comparison of service discovery protocols and implementation of the service location protocol. In *Proceedings of the EUNICE 2000, Sixth EUNICE Open European Summer School*, Netherlands.

Charles L., Clarke, A., & Gordon V. (2000). Shortest substring retrieval and ranking. *ACM Transactions on Information Systems, 18*(1), 44-78.

Chen, H. (2000). *Developing a dynamic distributed intelligent agent framework based on Jini architecture*. Master's thesis, University of Maryland, Baltimore County.

FIPA.(2002). *Agent Management Specification*. Retrieved from http://www.fipa.org

Gray, R., Cybenko, G., & Kotz, D. (2002). D'Agents: Applications and performance of a mobile-agent system. *Software—Practice and Experience, 32*(6), 543-573.

Guttman, E., Perkins, C., & Veizades, J. (1999). Service Location Protocol, Version 2, White Paper.

Hashman, S., & Knudsen, S. (2001). *The application of Jini Technology to enhance the delivery of mobile services*. White Paper. Retrieved from http://wwws.sun.com/

John, R. (1999). *UPnP, Jini and Salutaion: A look at some popular coordination framework for future network devices*. Technical Report, California Software Labs.

Klusch, M., Lodi, S., & Moro, G. (2003). The role of agents in distributed data mining: Issues and benefits. In *Proceedings of the IEEE/WIC International Conference on Intelligent Agent Technology (IAT'03)*, Halifax, Canada (pp. 211-217). IEEE Computer Society Press.

Lange, D., & Ishima, M. (1998). *Programming and deploying Java, mobile agents with aglets*. Boston: Addison-Wesley.

Li, X. (2001). IMAGO: A Prolog-based system for intelligent mobile agents. In *Proceedings of Mobile Agents for Telecommunication Applications (MATA'01)* (LNCS 2164, pp. 21-30). Berlin: Springer Verlag.

Li, X. (2006). On the implementation of IMAGO system. *International Journal of Computer Science and Network Security, 6*(2a), 107-118.

Li, X., & Autran, G. (2005). Inter-agent Communication in IMAGO Prolog. (LNAI 3346, pp. 163-180).

Milojicic, D., Breugst, M., & Busse, I. (1998). MASIF: The OMG mobile agent system interoperability facility. In *Proceedings of the Second International Workshop on Mobile Agents* (pp. 50-67).

Mitsubishi Electric ITA. (1998). *Mobile agent computing. A white paper. UDDI White Paper*. Retrieved from http://www.uddi.org

Park, B., & Kargupta, H. (2002). *Distributed data mining: Algorithms, systems, and applications, data mining handbook*. In N. Ye (Ed.), *Data mining handbook* (pp. 341-358). IEA.

Ravi, N. (2001). *Service discovery in mobile environments*. Technical Report. Department of Computer Science and Engineering, University of Texas, Arlington.

Recursion Software Inc. (2005). Voyager Product Documentation. Retrieved from http://www.recursionsw.com/voyager_Documentation.html

Rubinstein, M., & Carlos, O. (1998). Service location for mobile agent system. In *Proceedings of the IEEE/SBT International Telecommunications Symposium (ITS'98)* (pp. 623-626).

Salutation Consortium. (1998) *Salutation Architecture Overview.* White Paper. Retrieved from http:// www.salutation.org/whitepaper/originalwp.pdf

Sun. Technical. (1999). *Jini Architectural overview.* White Paper. Retrieved from http:// www.sun.com/jini/

Universal Plug and Play Forum. (2000). *Universal Plug and Play device architecture, Version 0.91.* White Paper.

Chapter X

Integration of Management of Quality of Web Services in Service Oriented Architecture

M. A. Serhani, United Arab Emirates University, UAE

M. E. Badidi, Uni ted Arab Emirates University, UAE

A. Benharref, Concordia University, Canada

R. Dssouli, Concordia University, Canada

H. Sahraoui, Université de Montréal, Canada

Abstract

With the proliferation of Web services and their wide adoption as a novel technology for business-to-business interactions on the Web, quality of Web services (QoWS) management has witnessed considerable interest in recent years. Most of the existing works regarding this issue do not provide support for the overall QoWS management operations and are very often limited to a subset of these operations. Some of these works propose QoWS solutions for only basic Web services, while others propose solutions for composite Web services. In this chapter, we propose to extend the service-oriented architecture (SOA) with a framework for QoWS management in which services may be basic or composite Web services. The framework uses a layered approach to provide support for the most common QoWS management operations, which include QoWS specification, QoWS verification, QoWS negotiation, and QoWS monitoring. These operations are supported at both the design and the development phases of Web services.

Introduction

Web services are increasingly used as a new paradigm for providing and/or consuming service artifacts via the Internet. The Web services approach presents fundamental changes in the way systems are designed, developed, deployed and managed. At the earlier stages of the emergence of Web services as a new paradigm, the focus was on the definition of protocols, standards, development environments and interfaces. A lifecycle of Web services needs to integrate features such as QoWS-driven Web services selection, QoWS management, and QoWS composition enforcement and management. These features need to be addressed in earlier phases of the Web services development process, especially during the design phase, and then ultimately in the implementation phase. QoWS has to be first specified then published so that it can be later discovered by clients through the Web service interface description. QoWS is becoming a key differentiator in Web services competition as it allows for the differentiation between providers of similar services. The provision of QoWS involves a number of QoWS management functions including QoWS specification, QoWS verification, QoWS negotiation, and QoWS monitoring.

Nowadays, QoWS management for Web services is drawing considerable attention in both industry and academia. Most research on Quality of Service (QoS) management has been performed in the context of distributed multimedia systems delivering multimedia documents (e.g., video/audio streaming). QoS management mechanisms were also applied to Web-based applications such as electronic commerce where users have access to online catalogues which may contain multimedia information. In the past recent years, research on Web services focused more on functional and interfacing issues, such as simple object access protocol (SOAP), Web service description language (WSDL), and the universal description, discovery, and integration (UDDI). Most of today's Web services do not generally consider the level of QoWS they can deliver to their users. QoS support in Web services is still at the earlier stages of maturity as a research area where most of the efforts target the enumeration of QoWS requirements and mechanisms for QoWS management. Only recently, QoS issues have begun attracting more attention from the Web services community. QoWS is expected to become a value-added capability of emerging Web services as providers will be able to advertise their Web services in QoWS enabled registries to differentiate themselves from their competitors.

The need for QoS guarantee has been recognized as an important issue since the early stage of Web development. Web services add more challenges as their contexts are dynamic and their environments are heterogeneous and continuously changing.

Currently, QoS for Web services is not managed in a well-structured manner and lacks management of important aspects such as QoWS certification, verification, negotiation, adaptation, composition, and renegotiation. The consideration of these key features by any QoS management architecture raises many challenges as they need to be performed dynamically and may involve more than one participant (clients, providers, and third party entities). The provision of acceptable QoWS is a challenging task due to the dynamic and unpredictable nature of the Web. In contrast to QoS management in centralized systems, QoWS management in distributed systems is very challenging as it depends on many factors such as the performance of the underlying network, the speed of the servers, response time of database systems, and the dynamic and unpredictable nature of business applications and Internet traffic.

Web services are sometimes referred to in the literature using different terms. Some authors use the term "XML Web Services," other use Web Services and capitalize the beginning letters "W" and "S," also some other authors use "service" is singular instead of "services." We will use the term "Web services" throughout this chapter. The term QoS is often used in the context of networking, multimedia applications and telephony which may not represent the same meaning in the context of Web services. In this chapter, we use the term quality of Web services (QoWS) to emphasize the QoS context of this research. We address the issue of QoWS management for basic and composite Web services. We focus first on describing a systematic way for developing Web services that takes into consideration QoWS management.

The goal of this work is to design and develop a framework that provides a structured approach for Web services development, and which captures important characteristics of Web services regarding QoWS management. The proposed framework provides QoWS management operations for both service providers and consumers. Web services providers are supported in the publication and verification of QoS rendered by their Web services while they are supported to express service specific requirements when selecting Web services. The process of quality of service management within the framework is conducted through a set of phases ranging from the specification of QoWS parameters, selection of QoWS-aware Web services, QoWS monitoring and guarantee, and QoWS composition management.

Related Work

QoS has been extensively studied in the areas of software engineering, network management, and distributed applications and systems. QoS from the networking point of view refers to the capability of a network to provide an acceptable service to selected network traffic over one or heterogeneous networks (e.g., IP-based, ATM, VoIP, etc.). Supporting end-to-end QoS through the network was widely covered in literature and industry. Hence, diverse solutions were developed to implement QoS support at the network level (Barden, Clark, & Shenker, 1994; Blake, Black, Carlson, Davies, Wang, & Weiss, 1998; Rosen, Viswanathan & Callon 1999; Stattenberger & Braun 2003). QoS management in distributed systems received great interest in the past few years. Numerous architectures have been proposed to manage the QoS for distributed applications (Braden, Clark, & Shenker, 1994; Campbell, Coulson, & Hutchison, 1994; Benerjea, Ferrari, Mah, Oran, Verma, & Zhang, 1996; Campbell, Aurrecoechea & Hauw, 1997; Fischer, Hafid, Bochmann, & De-Meer, 1997).

In the context of Web services, considerable attention was brought to the QoS support. A number of works were proposed to categorize, specify, measure, and evaluate QoS for Web services (Mani, & Nagarajan, 2002; Menascé, 2002; Liangzhao et al., 2003; Li, Ding, Chen, Liu, & Li, 2003; Shuping, 2003).

The approaches that have been proposed to provide QoWS support and management for Web services can be classified into two categories: (1) approaches that have been proposed for managing QoS of basic Web services, and (2) approaches that have been developed for managing QoS of composite Web services.

In the first category, numerous works present solutions for one or more of the following QoWS management operations: QoWS verification, QoWS discovery and selection, QoWS negotiation, QoWS monitoring, and QoWS adaptation. Approaches for QoWS-driven Web services discovery, selection, and verification were proposed initially by Shuping Ran in Shuping (2003). The author proposes a generic model for Web services discovery that includes the functional and non-functional requirements of Web services (i.e., QoWS). The model proposes certifying QoWS claims for providers and verifies these QoWS claims for clients. With main focus on addressing the issue of Web service selection, Maximilien et al. (2004) proposed a framework and ontology for dynamic Web services selection. The framework incorporates service selection agents that use the QoWS ontology and an XML policy language that allows service consumers and providers to expose their quality preferences and advertisements. It lets providers, consumers, and agents collaborate to determine each other's Web service quality and trustworthiness. Chen et al. (2003) presented a description and an implementation of a broker-based architecture for controlling QoS of Web services. The broker acts as an intermediary third party, which performs Web services selection and QoS negotiation on behalf of the client. Some similar broker-based architectures have been presented in Tian, Gramm, Naumowicz, Ritter, and Schiller (2003) and Tian, Gramm, Ritter, and Schiller (2004); they focus more on the QoS specification using XML schema, and the dynamic QoS mapping between Web server and network performance.

In summary, the solutions presented above for QoS management of basic Web services present some substantial limitations that are related to one or more of the following issues:

1. Most of the performed QoWS management operations are often restricted to Web services selection based on QoWS, even through other management operations such as QoWS verification and certification, QoWS negotiation, QoWS monitoring, and QoWS adaptation are also highly needed.

2. None of these solutions considers the performance of the entity responsible of managing QoWS (e.g., Broker). However, the performance of the broker can affect the whole architecture if it is not behaving as expected.

3. Most of the proposed solutions do not support several categories of the same service. They restrict the provider to delivering services to one category of clients. However, clients may have different and continuously changing requirements.

4. The monitoring operations proposed in the above solutions for QoWS management of Web services are often performed in one location and by a single component. However, monitoring information needs to be combined from different sources and performed at different locations.

In the second category of approaches for QoWS management, several research initiatives have been carried out to tackle the issue of managing QoWS of a composite Web service. Jaeger et al. (2004; 2005) focus on defining and extending abstract composition patterns with the consideration of Web services dependencies. Also, they propose to use the pattern-based aggregation in the monitoring process during run time. In the same direction, Cardoso et al. (2004) proposed a mathematical model for QoS aggregation in workflows. Their model uses a QoS computation algorithm that applies a set of reduction patterns to the workflow in order to obtain a valid and final workflow task. Zeng et al. (2004) proposed a QoS-based framework for selecting Web services to build composite Web services. Their model evaluates the overall QoS of Web services using a local optimization approach and a global planning approach. These approaches are used for selecting Web services that will execute a specific task in the composition. Canfora et al. (2005) proposed an approach to trigger and perform composite service re-planning during execution. Re-planning is triggered as soon as it is possible to predict the actual Web service QoS and detect whether the QoS will deviate from the initial estimate. Then, the part of the Web service workflow that still has to be executed will be determined and replanned. Baresi et al. (2004) presented an approach for monitoring the execution of composite Web services. The composition process is annotated by the provider of composite Web service using assertions, but there is no prior validation of these annotations. The monitoring conducted aims to assess the correctness of Web services composition. It focuses only on the monitoring of functional contract, the timeout, and exception handling.

With reference to the above solutions for QoS composition management of composite Web services, there are still some important issues to be addressed. Indeed, to enable a reliable and trustable QoS composition, we need a dynamic framework to verify and monitor the QoS composition.

Service-Oriented Architecture Overview

Standards and Protocols

The Web services architecture defines interactions between three roles: service provider, service registry and service requester (Gisofli, 2001; Kreger, 2001). The interactions between these roles involve three operations: publish, find, and bind, which are illustrated in Figure 1.

- A "Service Provider" is a network node that provides an interface to the Web services it is providing; and responds to requests for using its service.

Figure 1. Web services architecture

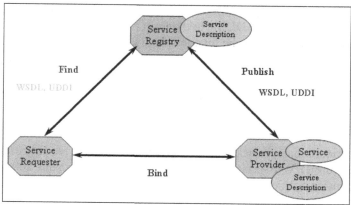

- A "Service Requester" is a network node that discovers and invokes Web services to realize a business solution.

- A "Service Registry" or service broker is a network node that acts as a repository for the description of Web services interfaces that are published by service providers.

Service providers "publish" services to a service broker. Service requesters "find" required Web services by using a service broker, and then "bind" to these services (Gisofli, 2001).

The Web services programming stack is a collection of standardized protocols and application programming interfaces (APIs) that are used to define, locate, implement, and make Web services interact with each other. The Web service protocol stack is mainly composted of four layers:

1. **Service transport:** This layer is responsible for transporting messages between network applications. It can be based on HTTP, SMTP, FTP, as well as the more recent BEEP (Block Extensible Exchange Protocol, 2001). Other network protocols, such as the IIOP (Internet Inter-ORB Protocol, 2004) or the IBM MQSeries (IBM MQSeries, 2005), may also be used.

2. **XML messaging:** This layer is responsible for encoding messages in a common XML format so that messages can be understood at each end of the network connection. Actually, this area includes protocols such as XML-RPC, and SOAP (XML Remote Procedure Call, 2003; World Wide Web Consortium, 2003). All of these protocols facilitate publish, find, and bind operations.

3. **Service description:** This layer is used for describing the public interface of a Web service. WSDL is typically used for this purpose. WSDL is often used in combination with SOAP and XML-Schema to provide Web services over the Internet. Before connecting to a Web service, a client parses first the WSDL to find out published functions. User-defined data types used within the interfaces are embedded in the WSDL file in the form of XML-Schema. The client can then use SOAP to invoke the functions listed in the WSDL document.

4. **Service discovery:** Services descriptions are centralized in a common registry so that Web services' providers may publish the description of their services, and clients may be able to dynamically discover available services. The UDDI registry is now the standard for Web services publication and discovery.

The Web services protocol stack also includes a whole range of recently established standards (Figure 2): Web services flow language (WSFL) (Leymann, 2001), SOAP security extension with digital signature (SOAP-DSIG) (SOAP Digital Signature,

Figure 2. Web services programming stack

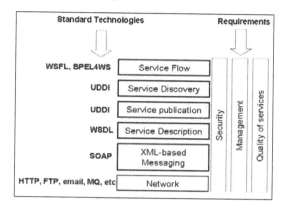

2001), and BPEL4WS (Business Process Execution Language for Web Services, 2003).

In order to meet the rigorous demands and requirements of today's e-business applications, an enterprise Web services infrastructure must be provided. This infrastructure should include, in addition to the above areas aspects new functionalities to deal with security, Web services management, and quality-of-service management. These infrastructure components, represented on the right side of Figure 2, have to be addressed at each layer of the stack. As the Web services paradigm is increasingly adopted throughout the industry, these issues are already undergoing standardization (Gottschalk, Graham, Kreger, & Snell, 2002; Della-Libera, et al., 2005).

SOA Features

Unlike traditional point-to-point architectures, SOA comprises loosely coupled, highly interoperable entities. The SOA enhances the interoperability of distributed systems through the integration of heterogeneous languages and protocols to ease the publication, discovery, and binding to Web services. Web services interoperate, thanks to a proper definition that is independent from the underlying platform and programming language (e.g., WSDL). The interface definition hides details of the service implementation and makes Web services very reusable as they are defined in a standards-compliant manner.

The rationale behind the success of SOA is the large support it has gained from all major IT vendors (IBM, HP, Oracle, Sun, etc.). Web services technology allows faster development, deployment, integration, and maintenance of business applications. Web services benefit from the adoption of widely known and used standards such as HTTP, XML along with other new XML-based standards (e.g., WSDL, and SOAP). Web services technologies benefit also from the experiences of previous distributed technologies such as CORBA, DCOM, EJB, RMI, JINI, and so forth. High-level languages, such as BPEL4WS, extend the Web service concept by providing a method for defining and supporting the composition of Web services to create large scale Web services. These languages use the concept of workflow and provide features to represent partners and orchestrate their interactions. As a result of these developments, the Web services concepts and technologies are becoming one of the most important existing distributed computing standards and their adoption is expected to rise in the near future.

QoWS Overview

QoS was recognized early in industry and academia and has been widely investigated for distributed and continuous media communications such as Voice over IP (VoIP). QoS for Web services is defined as the non-functional properties of the service being provided to users. These properties are also known as metrics. Common quality attributes for Web services are response time, availability, latency, cost, and throughput (Ran, 2003; Menascé, 2002). In SOA, both Web services' providers and Web services' clients should be able to consider QoS related statements to enable QoS-aware service publication and discovery. In composite Web service, increased requirements are placed upon QoS support as these applications might be very demanding in terms of performance guarantee and delivery assurance. In addition, different clients might require different levels of performance from the composite Web services they use.

The first step toward supporting QoWS is a precise definition of quality metrics related to Web services. A set of quality attributes for Web services have been proposed recently (Mani, 2002; Ran, 2003; Serhani, 2005). Quality attributes are classified and defined according to users' QoS requirements (different requirements

Table 1. Differentiated class of Web services

Class of WS / QoS Parameter	Class 1	Class 2	Class 3	....	Class n
Response Time	N/A	0.7 ms	0.5 ms		0.1ms
Latency	N/A	N/A	0.1 ms		0.01 ms
Throughput	N/A	N/A	N/A		300 requests/s
Availability	N/A	80%	95%		100%
Reputation	NN/A	4 /A	/5		5/5
Cost	00.10 $	0 .2 $	.25$		0.35$

for different users' profiles). These attributes and their related internal properties are identified and described by accurate and valid metrics. Classes of QoWS attributes may also be defined, and each class of service has different QoS attributes with different values.

Table 1 depicts examples of QoS classes for Web services based on a set of QoS attributes. A brief definition of each of the QoS attributes presented in Table 1 is provided below:

- **Response time (RT):** The time a Web service takes to respond to the client request. It represents the time interval between the time when the request is issued and the time the answer is received. The response time value includes the round-trip communication and the processing delays in servicing the client request (Menascé, 2002; Ran, 2003). RT attribute is measured either at the client's site or at the provider's site.

- **Service charge (cost):** The cost charged for using the Web service. This cost can be charged based on the number of invoked operations or the volume of data, or based on a combination of both.

- **Availability:** The probability that the Web service is accessible or available. It can also be defined as the percentage of time that the Web service is operating (Menascé, 2002). To compute this parameter, the Web service is observed over a period of time to measure its availability as the percentage of uptime during this observation period. A longer period of observation gives a more accurate approximation of the Web service availability.

- **Latency:** The amount of time taken between the time a service request arrives and the time the corresponding response is generated (Ran, 2003). This metric is computed at the provider site.

- **Throughput:** The rate at which a Web service can process requests (Menascé, 2002). It corresponds to the number of processed requests over a specified time period. It is related to latency (Ran, 2003). QoS measures can include the maximum throughput or a function that describes how throughput varies with load intensity.

- **Reputation:** A qualitative measure of Web services trustworthiness. It depends on the end users' experiences in using a Web service. Different users may have different opinions on the same Web service. The reputation values the average ranking given to the provider of the Web service by end users (Ran, 2003). For example, in Amazon.com, the range is [0 to 5].

A QoS Management Framework for Web Services

The initial specifications of Web services technology were focused on the functional and interfacing aspects to deal with the issues of service publishing and service discovery. The SOA was proposed to position the key players in this new paradigm, and technologies such as SOAP, WSDL, and UDDI were mainly designed to support interactions among these players. SOA in its initial form do not provide support for a complete development lifecycle of Web services that deals with the issues of performance, security, and management. However, new specifications are being proposed to incorporate transactions, reliable messaging, security, interoperability, quality of service, orchestration, and choreography. Some of these aspects are already undergoing standardization (Evans, et al., 2003; Peltz, 2003; Web Services Transaction, 2003).

With the above developments in mind as well as the limitations of the research works, which we described in the related work section, regarding the issue of QoWS management of Web services, we set out to develop a new framework that intends to capture most of the QoWS management operations we stated previously, and to extend SOA to provide support for Web services management, QoWS management, for both basic and composite Web services. The framework objectives are as follows:

1. Provide support for the composition of classes of QoS in Web services.

2. Validate the QoWS composition for both clients and providers before and after selecting a composite Web service.

3. Provide support for runtime distributed monitoring of both composite QoS and participating Web services. Most of the proposed solutions monitor the QoS composition at the final Web service. However, a violated QoS by the composite Web service may be caused by a basic Web service. Therefore, it will be more pertinent if the monitoring is performed at different locations, and information is collected from different sources.

4. Allow verification of QoWS composition, which will be useful for both clients and providers. Clients will ensure that the composite Web service meets their QoS requirements. On the other hand, providers of composite Web services will test and verify their QoS composition before they publish it to clients.

5. Should provide the means to monitor both the final Web service as well as its basic Web services to be able to locate where the originated QoS violations occurred, and identify the Web services responsible of the violation, so that they can be replaced or their QoS be adapted.

Figure 3. QoWS Management Framework

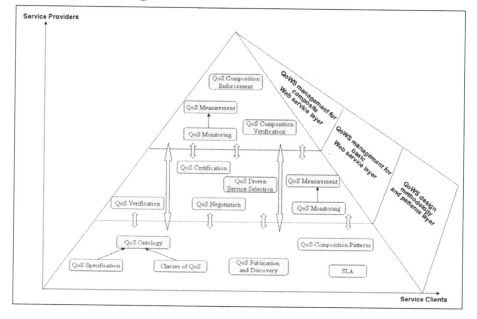

6.   Allow to evaluate and estimate the overhead of the management of QoS composition of Web services. This issue is not often studied. For example, some solutions can be very costly in terms of the load generated from the execution of management operations.

Components of the Framework

To meet the above requirements and to extend the service oriented architecture with QoWS management, we have chosen a layered approach for our framework. The framework promotes the integration of various QoWS mechanisms in both the client's and provider's environments to meet end-to-end needs. Figure 3 depicts the main layers and components of the framework. Components of the framework are designed to provide support for verification, certification, selection, negotiation and monitoring of end-to-end QoWS for both basic and composite Web services.

The proposed framework is divided into three layers:

1.   QoWS design methodology and composition patterns layer
2.   QoWS management for basic Web services layer
3.   QoWS management for composite Web services layer

The first layer deals with design principles and a methodology for QoWS specifica-tion, QoWS management, QoWS negotiation, and QoWS composition management. The second layer is concerned with operations for QoWS management of basic Web services, which mainly include QoWS verification and certification, QoWS negotia-tion, and QoWS monitoring. The third layer is concerned with QoWS management operations for composite Web services essentially those related to verification and monitoring of QoWS composition.

We have considered a bottom-up approach for the design of the framework, which has been guided by the following concerns:

1.   Specify how QoWS may be integrated in the development lifecycle of both basic and composite Web services
2.   Develop solutions for QoS management of basic Web services
3.   Develop solution for QoWS management of composite Web services

The management of composite Web services is more complex than the management of basic Web services. This complexity is due to the fact that a composite Web ser-vice aggregates a set of basic Web services to provide a more complex service. In addition to the management of the composite Web service in its own, management of basic Web services must be performed accordingly and all management entities should share management information.

Integration of QoWS in the Basic Web Services Lifecycle

Our motivation for considering the integration of QoWS in the Web services lifecycle is that existing models, described in the related work section, do not fully capture all activities and operations related to the quality of Web services such as QoWS specification, QoWS management, and management of QoWS composition. Our approach, described in Serhani, Dssouli, Sahraoui, Hafid, & Benharref (2005), in-vestigates how to augment the development process of Web services with the above activities. Greater consideration of QoWS, as perceived by providers and requesters, should be given during the development phases including design, implementation, development, testing, discovery, management, and composition of Web services.

Figure 4. WSDL document extended with classes of QoS ontology description

```
<?xml version="1.0" encoding="utf-8"?>
<definitions xmlns="http://schemas.xmlsoap.org/wsdl/" argetNamespace="http://... ">
.........
  <Class1>
    <QoS_Spec>
        <QoSOnto ontologyName="ResptimeOntserviceNames">
            <QoS name="response time">
                <QoS_Value>
                    <unit>milliseconde</unit>
                    <max>5</max>
                </QoS_Value>
            </QoS>
        </QoSOnto>
        ...
        <QoSOnto ontologyName="ThrouOntserviceNames">
            <QoS name="Throughput">
                <QoS_Value>
                    <unit>request per second</unit>
                    <max>500</max>
                </QoS_Value>
            </QoS>
        </QoSOnto>
    </QoS_Spec>
  </Class1>
  <Class2>
    <QoS_Spec>
        <QoSOnto ontologyName="ReputationOntserviceNames">
            <QoS name="reputation">
                <QoS_Value>
                    <unit>rank</unit>
                    <max>3</max>
                </QoS_Value>
            </QoS>
        </QoSOnto>
.........
    </QoS_Spec>
  </Class2>
</definitions>
```

Figure 5. QoWS management of a composite Web services

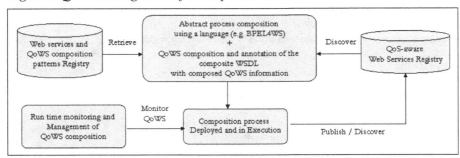

We strongly believe that QoWS features need to be described since earlier phases of the Web services development process, and especially during the design. They concern mainly QoWS specification, publishing and QoS-aware discovery, QoS-aware composition, and QoWS management.

Our new Web services lifecycle (Serhani, Dssouli, Sahraoui, Hafid, & Benharref, 2005) overcomes the limitations of existing models. It extends the traditional lifecycle by providing support for QoWS description, and QoS-aware publishing and discovery of Web services. QoWS parameters as well as differentiated classes of QoWS may be specified during the design phase. A QoWS class defines a set of quality parameters the Web service is able to provide. Figure 4 presents and example of WSDL document of a Web service extended with two classes of QoS description.

Integration of QoWS in the Composite Web Services Lifecycle

The composition of Web services is the process of aggregating a set of Web services to create a more complete Web service with a wide range of functionalities. Aggregating Web services together has to be done according to a set of design principals and by following a set of phases. We strongly believe that Web services composition is a separate lifecycle in its own as it is often a dynamic and complex process that presents new requirements when compared to the lifecycle of a basic Web services. Figure 5 illustrates our approach for integrating and managing QoS within the composite Web services lifecycle. The integration is achieved throughout the following phases: (1) QoS-aware Web services discovery, (2) abstract process and QoWS composition, (3) Web services and QoWS composition patterns registry, and (4) monitoring and management of QoWS composition.

Figure 6. Aggregation of Numeral QoS Dimension: QoWS composition patterns (Jaeger, Rojec-Goldmann, & Muhl, 2005)

# Pattern	Mean Execution Time	Mean Cost	Mean Reputation
Sequential Patterns			
1 Sequence	$x_a = \sum_{i=1}^{n} x_i$	$x_a = \sum_{i=1}^{n} x_i$	$x_a = \min \{x_1, ..., x_n\}$
2 Loop	$x_a = kx$	$x_a = kx$	$x_a = x$
Parallel Patterns			
3 XOR-XOR	$x_a = \frac{1}{n} \sum_{i=1}^{n} g_i x_i$	$x_a = \frac{1}{n} \sum_{i=1}^{n} g_i x_i$	$x_a = \frac{1}{n} \sum_{i=1}^{n} g_i x_i$
4 AND-AND	*n.a.*	$x_a = \sum_{i=1}^{n} x_i$	$x_a = \min \{x_1, ..., x_n\}$
5 AND-DISC	$x_a = \frac{1}{n} \sum_{i=1}^{n} h_i x_i$	$x_a = \sum_{i=1}^{n} x_i$	$x_a = \frac{1}{n} \sum_{i=1}^{n} h_i x_i$
6 OR-OR	*n.a.*	$x_a = \frac{1}{n} \sum_{i=1}^{n} h_i x_i$	$x_a = \min \{x_1, ..., x_n\}$
7 OR-DISC	$x_a = \frac{1}{n} \sum_{i=1}^{n} h_i x_i$	$x_a = \frac{1}{n} \sum_{i=1}^{n} h_i x_i$	$x_a = \frac{1}{n} \sum_{i=1}^{n} h_i x_i$

QoS-aware Web services discovery is the operation that allows the discovery and the localization of QoS-aware Web services that will participate in the composition process. It provides the requestor with the service description (WSDL document) that contains information about the service location and the QoWS it is providing. The requestor (abstract process composition) uses then this information to bind to the service, invoke its operations, and compose its QoS.

Abstract process composition is a formal definition of the composition process which identifies the services partners that are involved in a given composition, the specification and the orchestration of their interactions, the sequences of planned activities, and the generation of interface description of the composite Web service.

Web Services and QoWS composition patterns registry is a registry, which contains a set of design principles that may be applied while composing Web services and their offered QoWS. These patterns are defined according to the way Web services are invoked and derived from the composition process. A detailed description of these composition patterns is illustrated in Figure 6. They are also described in an XML document which is automatically explored when a composition is executed in order to apply the corresponding pattern.

QoWS composition and WSDL QoWS annotation. This phase enables testing the composition process during the design phase. It consists of verifying the BPEL document and applying both Web services composition patterns and QoWS composition patterns. The result of this phase leads to the extension of the WSDL interface of composite Web services with QoWS annotations.

Runtime Monitoring of QoWS composition of a composite Web service. In this phase, Web services concerned by the composition are fully deployed, and the composite service specifications is executed while striving to satisfy quality constraints, for example, availability, response time, cost, and other properties. Monitoring QoWS composition is a continuous process of observing delivered QoWS. A concise monitoring of composite QoWS requires monitoring the QoWS of all Web services involved in the composition.

Layer 2: QoWS Management of Basic Web Services

In our previous investigations work (Serhani, Dssouli, Hafid, & Sahraoui, 2005; Serhani, Dssouli, Sahraoui, Benharref, & Badidi, 2006), we have proposed an architecture to handle QoWS composition, validation, and monitoring. QoWS management of basic Web services is achieved by using a QoWS *Broker* based architecture. This architecture extends the SOA by employing a new mediator to provide support for the management and enforcement of QoWS delivery. Layer 2 of the proposed framework integrates perfectly the features provided by the above architecture, and that we can summarize as follows:

1.   Ability to define classes of QoWS to support increasing number of clients with different QoWS requirements, and well defined QoWS properties of Web services are made available to clients. QoWS model provides an integrated view for both service providers and requestors, though they do not have the same view. The QoWS attributes are classified according to QoWS user requirements (different requirements for different users). Each class of service is described by the set of QoWS attributes each Web service can offer.

2.   Support for QoWS management operations such as QoS-driven Web services selection, QoWS negotiation, QoWS verification and certification, and QoWS monitoring.

3.   Efficient selection and execution of Web services based on client requirements and QoWS verification and certification mechanisms.

4.   Online monitoring of QoWS provision to assure compliance with published or negotiated QoWS requirements, and provision of immediate QoWS user feedback. The monitoring techniques observe QoWS provision at runtime, and collect valuable information from the user and the provider using measurement techniques to dynamically evaluate QoWS metrics.

Layer 3: QoWS Management of Composite Web Services

It is relatively easy to glue Web services together in a composite Web service. However, it is more difficult to guarantee the global QoWS of a composite Web service made up of several basic Web services. Hence, it is critical to determine how the global QoWS property is related to the QoWS proprieties of individual Web services. We have developed in a previous work (Serhani, Dssouli, Sahraoui, & Benharref, 2006) a model to manage the QoWS composition, its verification, and its monitoring. The Verification and monitoring of QoWS composition is very useful for both clients and providers. Clients ensure that the composed Web service meets their QoWS requirements. On the other hand, providers of composed Web services are able to test and verify their QoWS composition before they publish it to clients.

With regards to QoWS composition and monitoring of composite Web services, the third layer of our framework provides the following features:

1. It specifies a set of QoWS composition patterns using an ontology, which allows categorizing the various patterns that may apply to a given QoWS composition.

2. It defines and formulates an ontology for classes of QoWS to facilitate the description of QoS knowledge in the services interface of each basic Web services taking part in the composition.

3. It extends the interface description of a composed Web service with QoS composition information.

4. It supports the description of classes of QoWS composition of composite Web services. Most of the existing solutions are restricting the QoWS composition to one type of QoWS for one category of clients. However, clients may have different and continuously changing QoWS requirements.

5. It monitors the behavior of all Web services taking part in the composition to identify eventual QoS violation, and identify the Web services, which are responsible of the violation.

Implementation and Evaluation

A prototype of our proposed framework is under development. Many of the features and components of the framework, we described in previous sections, have been implemented. They concern essentially the QoWS management schemes, including specification, composition, and monitoring, of basic and composite Web services.

Figure 7. Application support for QoWS specification

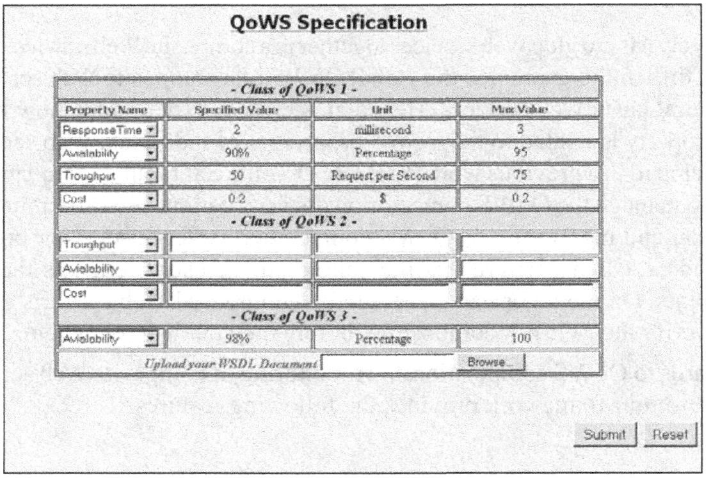

The following subsections present details about the implementation of the features of each layer of the framework.

Specification of Classes of QoWS

The WSDL of a QoS-aware Web service comprises the definition of functions in addition to a description of QoWS classes it can deliver. The integration of classes of QoWS in the WSDL document of a service is not straightforward. We have automated the process of QoWS specification, and we have developed an application interface to support the provider in specifying classes of QoWS of their Web services (see Figure 7). For each class of QoWS the provider specifies the QoWS property name, property type, and property value. Then, the provider has to upload the WSDL document of its Web service. Once the provider presses the submit button, the specified QoWS information is used by the application to automatically generate a new and "well formed" WSDL document that includes the specified classes of QoWS description provided by the provider through the application interface.

QoWS Publication and Discovery

To support QoS-aware Web services publication and discovery within our framework, we have chosen to use universal description, discovery and interaction extension

Figure 8 Validation of QoS before the publication process

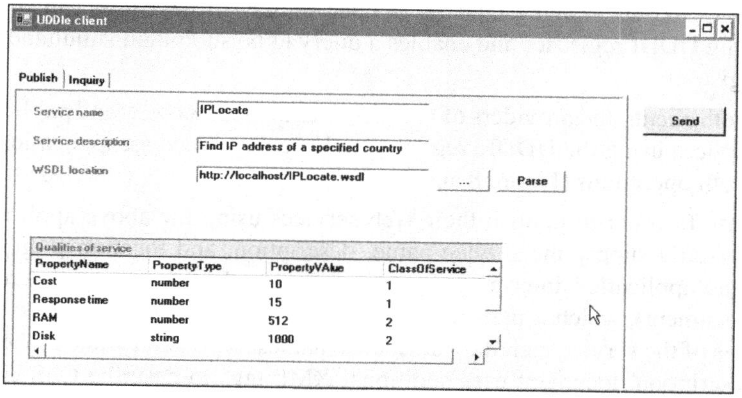

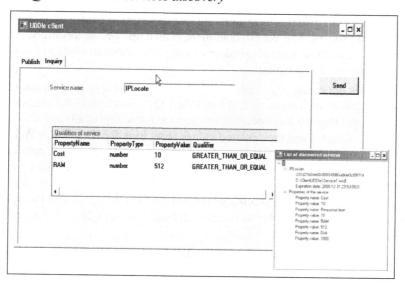

Figure 9 QoS driven Web services discovery

(UDDIe) (Shaikhl, 2003) as a Web services registry. This registry extends the classical UDDI registries by supporting QoS publication and discovery. UDDIe supports the concept of "blue pages" to record user-defined properties associated with a Web service, and to enable discovery of Web services based on these properties. Searches for attributes other than the name of a Web service are achieved by extending the Business Service class in UDDI with propertyBag, and by extending the find method to enable queries submitted to UDDIe to be based on numerical and logical (AND/OR) ranges. UDDIe, an open source software tool, can co-exist with existing UDDI registries and enables a query to be submitted simultaneously to both registries.

To guide both clients and providers of Web services in the discovery and publication of Web services using the UDDIe registry, we have developed an application that supports both operations (Figure 8 and 9).

Publication. In order to publish their Web services using the above application, providers should supply the service name, description, and location (Figure 8). Through the application interface, the provider uploads the service description (WSDL document), which is parsed to validate its content and to display the list of QoS classes of the service including attributes' names, types, and values. The Web service description document uses additional XML tags to describe QoS classes in terms of QoS attributes and their related values. The validation process of the WSDL document verifies the correctness of its published operations in addition to the QoS information. Using the application interface, the Web service provider can add or remove QoS attributes to/from its service description before going through the publication process. The WSDL document is then updated accordingly. At this stage, the WSDL document is validated and its provider publishes the QoS-enabled Web service interface description.

Discovery. This operation is available to Web service clients to guide them in the process of selecting Web services that meet their QoS requirements (Figure 9). A client queries the registry and specifies the service name (optional) and the set of required QoS attributes and their related values (e.g., look for IP_Locator Web services, that return the location of a given IP address; a client can specify conditions such as: cost less than $25 and response time less than 20 ns). The client has the possibility to fully edit the query before issuing it. A list of Web services' descriptions that fulfill the client's requirements is displayed via the application interface. The frame contains the list of QoS classes with their corresponding values, as well as the Web service definition.

An added value of this application is that it validates and verifies WSDL documents and their QoS. It also generates the client's request that specify QoS requirements, which is then submitted to the UDDIe. The result of the query is a detailed description of suitable Web services and their QoS. This significantly helps the client making decision and selecting the Web service that best meets his/her needs.

QoWS Monitoring

QoWS monitoring is a necessary management activity to sustain the contracted QoWS and to support other management activities such as QoS adaptation, QoWS

Figure 10. Scenario of RT monitoring for Tri_Stat Web service

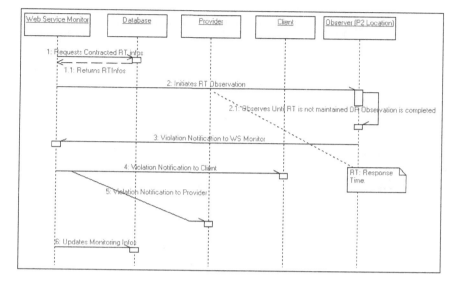

policing, and QoS re-negotiation. QoWS monitoring is the continuous observation of the level of QoS delivered to clients. Observation of QoWS is conducted through periodic measurements and computation of QoS parameters at certain observation points between the client and the Web service provider. If the measured value of a QoWS parameter does not meet the agreed upon value, a violation is detected and announced, indicating the violation and if possible the cause.

Monitoring QoWS relies on a well-designed component that gathers accurate measurements, models and analyzes the data over certain periods of time or when certain events occur. Provisioning of QoWS is highly affected by the Internet infrastructure as Web services are deployed and consumed via the Internet that is known as an unreliable network environment. This makes QoWS monitoring difficult to automate and manage.

We have considered all of the above constraints to monitor the QoWS at different observation locations: client site, provider site, and/or somewhere between them. The location of the point of observation has to be chosen very carefully, depending on the nature of the QoWS attribute to be measured. For example, in the case of the response time parameter, when it is measured at the provider site (PS), the delay and latency of the underlying network are not considered. However, when it is measured at the client site (CS), it is affected by the delay introduced by the underlying network infrastructure as it will be perceived by the client.

QoWS monitoring is achieved by a third component (e.g., Monitor), which instantiates observers at some points of observation (PS and CS). To measure the response time (RT) for example, the observer at CS captures the time stamp when the request leaves the client and the time stamp when the response is received by the client. The QoWS monitor then calculates the response time by determining the difference between the two time stamps, and stores the measured values in the monitor database or writes them to a log file. A violation is detected by the QoWS monitor if the measured value is above the threshold value agreed upon with the provider. Figure 10 describes a scenario of monitoring a Tri_Sat Web service (Serhani, Dssouli, Hafid, & Sahraoui, 2005).

For QoWS computation and monitoring, the observers deployed by the monitor are called SOAP handlers. Handlers are Java interfaces that can be developed and easily deployed to support a set of functionalities. These handlers are supported by the BEA platform (Taleb, 2005). SOAP handlers can be deployed within the provider environment. Also, the client can be set up to support the deployment of these handlers when QoS computation at the client site is required for certain QoS attributes. SOAP handlers are used by the monitor to observe the messages between Web service providers and their clients. A SOAP handler is used in our framework to monitor QoWS by performing the following actions:

1. Initiate timers when an event occurs (reception of a request or generation of its response).

2. Intercept messages arriving to and/or leaving from the component under observation (Web service or client application).

3. Forward messages to third party components (e.g., monitor).

4. Collect and write traces to a log file, these traces are analyzed to detect any misbehavior of observed Web services.

5. Measure some QoWS attributes such as the time consumed in processing each client request (latency).

6. Forward measured values of QoS to a third party broker for example and/or write them to a log file.

Handlers implement timers to compute response time and processing time. We have chosen to compute QoS values directly with the handler instead of getting values from the handler and analyzing them by the monitor.

In our example, the SOAP handler sends every event in a UDP Datagram to the monitor. The data received from the handlers are then collected and analyzed periodically by the broker to check if the contracted QoS values are being maintained.

Figure 11. Generated WSDL of a final Web service within the composite QoS description (Serhani, Dssouli, Sahraoui, & Benharref, 2006)

```
<? xml version="1.0" ?>
<definitions name = "Call COnference"
        targetNamespace = http:// .../CallConference.wsdl>
. . .
-------------------------------------------------------------------

        <composedResultsClass1>
                <ResptimeOntserviceNames>8.0</ResptimeOntserviceNames>
                <AvailOntserviceNames>92.1199</AvailOntserviceNames>
                <CostOntserviceNames>1.0</CostOntserviceNames>
                <ThrouOntserviceNames>300.0</ThrouOntserviceNames>
        </composedResultsClass1>
        <composedResultsClass2>
                <ReputationOntserviceNames>3.0</ReputationOntserviceNames>
                <AvailOntserviceNames>95.0</AvailOntserviceNames>
                <CostOntserviceNames>1.4</CostOntserviceNames>
        </composedResultsClass2>
-------------------------------------------------------------------
. . .
</definitions>
```

Management of QoWS Composition
for a Composite Web Service

The management of QoS of a composite Web service is a very complex task when compared with the management of the QoS of basic Web services, which is itself not an easy task. It is affected by the way the QoS of basic Web services is managed. For example, a higher response time of the composite Web service may be caused by a Web service taking more time than expected to respond. This Web service should be identified and its response time reduced. Also, a low availability of the composite Web service might be due to one or more basic Web services that are unavailable when requested. Therefore, the QoWS management of composite Web services is tightly coupled to the management of QoWS of its basic Web services. It requires continuous sharing of management information between the composite Web service and its basic Web services. Management of QoS for composite Web services includes: QoWS composition, and QoWS monitoring.

QoWS values of a composite Web service are a function of QoWS values of its basic Web services. Hence, the composite QoWS properties and their values are

Figure 12. Monitoring the QoWS of the CWS

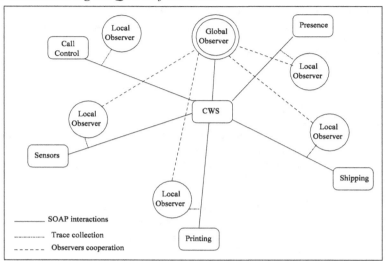

calculated from the WSDL of basic Web services and added to the WSDL document of the composite Web service after applying appropriate composition patterns (see Figure 6). The specification of the calculated composite QoWS is introduced in the WSDL document using the same ontology described in Figure 4. It also takes into account the composition of classes of QoWS. The number and the type of computed composite QoWS properties in the new WSDL document of the composite Web service should be the same as those described in the WSDL documents of basic Web services. Moreover, each composite class of QoWS holds QoWS information similar to those described in the WSDL documents of its basic Web services. This information concerns: QoWS properties names, threshold values, and the unit (e.g., millisecond, request/second). Figure 11 presents an example of an extended WSDL of a composite Web service with composite QoWS description. The composite value of the QoWS property "availability" of Class1 is 92.1199 and the composite reputation value of Class2 is 3.0.

We use an agent-based monitoring approach to monitor, validate, and enforce the aggregated QoS of a composite Web service. More details can be found in our previous work (Serhani, Dssouli, Sahraoui, & Benharref, 2006). The QoWS monitoring process detects any QoWS violation and the Web services responsible of the violation. This architecture is demonstrated through a case study for verifying and monitoring the QoWS of a composite teleconferencing Web services in a 3G network. The network load generated by the QoWS verification and monitoring is measured.

We use two observation configurations a single-observer configuration to observe a simple Web service, and a multi-observer configuration for composite Web services. Since the call conference Web service (CWS) is a composite Web service, a network of observers is used to monitor its QoS and the QoS of its basic Web services. This configuration is illustrated in Figure 12.

Discussion

Since Web services are operating in open and heterogeneous environments, the proof of concepts provided by the components of our QoWS management framework, presented in Figure 3, were very challenging. The first step toward evaluating our approach is to implement the components and interfaces of the models. The second step consists of (1) evaluating the operations provided by the framework by using real Web services, and (2) evaluating and measuring the interactions between the components of the framework.

The framework offers QoWS management operations that are unique when compared to other architectures for QoWS management. It provided a formalism to describe QoWS attributes in Web services interfaces, and tools to verify QoWS claimed by providers.

It also provides guidance for QoWS publication and discovery. During the QoWS provision, the framework offers a monitoring optional feature for both basic and composite Web services to detect any occurrence of QoWS violations.

The graphical interface of the prototype allows the client and the provider to execute a wide variety of functions, such as checks, updates, deletions and additions of QoWS information in the Web service interface prior to publication and discovery of Web services. These two features allow flexible and efficient support of QoWS in the publication and discovery processes. We have tested these two features by using the validation application with a number of Web services users. The results of these preliminary tests have been very satisfactory. Other results of our experiments have been published in (Serhani, Dssouli, Hafid, & Sahraoui, 2005) and concern the operations provided by the broker component regarding QoS verification, certification, and monitoring.

Further experiments were conducted in another work (Serhani, Dssouli, Sahraoui, & Benharref, 2006) to evaluate the QoWS monitoring of a composite call conference Web service in 3G networks. The simulations we have performed using a network of mobile observers (agents), have shown an optimum load is generated by the monitoring activities. The monitoring of the composite call conference Web service has shown that there have been some violations of response time, processing time, availability, and throughput of basic and/or composite Web services, and the Web services responsible of these violations have been identified.

These experiments have allowed us to validate our design and implementation of the framework components and have shown that it is possible to go through the overall process flows of the proposed QoWS management schemes (specification, composition, and monitoring) for basic and composite Web services. The implementation has allowed us to:

- Evaluate the applicability of our framework in managing QoWS of basic and composite Web services.

- Show that it is possible to integrate the management phases of QoWS (QoWS Specification, publication/discovery, composition, and monitoring) within a coherent lifecycle.

- Show that the framework enables a certain level of trust between service consumers and providers and a certain level of autonomy.

- Illustrate how QoWS monitoring is achieved for both basic and composite Web services.

- Demonstrate that the QoWS of a composite Web services can be verified and monitored effectively.

The framework we present throughout this chapter may be the subject of further improvement and extensions, such as:

- Improvement of QoWS specification to include a wide range of properties and their relationships.

- Integration of alternative solutions to adapt QoWS composition of a composite Web service within its lifecycle once some QoWS are violated. This can be done by taking into account feedbacks from monitoring of composite QoWS, or by dynamically replacing a faulty Web service or by scaling available resources at the provider environment.

- Implementation of additional monitoring scenarios of different QoWS properties.

- Development of additional tools that will support other QoWS management operations such as QoWS monitoring operation.

Conclusion

Web services are a new emerging paradigm for developing and/or consuming services over the Internet. As these services are becoming omnipresent on the internet, it is obvious that the QoWS support and management of these Web services based applications become a hot topic in the Web services community.

QoWS management has been recognized as being indispensable for Web services providers seeking to achieve a higher degree of competitiveness. However, its implementation is very challenging due to the dynamic nature, the heterogeneous environment, and the autonomy of the Web services.

Our main objectives in this research are to automate the QoWS management for both basic composite Web service. An important concern has been how to provide both clients and providers with an automated solution that provides support for QoWS management operations such as QoWS description, QoWS publication, QoWS selection, QoWS verification, and QoWS monitoring.

To attend these goals, we have proposed a framework for QoWS management, which is capable of handling an increasing number of clients with different QoWS requirements. We have considered a layered approach in the design of the framework. The first layer provides a QoWS design methodology and patterns for basic and composite Web services. The second layer provides an approach to automate and support QoWS management operations for basic Web services that are: (1) verification and certification of QoWS,(2) support of QoWS driven Web services selection, and (3) QoWS monitoring. The third layer provides an approach for management of QoWS composition of a composite Web service, which is based on the deployment of several observers to monitor and enforce the QoWS composition of a composite Web service.

A prototype of the framework has been developed and the set of experiments have been conducted to evaluate our approach regarding QoWS management operations (QoWS specification, QoWS-aware selection, QoWS verification, and QoWS monitoring).

As a future work, we intend to enhance the framework by providing support to other QoWS management operations such as QoWS adaptation. Work is in progress to implement the remaining components of the framework and to evaluate the overall features of the framework on a large scale Web services environment.

References

Baresi, L., Ghezzi, C., & Guinea, S. (2004). Smart monitors for composed services. In *Proc. of the 2nd International Conference on Service Oriented Computing*, New York.

Benerjea, A., Ferrari, D., Mah, B. A., Oran, M., Verma, D., & Zhang, H. (1996). The Tenet real-time protocol suite: Design, implementation and experiences. *IEEE/ACM Transactions on Networking.*

Blake, S., Black, D., Carlson, M., Davies, E., Wang, Z., & Weiss, W. (1998). *Architecture for differentiated services.*

Block Extensible Exchange Protocol (BEEP). (2001). Retrieved from http://www.beepcore. org/

Braden, R., Clark, D., & Shenker, S. (1994). *Integrated services in the Internet architecture: An overview.*

Business Process Execution Language for Web Services (BPEL4WS). (2003). Retrieved from ftp://www6.software.ibm.com/software/developer/library/ws-bpel.pdf

Campbell, A., Aurrecoechea, C., & Hauw, L. (1997). A review of quality of service architecture. *ACM Multimedia Systems Journal.*

Campbell, A., Coulson, G., & Hutchison, D. (1994). A quality of service architecture. *ACM Computer Communication Review.*

Canfora, G., Di Penta, M., Esposito, R., & Villani, M. (2005). QoS-aware replanning of composite Web services. In *Proceedings of the IEEE International Conference on Web Services.*

Cardoso, J., Sheth, A.,Miller, J., Arnold, J., & Kochut, K. (2004). Modeling quality of service for work-flows and Web service processes. *Web Semantics Journal: Science, Services and Agents on the World Wide Web Journal.*

Chen, H., Yu, T., & Kwei-Jay L. (2003). QCWS: An implementation of QoS-capable multimedia Web services. In *Proceedings of the IEEE Fifth International Symposium on Multimedia Software Engineering.*

Della-Libera, G., et al. (2005). Web Services Security Policy (WS-SecurityPolicy). Retrieved from http://www-106.ibm.com/developerworks/library/ws-secpol/

Evans, C., et al. (2003). Web Services Reliability (WS-Reliability). Retrieved from http://www.oracle.com/technology/tech/webservices/htdocs/spec/WS-ReliabilityV1.0.pdf

Fischer, S., Hafid, A., Bochmann, G., &. de Meer, H. (1997). Cooperative QoS Management in Multimedia Applications. In *Proceedings of IEEE International Conference on Multimedia Computing and Systems (ICMCSO97)*, Ottawa, Canada. IEEE Computer Society Press.

Gisofli, D. (2001). *Web services architect: Part1. An introduction to dynamic e-business.* IBM Software Group, White Paper.

Gottschalk, K., Graham, S., Kreger, H., & Snell, J. (2002). Introduction to Web services architecture. *IBM Systems Journal, 41*(2), 170-177.

IBM MQSeries. (2005). Retrieved from http://www.mqseries.net/

Internet Inter-ORB Protocol (IIOP). (2004). Retrieved from http://www.omg.org/technology/documents/formal/corba_iiop.htm

Jaeger, M., Rojec-Goldmann, G., & Muhl, G. (2004). QoS Aggregation for Web Service Composition using Workflow Patterns. IEEE Enterprise Distributed Object Computing.

Jaeger, M., Rojec-Goldmann, G., & Muhl, G. (2005). QoS Aggregation in Web service compositions. In *Proceedings of the IEEE International Conference on e-Technology, e-Commerce and e-Service.*

Kreger, H. (2001). *Web Services Conceptual Architectures (WSCA 1.0)*. IBM Software Group, White Paper.

Leymann, F. (2001). Web Services Flow Language (WSFL 1.0). Retrieved from http://www-306.ibm.com/software/solutions/webservices/pdf/WSFL.pdf

Liangzhao, et al. (2003). Quality driven Web services composition. In *Proceeding of WWW2003*, Budapest, Hungary.

Li, Y., Ding, X., Chen, Y., Liu, D., & Li, T. (2003). The framework supporting QoS-enabled Web services. In *Proceedings of the International Conference on Web Services*, Las Vegas, Nevada.

Mani, A., & Nagarajan, A. (2002). Understanding quality of service for web services. Retrieved from http://www-106.ibm.com/developerworks/library/ws-quality.html

Maximilien, E., & Sing, M. (2004). *A framework and ontology for dynamic Web services selection*. IEEE Internet Computing.

Menascé, D. (2002). QoS issues in Web services. IEEE Internet Computing.

Peltz, C. (2003). *Web Services orchestration, a review of emerging technologies, tools, and standards*.

Ran, S. (2003). A Framework for discovering Web services with desired quality of services attributes. In *Proceedings of the International Conference on Web Services*, Las Vegas, Nevada.

Rosen E., Viswanathan, A., & Callon, R. (1999). *Multi-protocol label switching architecture*.

Serhani, M., Dssouli, R., Hafid, A., & Sahraoui, H. (2005). A QoS broker based architecture for efficient Web services selection. In *Proceedings of the IEEE international conference on Web services*. Orlando Florida.

Serhani, M., Dssouli, R., Sahraoui, A., & Benharref, A. (2006). CompQoS: Towards an Architecture for QoS composition and monitoring (validation) of composite Web services. In *Proceedings of the International Conference on Web Technologies, Application, And Services (IASTED)*, Calgary, Alberta, Canada.

Serhani, M., Dssouli, R., Sahraoui, H., Hafid, A., & Benharref, A. (2005). Toward a new Web services development life cycle. In *Proceeding of the International Multi-Conferences in Computer Science & Computer Engineering, International Symposium on Web Services and Applications*.

Serhani, M., Dssouli, R., Sahraoui, A., Benharref, A., & Badidi, E. (2006). VAQoS: Architecture for end-to-end QoS management of value added Web services. *International Journal of Intelligent Information Technologies, 2*(4), 37-56.

Shaikhl, A., Rana, O., Al-Ali, R., & Walker, D. (2003). UDDIe: An extended registry for Web services. *Workshop on Service Oriented Computing: Models, Architectures and Applications at SAINT Conference*. Florida.

Shuping, R. (2003). A Framework for discovering Web services with desired quality of services attributes. In *Proceedings of the International Conference on Web Services*, Las Vegas, Nevada.

SOAP Security Extensions: Digital Signature (SOAP-DSIG). (2001). Retrieved from http://www.w3.org/TR/SOAP-dsig/

Stattenberger, G., & Braun, T. (2003). *Performance of a bandwidth broker for DiffServ networks.* TR, Institute of Computer Science and Applied Mathematics, University of Bern, Switzerland.

Taleb, I., Hafid, A., & Serhani, M. (2005). QoS-Aware multimedia Web services architecture. In *Proceedings of the International Conference on Web Information Systems and Technologies*, Miami, USA.

Tian, M., Gramm, A., Naumowicz, T., Ritter, H., & Schiller, J. (2003). A concept for QoS integration in Web services. In *Proceedings of the 4th International Conference on Web Information Systems Engineering*, Rome, Italy.

Tian, M., Gramm, A., Ritter, H., & Schiller, J. (2004). Efficient selection and monitoring of QoS-aware Web services with the WS-QoS framework. In *Proceeding of the IEEE/WIC/ACM international Conference on Web Intelligence*, Beijing, China.

Web Services Transaction (WS-T). (2003). Retrieved from http://www-106.ibm.com/developerworks/library/ws-transpec/

World Wide Web Consortium. (2003). SOAP (Simple Object Access Protocol) Version 1.2. W3C Recommendation. Retrieved from http://www.w3.org/TR/soap/

XML Remote Procedure Call (XML-RPC). (2003). Retrieved from http://www.xmlrpc.com/

Zeng, L., Benatallah, B., Ngu, A., Dumas, M., Kalagnanam, J., & Chang, H. (2004). QoS-aware middleware for Web services composition. IEEE transactions on Software Engineering.

Section IV

Semantic Technologies

Chapter XI

Using Semantic Technologies for the Support of Engineering Design Processes

Sebastian C. Brandt, RWTH Aachen University, Germany

Marcus Schlüter, aiXtrusion GmbH, Germany

Matthias Jarke, RWTH Aachen University and Fraunhofer FIT, Germany

Abstract

The design and development processes of complex technical systems are of crucial importance to the competitiveness of a technology-oriented enterprise. These processes are characterized by high creativity and strong non-deterministic dynamics. Established information science methods, however, are intended for more deterministic work processes. They cannot be effectively applied to support creative activities like conceptual synthesis, analysis, and decision-making. Therefore, methods of experience management need to be exploited here. This chapter presents a new integrated approach to such design process guidance based on capturing the process traces in a Process Data Warehouse (PDW). Both the products to be designed and the process steps that correspond, are structured and stored as extended method traces. This trace capture facilitates the processing and subsequent reuse of the information through a process-integrated development environment. The concept of the PDW has been evaluated in several engineering design case studies. One of those, which focuses on the conceptual design of a chemical production plant, will be described in more detail.

Introduction

Knowledge about engineering design processes constitutes one of the most valuable assets of modern technology-oriented enterprises. This is especially true for creative and non-deterministic design processes, as treated in this publication. Those processes are only marginally supported by established product lifecycle management (PLM) systems and similar approaches. Information items from the early phases of the product lifecycle are only weakly structured and usually not integrated. The knowledge of these design processes is normally only known *implicitly* to the participating designers and teams, relying heavily on the personal experience background of each designer. To fully exploit this important intellectual capital, it must be made *explicit* and shared among designers and across an enterprise. A comprehensive and consistent *knowledge management* framework needs to be established, to capture and integrate the individual knowledge items emerging in the course of an engineering design project, and thus to drive experience reuse processes.

Typically, a vast amount of design information is manipulated by legacy tools and stored in highly heterogeneous sources, such as electronic documents, files, and data bases. Thus, any knowledge management system (KMS) needs to provide a comprehensive representation of the contents of these sources, thereby correlating the scattered knowledge items and providing a single point of access to design knowledge. As such, a comprehensive representation cannot be complete (for practical reasons); the KMS should employ mechanisms to easily locate the original knowledge sources, where more detailed information can be retrieved. To this aim, (meta) information about the sources (e.g., type, structure, version history, storage location) has to be combined with information about their contents.

To support the *direct reuse* of the knowledge applied in design processes, the *traces* of these processes need to be captured. These traces can then be searched and reused as some kind of *experience knowledge* in similar situations. In addition to capturing the *products* of the design processes, that is, the documents, diagrams and other resources created and modified during the work processes, it is necessary to capture these *processes* themselves. This allows providing information about the circumstances in which the individual knowledge items have been created. In particular, recording of the decision making procedures allows recalling the design rationale applied at that time. Thus, the experience information that is suitable for a particular situation can be systematically retrieved, and its applicability to the current working context evaluated. Moreover, *best practices* abstracted from the recorded work processes can be exploited for *direct process support* (i.e., the partially automated enactment of routine tasks in design tools). To achieve all this, the recorded traces and the correlated experience knowledge need to be structured and formalized to a certain degree, for example, by using ontological models.

On this background, the aim of the research presented here is to improve the work situation of the engineers participating in these design and development processes. As an example domain, the authors of this publication have been working on the support of *basic chemical engineering*. For this aim, they have developed the concept of the *Process Data Warehouse* as an engineering product and process repository, to allow the tracing and reuse of complex design processes.

This chapter is organized as follows: The next section will investigate the possibilities of supporting technical design processes by experience management. In the section afterwards, the concept of the Process Data Warehouse for trace capture and experience reuse will be explained in more detail. The following section will illustrate how these concepts have been applied in a case study in the domain of chemical engineering. Also, a short overview on other case studies will be given. Finally, conclusions are provided including further on-going and future research.

Support for Dynamic Design Processes

The inherent dynamics of the work processes pose one of the main problems when trying to support engineering design and development with computer and information science methods. In these processes, the requirements and other parameters change from one project to the next, and will also evolve during the lifetime of a single project. Often, these changes are directly influenced by finished steps, requiring iterative repetitions. As no methods in the sense of "best practice" are known, the driving influence in engineering design is the personal experience of the system designers.

To transfer this implicit (experience-) knowledge between the participating experts, it is necessary to convert it into an explicit form. Otherwise, the process of knowledge transfer consists prominently of more or less successful trials and errors. Nonaka and H.Takeuchi (1995) describe the cycle of organizational learning, which uses four steps to describe the dissemination of implicit knowledge in an organization. During *socialization*, the knowledge is shared by personal communication and common experiences. It can then be converted into in *explicit* form, and *combined* by using the available knowledge sources and repositories. Finally, the knowledge is again *internalized* by the experts concerned. This model primarily describes processes of personal knowledge creation, independent of any kind of computerized support. This is similar to the concept of *organizational memory*, as described, for example, by Conklin (1993).

If work processes are already supported by computerized tools, the *product* information (documents, diagrams, and such) is commonly recorded and stored automatically, offering an additional advantage. On the other hand, the *work processes* themselves, which describe the work context that resulted in the creation of the products, are rarely captured.

This computerized recording of product information allows to base common approaches to knowledge management on offering information to the expert which has been recorded in earlier executions of the same or a similar task. In this way, each expert can use his own experience and that of his colleagues to improve both his work situation and the quality of his work, while also enhancing his autonomy. This information allows the construction of some kind of "best practice" rules by analyzing the different steps of previous or finished design processes. These methods of knowledge management are usually applied in processes where no algorithms or other kinds of well-defined problem solving processes are available, no complete domain models have been—nor can be—established, and specific expert knowledge is more important than large amounts of common sense (Bergmann, 2002).

For some engineering domains, technical solutions have already been established. During the last decade, many manufacturing enterprises have started using Product Data Management (PDM) systems for managing the information about the products from design to production. Product lifecycle management (PLM) systems are being used as their successors to manage the complete lifecycle of a product. The goal of these systems is to integrate the manufacturing processes with product design activities on the one hand, and the business and logistics processes (Enterprise Resource Planning, ERP) on the other hand.

The PDM and PLM systems available today still lack essential aspects needed for supporting phases of conceptual design, such as adequate information models and support for knowledge or experience management (e.g., Szykman et al., 2001). Also, these systems have largely focused on the support of micro-level processes on the administrative level, such as versioning or engineering change management (Mesihovic et al., 2004). They lack the functionality to capture and support complex work processes and decisions, as well as capabilities for direct process support (Brandt et al., 2007).

While PLM systems are widely used in the manufacturing industries, they are less common in the chemical engineering domain. Instead, specialized *computer aided engineering (CAE)* systems are used, which resemble classical PDM solutions but are specifically adapted to the needs of the chemical process industries. Information models of CAE systems suffer the same aforementioned deficiencies as PDM systems, that is, the lack of well-structured models for product representation, especially for the early design phases (e.g., Bayer & Marquardt, 2003).

Some more recent approaches exist to extend these systems with current information science concepts. Kim et al. (2001) have integrated concepts of artificial intelligence into a commercial PDM system. They use a flexible workflow model which enables the dynamic and integrated management of task processes and information flows. Semantic technologies allow querying and manipulating the system based on types and relationships. The system requires relatively well-understood and well-documented processes which are not available in conceptual process engineering.

Gao et al. (2003) extend a commercial PDM system with the ontological methods offered by the Protégé ontology editor (Stanford, 2007), to provide knowledge management capabilities for the conceptual design stage. This allows the manual entering of knowledge, based on the defined ontology models, instances and rules; however, *experience* knowledge is not automatically captured. Again, this approach relies on a domain where the processes are better understood than in conceptual process engineering. In Grabowski et al. (2001), a knowledge-based approach for product design is examined, based on integrating partial domain models and using patterns to represent the non-deterministic behavior of design processes.

Some other approaches from non-engineering domains such as software development also need to be mentioned here. To support, and thus to improve creative and non-deterministic design processes, experience and understanding of one's own work is necessary; only this way, can process evolution and improvement be achieved (Humphrey, 1990). This insight has resulted in several approaches based on the basic concept of knowledge management and *experience reuse*. For example, as part of the TAME project, Basili and Rombach (1988) propose a process model for supporting creative software development processes, which is based on their own experiences in software requirements engineering. Their approach focuses strongly on quantitative and metrics-based method evaluation for the later steps of software engineering. In the *Experience Factory* approach, an independent logical organization is responsible for gathering the knowledge and core competencies of a development group and offering this information for reuse (Basili et al., 1994). Another project has developed a process platform which supports the experience-based management and reuse of coarse-grained aspects of software development processes (Münch & Rombach, 2003).

Another set of well-researched methods for the domain of artificial intelligence is based on the definition and reuse of *cases* which represent knowledge, based on certain problem characterizations and the lessons applicable for reusing this knowledge. The possibilities offered by Case-Based Reasoning (CBR), and their limitations, are described, for example, in Aamodt and Plaza (1994).

Common to the approaches described so far is their placement in domains like automotive engineering where the design processes are relatively well-documented, strict and deterministic. The same situation applies to the later phases of chemical process engineering (CAPE), the detail engineering. This stands in contrast to conceptual design and basic engineering as treated in this chapter, where the process dynamics described above inhibit such deterministic modeling approaches. In such dynamic settings, only the recording of the work processes and work contexts in addition to the manipulated products allows achieving successful support functionalities.

The Process Data Warehouse

From the problems described so far, and the shortfalls of the existing solution approaches, the need for *integrated* technical support for the early phases of creative system design can be derived. Therefore, the authors' research group has examined the possibilities offered by recording and reusing the traces of work *processes* in technical design. The project activities have been performed as part of the Research Centre on Cooperative Computer-Aided Process Engineering (SFB/CRC 476 IM-PROVE, Marquardt & Nagl, 2004).

In the scope of this research, concepts of *direct process support* and integrated method guidance have been realized, strongly intertwined with product support and reuse. This has been primarily achieved by the strategy of *process integration* (Pohl et al., 1999) and *process data warehousing*. The Process Data Warehouse (PDW) has been defined by Jarke et al. (2000) as a knowledge-based metadata repository for tracing and driving heterogeneous work processes in engineering. It captures and analyzes the traces of design processes: products, process instantiations and their interdependencies. The main concept has been to capture the artifacts (the technical system) to be designed and modified during the processes, and to relate them to the processes which perform these modifications. From these semantically structured product and process traces, the relevant information can be extracted in an *analysis* step, and then *reused* in further process executions.

The primary function of the PDW is given by buffering the results of earlier design cycles and steps, for example, simulation results, and the management of historical data. This is similar to the well-known and well-researched area of data warehouses (e.g., Jarke et al., 2003) and business intelligence, where large amounts of fixedly structured data (e.g., from sales or accounting) are aggregated and analyzed, commonly based on relational schemata. Yet to achieve this functionality in the context of creative and non-deterministic processes, several changes are necessary that will be described in the following.

Interleaved Recording of Process and Product Traces

The central problem of the approach described here is how to support *traceability*. To enable traceability, first of all, the conceptual relations and dependencies between products and processes need to be examined. Therefore, Ramesh and Jarke (2001) abstracted a *traceability reference model* from a large number of industrial case studies. This model distinguishes between *product-oriented* and *process-oriented* trace objects, as already mentioned in the introduction. The former describe the properties and relationships of concrete design objects, while the latter represent the *history* and *rationale* of actions that led to the creation and modification of the product objects. The reference model also shows that recording the process traces needs to include all related influence factors, like the actual problem situation, the resulting artifacts, and the decisions that led to the final results. Also, the role of the stakeholders who participate in the processes and the sources that contain the information need to be taken into account. All these aspects and their dependencies cannot be reasonably separated, as each one strongly depends on the others.

The recording of the *product* information is normally realized inside the tools that compose a development environment. On the other hand, special steps need to be taken for recording and relating *process* traces and supplementary information like decisions and arguments. It is therefore necessary to enrich the application environment with tools to enable a consistent automated and partially manual trace capture. This enrichment has been realized based on the idea of *a-posteriori integration*. The experts can still use the tools they are accustomed to, while additional value is provided by the integration.

To achieve the necessary integration and interleaving of product and process traces, the process-integrated development environment PRIME has been developed; it realizes the authors' vision of *integrating* development tools, product data, process guidance, and trace capture. The concept of process integration was derived from the idea of process-centered environments (PCE, see Dowson & Fernström, 1994), which are based on the three domains of modeling, enactment and performance. The concepts of PRIME enhance the interaction between these domains. Especially a tight integration between the enactment domain (where method fragments are executed) and the performance domain (where the user interacts with the tools) was realized. More information about this topic can be found in Pohl et al. (1999).

The PDW forms a central part of this process-integrated environment. It captures the traces of the supported design and development processes in a structured, reconstructable, and reusable way. This requires high flexibility concerning both information modeling and runtime data integration. Common Data Warehouses cannot achieve this, due to their construction on top of fixed structures. Instead, (a) the models of the PDW are explicitly defined in an ontology-based language, and (b) the complete model consists of loosely connected *partial models*, each of them modeling a certain conceptual area or usage environment. Thus, the conceptual model of the PDW is composed of a number of models (or ontology modules) which are held together by a central model, the so-called *core ontology*. In addition to incorporating the process aspect, this also allows to integrate the complex, diverse, and often changing domain models.

This way, the information from diverse tools, workplaces and disciplines is integrated into one central repository. Other external data sources and repositories are indirectly integrated, with the PDW taking the role of a semantic data mediator. To find and reuse experience traces, the current process state, the situation of the selected products and the attributes of other objects in their vicinity can be used to formulate queries on the experience base. It is possible to use *semantic search* mechanisms on the integrated model of the PDW, as it is based on ontological concepts and ontology- and logic-based languages. This enables the retrieval of objects and their attributes based on relationships, attribute values, classifications, and other constraints. Due to the explicit definition of the concepts and their relationships in the ontology modules, classifications, subsumption and similar characteristics can be automatically inferred. Attribute ranges and other meta-concepts can also be used to achieve similarity comparisons and searching.

The Conceptual Framework of the Process Data Warehouse

As already mentioned, the conceptual model of the Process Data Warehouse is based on a set of loosely connected partial models. These are interconnected through the *core ontology* which will be introduced here. In particular, it comprises the process models, product and dependency models, models for decision support and documentation, for the description of content and categorizations, and other integration models.

Around these fundamental and domain-independent models, *extension points* are placed that can be used to add the models of a specific application domain or other specializations. Details about the Core Ontology can also be found in Brandt et al. (2006a).

Four prominent areas of conceptualization are arranged around the *object* as the abstract central concept. They are shown in Figure 1.

Product area. The product area (top) contains concepts for the description of the type and version history of electronic documents and other information resources, as well as their mutual dependencies and their structural composition. The Product concept denotes all kinds of information elements, such as data items, diagram elements, or the arguments or positions of decisions. Products can be bundled by a Version Set and aggregated into the different Document Versions of one (logical) Document.

Figure 1. Simplified view of the core ontology and some peripheral ontology modules

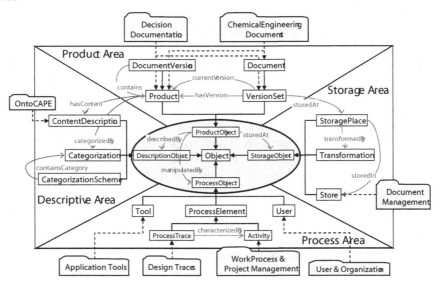

Storage area. The storage area (right) describes at which Storage Place a particular Version Set is located, that is, in which data base, document management system, or external tool the "physical" original is stored. A Storage Place forms part of a Store, such as a document management system. This allows a tight integration with document management systems, including the direct propagation of document and data changes from and to the PDW.

Descriptive area. The descriptive area (left) contains basic concepts for describing the content or the role of Product Objects on a high semantic level. This includes Content Descriptions and Categorizations, which are grouped into Categorization Schemes. Thus, the descriptive area provides the vocabulary necessary for the content-based retrieval of data and documents.

Process area. The process area (bottom) contains the concepts needed to represent the processes (Process Objects) that create, use, or modify the product information (Product Objects). They comprise general process definitions (Actions) as well as Process Traces resulting from concrete executions of the Actions. Users and organizational structures like companies and workgroups are also placed here.

Three important relationships between the elements of different areas should be described exemplarily in more detail. DescribedBy relates the product objects with descriptive elements that describe their type, content or category; storedAt represents the storage of products and documents in physical places like file systems or repositories; and manipulatedBy describes how the product objects are created, used and modified by the users in process activities.

All areas offer the extension points which have been mentioned above. Here, the partial models of an application domain or other specializations can be added. As examples, some of these models are introduced here, as they will be needed for the case studies described in the next section.

- The most elaborate of these extensions is *OntoCAPE* (Yang & Marquardt, 2004; Morbach et al., 2007), a large-scale ontology developed for the domain of computer-aided process engineering. It consists of a set of interconnected partial models which are hierarchically organized across several levels of abstraction. Important areas covered by OntoCAPE are substances and their thermophysical properties, unit operations and plant equipment, as well as mathematical modeling. OntoCAPE has been mainly integrated into the Core Ontology by extending the ContentDescription concept. This is described in more detail in Brandt et al. (2007).

- Models for the domain of plastics engineering, especially the design and realization of compounding extruders by functional zones and screw elements, are integrated by extending the Product and TypeDefinition concepts (Brandt et al., 2006b).

- To access documents and files that are stored inside a Document Management System, the storage area has been extended with the appropriate concepts and some specific implementations. This has been realized for the commercial system Documentum (EMC, 2007), and the Open-Source system Slide (Jakarta, 2007).

- Models and systems for Enterprise Resource Planning (ERP), esp. SAP R/3 (SAP, 2007), and for the recording of plant operation data, have also been integrated into the storage area. This includes a generic transformer concept that imports the content of XML and OWL-based data sources into the PDW.

Theses partial models, or ontology modules, are explicitly implemented in a semantic modeling language similar to the realization of ontologies as part of the Semantic Web effort (RDF, OWL, see Berners-Lee et al., 2001). The standardized OWL language (Bechhofer et al., 2004) could not be used because of technical constraints concerning the persistent storage of large numbers of ontology instances. The RDFS-based KAON system (Oberle et al., 2004) has been used instead, because it allows executing semantic queries directly on the relational back-end storage. On the other hand, this resulted in the loss of some of the constraint and inference expressiveness of OWL. The conversion of models and instance data between OWL and the PDW has been realized.

Applications of the PDW

Based on the information and knowledge storage presented above, the PDW has been designed to support engineers and other experts in the following tasks. The application of the PDW onto concrete scenarios will be described later on, in the next section.

Design documentation. The PDW offers a unified and integrated access structure onto all types of design information, that is, the product and process traces of engineering design processes. During the development processes, this documentation already offers valuable possibilities and insights, for example, to facilitate the communication among distributed development teams. Additionally, this information can be used in later phases of the designed system's lifecycle, to support tasks such as maintenance, change management, or quality management. To enable this, the information must be kept accessible and presentable independently of the original sources and formats.

Content-based retrieval of resources. Using the content-based annotation of the information items, specific semantic queries can be formulated and submitted to the PDW. This allows, for example, to find all documents that specify or simulate a certain type of systems, and have been created as part of a certain project context. A graphical editor supports the construction of such queries in a "query-by-example" fashion. Concepts, relationships, and already known instances from the ontology can be connected into a semantic network that represents the characteristics of the information searched for. Since the semantics of the query terms have been formally defined within the ontology, the computer "understands" the meaning of the query and is therefore able to retrieve the appropriate documents, even if they are represented by different (but semantically equivalent) ontological concepts within the PDW. Also, these queries can be executed and answered on top of a view that is not available in the original sources alone, as the PDW is able to connect information from all available data sources.

Documentation of organizational context. The process objects introduced above represent the various workflow actions and activities. They are traced in direct association with the products that were created, changed or used as part of these process steps. This allows documenting and thus, retrieving information about the organizational context in which the products were created originally, including related work processes and decision documentation. Queries can be formulated, like "*What has this document been used for?*" or "*Which decisions have been taken based on this data?*" Moreover, by analyzing the process traces of finished projects, a user can identify the expert who already solved a certain problem, and can contact him or her directly.

Experience reuse. As already mentioned, a less experienced expert can search for, retrieve and thus reuse information from earlier project executions, when a more experienced expert solved a similar problem. Similar to the concepts of Case-Based Reasoning, the comparison and adaptation of the retrieved cases enables their direct reuse. To simplify the search mechanism, the integrated tools can directly query the experience repository based on their current situation or context. This also offers the possibility of analyzing the data to detect recurring fragments. Fine-grained process support can then be offered to the user, based on modeled process fragments (see PRIME in the beginning of this section, and Pohl et al., 1999).

Cross-organizational cooperation. Information often needs to be passed to a co-operation partner, based on strict rules of intellectual property and need-to-know. Besides the problems of business agreements, communications and the technologies for information transfer, other aspects need to be addressed here. Only very select information may be released, and then passed across organizational boundaries. The cooperation partner may only be allowed a restricted and well-controlled *view* onto the repository. In many cases, vital information may be recognized to be missing at the cooperation partner's site. Then, additional information needs to be released and transferred to allow the partner to solve the given task. Based on the traces recorded earlier, the PDW allows revising the initial decision; also, in case of repeated cooperation, these problems can be avoided from the beginning.

Architecture of the PDW

In the following, the architectural structure of the PDW *experience repository* as a trace recording and reuse framework is shown. Furthermore, it is described how the PDW interacts with the software environment it is realized in. Following the authors' concept of a-posteriori integration, the existing software tools are augmented by integrating them with the PDW framework. While the engineers can go on working with the tools they are accustomed to, additional support functionality is offered by the integrated environment.

Figure 2 shows how the experience repository of the PDW is embedded into its usage environment. The PDW server itself can be seen on the right of the figure. The KAON *ontology framework* (Oberle et al., 2004) is responsible for managing the ontology classes of the PDW and the corresponding instances. All this data is stored in an SQL2-compatible relational database (PostgreSQL, 2007), mapping the flexible ontology structure onto a fixed relational schema. Additionally, KAON offers a query mechanism that is able to transform requests in a high-level semantic query language into SQL queries which can be performed directly on the relational

Figure 2. Overview of the architecture of the PDW

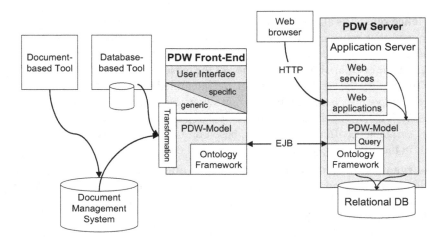

storage back-end. Thus, only those instances that either result from the query or are navigated to need to be loaded from storage.

Around this ontology framework, the PDW-Model forms an implementation wrapper that represents the core ontology and offers other specialized functionality. It gives access to the ontological concepts both in a generic way (as classes, instances, association types, and relations), and by specialized interfaces.

The realization of the server as described here is placed in an application server based on the Java Enterprise Edition programming language and platform (Sun, 2007a). This enables the PDW to offer services based on various standardized communication protocols:

- Web services are, nowadays, often used for service-based integration of enterprise applications, thus offering company-spanning workflows that can be dynamically composed. Especially in a cooperative setting, this allows to extend the PDW with well-defined and standards-based service interfaces.

- Access for thin clients (i.e., Web browsers) is provided by Web applications that are using the technologies of Servlets and Java Server Pages (Sun, 2007a).

- Access to the server from rich clients (i.e., stand-alone client applications) is realized via Enterprise Java Beans, EJB (Sun, 2007a).

In the centre of Figure 2, such a rich client application can be seen. This application, the PDW front-end, forms the primary means of accessing the PDW experience server and repository. The front-end contains a client-side representation of a part of the PDW's classes and instances, thus reflecting the current state of information inside the server. Changes to the client-side data are transferred to the server and persisted in a database transaction. All those changes are then communicated to the running clients, allowing the clients to synchronize with the current state of information, and, possibly, display the newly created or changed information.

Three different kinds of graphical user interfaces are offered by the PDW front-end. The *generic* display is based on UML notation (OMG, 2004) of the classes and instances of the ontological models. It displays classes and instances as blocks of different colors with their attribute types and values, and relations as links between them. This view is mainly aimed at the ontology engineer responsible for modeling and integrating a particular domain into the system, and for rapid prototyping of possible use cases. *Specific* user interfaces need to be created for the various application cases, so that the domain users can work with customized interfaces that offer appropriate solutions for their problems. *Semi-specific* interfaces can be used to uniformly visualize different concepts of the ontology that have similar characteristics. This allows defining general rules for presentation as model annotations, for example, to display composition hierarchies or networks of blocks and streams of various kinds, using the same user interface.

The PDW system is in several ways integrated with its external environment. As already mentioned, this external environment is mainly kept unchanged; it is only extended. A Document Management System, such as Documentum (EMC², 2007) or Jakarta Slide (Slide, 2007), is responsible for supporting document-based storages, offering version management and change notification support. When an expert checks in a new version of a document into the DMS, the PDW front-end running on his or her workplace is notified. The ontology instances corresponding to the document, its new version, and its storage place are created or updated and shown to the expert. The document instance can then be enriched semi-automatically with the current organizational context. Possibly, the content of the document can be transformed from the external tool's format into a representation inside the PDW's repository, provided that the format can be automatically interpreted.

Other external tools, mainly those that use repositories or databases for storage purposes instead of simple files or documents, can be integrated as external data sources as well. This often applies to ERP or CAE systems. Their data can usually be accessed by the programming interfaces offered by these tools, read and converted into PDW storage, enriched with semantic information, and transferred to and from other tools for subsequent design steps. A generic mechanism for integrating external data sources has been implemented using XML (W3C, 2006) as an exchange format, and XSLT (W3C, 1999) to transform the intermediate files into a form that matches the conceptual representation of the PDW.

Case Studies

Following the general description of the concepts of the PDW, and its uses for supporting creative design and development processes, two case studies will be described that show the application of the PDW experience reuse environment onto real-world engineering issues. The case studies have been conducted and evaluated in different domains of engineering. The primary case study is an excerpt from a scenario of designing a plant for the production of polyamide 6 (nylon). The second study describes the support of complex production processes that cannot be described by mathematical models and are thus, mainly driven by operators' experience. Due to space constraints, only the first case study will be described in detail.

A further case study that describes special aspects of cross-organizational delegation can be found in Brandt et al. (2006b). It is based on delegating certain steps of the design and realization of compounding extruders from a process engineering company to a plastics engineering contractor. Other aspects, like the visualization and handling of multimedia-based simulation results, have been treated there as well (Jarke et al., 2004; 2006).

Designing a Chemical Plant

The sample scenario described in this section is a simplified version of designing a plant for **polyamide 6** (nylon) production. The scenario was developed in an industrial workshop with several German partners (e.g., Bayer AG). The plant to be designed produces polyamide 6 by hydrolytic polymerization out of the reactants ε-caprolactam and water. Only a small part of the scenario will be extended here for the use with the PDW. The elaboration of the cooperative scenario and the requirements for the productions processes and the product itself, are described in Marquardt and Nagl (2004). The engineering side of the experience-based support is also described in more detail in Brandt et al. (2007).

In the domain of polyamide production, no integrated and thorough design environments yet exist. Topics such as tool integration and work process support have hardly been implemented in industrial application, and are still of great interest for research. This stands in contrast to other chemical engineering domains like petrochemicals. Therefore, a scenario from this domain has been taken as base for the authors' research.

In the following, an example session will be described that shows the possible interactions of a design engineer with the PDW. Such a session usually consists of three important logical steps:

1. **Retrieval of experience knowledge:** The user searches the PDW for experience knowledge matching his/her current task. The user may either actively search the PDW by composing queries manually, or s/he may rely on the PDW's ability to automatically derive queries from the current work context of the application tools (context-sensitive knowledge retrieval).

2. **Review and reuse of retrieved experience knowledge:** The retrieved information needs to be reviewed by the user who can then decide on reusing some or all of the experience knowledge in the tools that form the current work context.

3. **Knowledge capture:** The design knowledge created by the user when processing the current task is recorded and stored in the PDW in order to increase the knowledge base, and to enable step 1 in the first place.

We will now discuss how these three steps are carried out in this particular application scenario. The models used here are based on the lifecycle ontology OntoCAPE (Morbach et al., 2007), already introduced above as one of the most important extension modules.

At the outset of the application scenario, the engineer is assigned the task of developing a conceptual design for the polyamide 6 reactor. The only specifications given at this point are the feedstock—polyamide 6 is to be produced from water and caprolactam—and the desired amount and material properties of the polyamide 6 product. After selecting a suitable reactor device (here: a VK tube), the engineer

Figure 3. The application scenario of the chemical plant design with PDW support

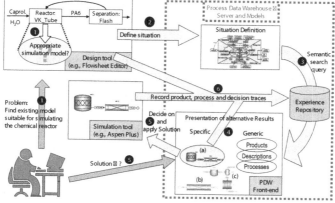

needs to perform simulation experiments to determine certain design parameters. To this aim, he wants to query the PDW for mathematical models that can be reused to simulate the physicochemical behavior of the VK tube. In Figure 3, the Process Data Warehouse and its surroundings are shown, as used in this application scenario.

Situation-based query for experience traces. Supported by the expert, the design environment is able to derive a semantic query from the current work context of the application tools, thus providing reusable product or process knowledge that matches the current situation. To this end, the PDW needs to be integrated with the (legacy) application tools used by designers. To demonstrate the feasibility of this approach, a prototypical experience reuse framework has been realized, consisting of the Process Data Warehouse, the process-integrated development environment PRIME (Pohl et al., 1999) and a proprietary Flowsheet Editor (Bayer et al., 2001), which is an advanced prototypical design environment for process flowsheets.

An initial Process Flow Diagram has been created in the Flowsheet Editor, reflecting the main process steps and interconnecting material streams of the polyamide 6 process (Figure 3, item 1). The search for an appropriate mathematical model is triggered by clicking on a menu item "find simulation model" and selecting the section of the flow diagram that is to be simulated (Figure 3, item 2). The semantic query is now composed of concepts from several areas of the core ontology:

- The product part of the query defines the type of document (i.e., a model file) to be retrieved as well as optional further constraints such as the desired format (e.g., a simulation model file).

- The descriptive part of the query specifies the content of the model by using concepts from OntoCAPE. In this particular case, the specification comprises the type of model (steady-state, rigorous), the type of the modeled reactor (VK tube), and the material streams flowing into and out of the reactor.

- The most important process element is the user's intention in this situation, that is, "find simulation model," given by the menu item. This also determines the desired document type, a simulation model file (see above).

This situation definition can then be passed on to the Process Data Warehouse to search for matching experience information (Figure 3, item 3).

Review and reuse of retrieved experience knowledge. In the example scenario, several different mathematical models for the simulation of a polyamide 6 reactor are found and returned. The models are combinations of different standard model blocks, such as flash units, Plug Flow Reactors (PFR), or Continuous Stirred Tank Reactors (CSTR), which are interconnected via process streams. This information is then presented to the user via the front-end of PDW (Figure 3, item 4). Two different visualizations as described together with the architecture of the PDW, can be

Figure 4. Generic (left) and specific (right) visualization of the search results

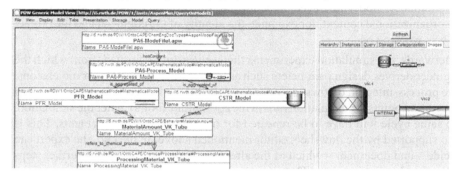

applied here: The generic representation shows the class instances, their attributes and relations in UML instance notation, while the specific representation in this case shows a graphical snapshot of the reactor models (see Figure 4).

Now the expert needs to decide which of the simulation models to reuse (Figure 3, item 5). The PDW supports this decision-making by providing additional information about the models in the descriptive area, such as the reaction kinetics and material properties data used in the model. Moreover, by browsing associated concepts from the process area (refinements of ProcessTrace) and related decision documentation, the user may find out more about the former usage of the models. For example, he may learn that a particular model was developed for an initial feasibility study (and is therefore likely to be rather simple and inaccurate), while another model was employed for detailed design calculations and was therefore validated against experimental data. Thus, in accordance with the present task, the engineer decides to reuse the latter model. The model is then retrieved from the PDW and adapted according to the specifications of the given design task.

Capturing Product and Process Traces. The solution (i.e., the mathematical model to be used for the simulation runs), and the path that led to it, are recorded in the PDW as experience traces (Figure 3, item 6). In addition to the product information (the adapted simulation model as well as the design specification in the Flowsheet Editor), the task-related working steps and situations are traced (semi-) automatically. Similar to the situation definition described above, concepts from all four areas are used and instantiated to describe the activities and product modifications that took place. This includes the documents, their version history and structural composition (e.g., VK tube) from the product area; descriptive elements like the chemical reaction with its reactants and products; and storage elements that represent the physical storage location of the documents. From the process area, all process steps and activities are recorded that led to the (re)use and adaptation of the simulation model are traced, including the situations and queries, and aspects of the organizational context, for example, the identity of the engineer, and the project he was working on.

Afterwards, the simulation experiments themselves are performed, from which the engineer derives design parameters such as temperature, flow rates, or dimensions. The process-integrated flowsheet editor and the PDW also serve as the starting and integration points for simulation runs in the appropriate tool(s). After the simulation, the same cycle will have to be repeated for other, alternative refinements. This is also supported by the flowsheet editor mentioned above. In the end, the expert can decide—and document—which of the alternatives should be kept for further steps in the development process. Then, arguments that have been entered earlier and the simulation results related to them can be directly reused by the PDW, to support the decision process here.

The repeated cycles of choosing a reactor realization, furthermore simulating the realization, documenting the results and entering some notes or arguments, and the concluding decision-making may be recognized as a single recurring method fragment, through analyzing the process traces. In a later analysis phase, a *method engineer* may decide to add a loosely modeled method fragment into the experience base that can be activated by the expert when facing this or a similar problem situation again, to guide him or her efficiently through these tasks. More about these aspects can be found in Miatidis et al. (2005).

Supporting Continuous Production Processes

This second application case exhibits two major differences from the previous one. Firstly, it treats the support of *production* processes, not *design* or development processes as before. Secondly, this subsection describes an industry project in which the developed software is permanently used during day-to-day operations, in contrast to the more abstract case study described above.

In plastics engineering, it has been found that certain kinds of continuous production processes for rubber profiles show characteristics similar to those of design processes. An operator is only able to efficiently start and control such a production line after having gained a lot of personal experience. Much variation can be found in the time necessary to achieve a stable production state. Common approaches for automation control do not suffice because of the complexity of the processes. Due to the length of the production lines (up to 250 m), and the slow speed of extrusion, the results of operating parameter changes can only be detected after a long time (up to 30 minutes), and after generating a lot of waste. This also makes it impossible to create explicit process models and thus to control and predict process behavior. In these extrusion processes, production costs are mainly determined by the consumption of raw materials. Unfortunately, vulcanized rubber cannot be reused if the final profile does not conform to specification.

In the scope of the project "MErKoFer – Management of Experience Knowledge in Continuous Production Processes," the approach of experience-based support for creative processes has therefore been extended to the support of operation personnel in profile extrusion, in cooperation with an industry partner. In contrast to the design processes treated up to now, these processes offer the advantage that process parameters and product quality can be automatically registered and measured quantitatively. The primary goals of the research were to improve the work situation of the machine operators, especially their autonomy, and to reduce the time spent in producing rejects, thus saving money and reducing environment impact. More about the general approach of the research and its preliminary results can be found in Raddatz et el. (2006).

In this project, the PDW has mainly been used for modeling all the information and data structures that influence the production processes themselves. This includes all the usual process parameters from automation control, but also some rather unexpected factors such as the weather (temperature, pressure, humidity), and the storage duration of the rubber mixtures before production. Due to several technical and usability reasons (e.g., the need for specialized touch-screen interfaces), it was not possible to directly use the PDW for operator support.

The PDW has shown its strengths in the rapid design and realization of a prototype for this environment. The domain models could be directly used for initial recordings of the information described above. As an extension to the initial (strict) implementation, the front-end of the PDW offered (a) a very good overview on the models; (b) the ability to directly display and browse through the instance data; (c) semantic queries could be formulated and executed, to answer questions such as *"In which productions of the profile XX-1234 on line YY-12 did the error 'dips' appear, and what were the countermeasures?"*; and (d) first analyses could be conducted about the correlation of profiles, various kinds of errors, and their countermeasures.

Lessons Learned

It has been found that the PDW can be powerfully used for reusing product and process traces, yet its ontology-based representation is not adequate for data analysis and data mining functionalities. It is possible to review a certain product or process trace and to analyze it together with its context, yet statistical analysis and other forms of data aggregation are hard to realize. Especially in the production scenario described above, it is necessary to aggregate and analyze the process traces, similar to the functionality offered by usual Data Warehouses and business intelligence systems. For this kind of analyses in production settings, the term *production intelligence* has been coined. Thus, the PDW will have to be extended with functionality similar to the ETL (Export, Transform, Load) processes of data warehouses, to extract, aggregate and then analyze the recorded process traces. Therefore, research is being done about integrating the ontology-based representation of the PDW, the conversion of the traces into relational and/or multidimensional storage, and the analysis functionality, using production intelligence methods based on the Pentaho framework (Pentaho, 2007).

A major problem of current ontology-based frameworks is the trade-off between *implementation efficiency* and *descriptive logical power*. Most existing ontology frameworks need to load the entire information into memory to work with it. As a result, these frameworks can handle only a relatively small amount of instance data. Thus, to develop a system usable for real-world application, it is necessary to use a back-end for database storage that is directly able to interpret at least some inference rules and semantic queries. The KAON system, which the PDW uses, has been realized this way.

On the other hand, the full expressive power of **ontology** and description-logics- (DL) based languages (Baader et al., 2004) would offer capabilities not available in the current PDW. While the PDW is only able to infer supertype and subtype relations, a full-fledged description logic system would be able to infer additional character-istics of classes and instances, based on semantic constraints and rules. This goes beyond the capabilities of semantic searching currently implemented in the PDW, as can be seen from the following simple example. If an inexperienced user enters information about a reactor, annotating it as an instance of the generic class Vessel only, the current PDW will *not* return this instance when queried for a Reactor. In contrast to that, a DL system might contain an inference rule "A Reactor is a Vessel in which a ChemicalReaction takes place." The system could then conclude that the above Vessel is in fact a Reactor, and return it when queried for such. Thus, the recall of the search (i.e., the proportion of relevant information retrieved out of all the relevant information in the collection) may be significantly enhanced.

Still, even with the current implementation, *scalability* remains an issue. The PDW offers a powerful prototype for demonstration and first application purposes in both design and industrial production settings. Based on its flexible models, it could be adapted and deployed very fast, and was easily adjusted for model extensions and changes.

Yet it has also been recognized that the PDW in its current ontology-based form does not scale well enough for industrial application. In production processes, a very large amount of data accumulates; at the same time, the complexity of the models and their relationships requires to employ many concepts and associations. The KAON system, on which the PDW is based, can only be used efficiently up to a certain number of concepts and instances. Using file-based ontology languages such as OWL, this limit would have been reached much sooner.

Therefore, it will be necessary to design a less flexible system to continue the MErKoFer project. Its models will have to be more strict, that is, changeable only during design, but not during runtime of the system. Yet this re-implementation will still have to (1) be based on the Core Ontology of the PDW, (2) be able to integrate existing and new semantic models (especially all the existing models and implementations), and (3) support a semantic query language. Currently, a new back-end implementation based on the Java Persistence API (JPA, Sun 2007b) is being developed, which still supports the same client-side interfaces as the current implementation, thus allowing to use one PDW implementation for design, rapid prototyping and customization, and the other one for regular production use.

Storing most of the information of the PDW in relational table models would also allow applying methods of data mining and business or production intelligence directly on the repository, avoiding additional integration and transformation steps.

Contrasting the two aspects of additional logical expressiveness on the one hand, and scalability on the other, the two aspects do not seem to be reconcilable. The only solution will be to use different emphases for the different aspects of the PDW framework. The knowledge acquisition side, both the automatic integration of external data sources and documents, and the manual entering of information by a user, will have to be based on a language with high description logic expressiveness. The standardized OWL language (Bechhofer et al., 2004) will be a good candidate for this purpose. At the same time, the storage back-end will be implemented in a more simplistic manner, allowing scalable applications in many industrial domains. Of course, it will be necessary to employ a query language that is both able to offer at least some of the expressiveness of common ontology query languages, and still be executable on a relational database storage.

Conclusion and Outlook

In this chapter, a traceability-based approach for supporting creative design processes has been described. By integrated and interrelated capture of the product and process artifacts of the work processes, their subsequent reuse as experience traces is enabled. The process data warehouse (PDW) is constructed as a set of loosely connected ontology modules that are arranged around the four areas of the core ontology, namely products, processes, descriptions, and storage. Domain models and other extension are placed around the concepts of these four areas. Based on the PDW, information and computer science support for engineering design and development processes has been facilitated. The approach has been validated in a case study of designing a plant for the production of polyamide 6 (nylon) by hydrolytic polymerization, and in industrial application in the domain of rubber profile extrusion.

These case studies have shown that the authors' approach of direct experience-based product and process support can be applied very well in various design and production settings. The PDW has been used as a powerful prototype, to allow the construction and validation of complex domain and application models. This also allowed supporting the later construction of more specific and explicit implementations to support a domain's end users.

It has been found that the PDW needs to be extended into two different, yet contradicting directions. On the one hand, some features of the description-logic based languages of the Semantic Web have to be integrated. On the other hand, scalability and stability are important issues in industrial application; thus, at least the storage back-end will have to be redesigned, to address these requirements.

For supporting similar processes in other domains, several extensions are being planned and under development. By extending the currently available methods for data acquisition, visualization and retrieval, an integrated view on different information sources is to be achieved. Among those, techniques of data mining are especially important to enable explorative data analysis. Also, document mining methods can be used to cluster large numbers of documents according to content similarities, and to integrate the resulting document and feature maps with the ontology-based view of the PDW. Thus, a multi-view-based user interface approach is created that is able to display, explore and search the information according to different visualization and usage paradigms, including business and production intelligence.

A further project is being initiated to transfer the often vast amounts of printed documentation resulting from the design and construction of a chemical plant, into digitized form. After scanning and text recognition, document mining tools are applied to visualize and structure the information. The Process Data Warehouse is used to semantically enrich and categorize these documents and their content. The resulting information repository can be used to enhance document access during plant operation, repair and modification.

Finally, in the domain of chemical engineering, the workflows of the full plant life cycle are going to be examined, from the design phase through plant operation, modifications and redesign or reengineering. The "freezing" and later restarting or continuing of design processes is also to be researched.

Acknowledgment

This work was supported by the German National Science Foundation (Deutsche Forschungsgemeinschaft, DFG) within the Collaborative Research Centre CRC/SFB 476 "Informatics Support for Cooperative Chemical Engineering—IMPROVE" (1997-2006, transfer till 2009), and by the German Ministry of Research within the project "MErKoFer—Management of Experience Knowledge in Continuous Production Processes" (2004-2007). Thanks are due to our colleagues from the projects, and to our students who implemented the Process Data Warehouse, PRIME, and the aiXPerience environment.

This is an extended version of the publication:

Brandt, S.C., Schlüter, M., & Jarke, M. (2006). A process data warehouse for tracing and reuse of engineering design processes. *International Journal of Intelligent Information Technologies*, *2*(4), 18-26.

References

Aamodt, A., & Plaza, E. (1994). Case-based reasoning: Foundational issues, methodological variations, and system approaches. *AI Communications, 7*(1), 39-59.

Baader, F., Horrocks, I., & Sattler, U. (2004). Description logics. In: S. Staab & R. Studer (Eds.), *Handbook on ontologies*. Berlin, Heidelberg: Springer Verlag.

Basili, V., Caldiera, G., & Rombach, H. (1994). The experience factory. In J. Marciniak (Ed.), *Encyclopedia of software engineering, Volume 1* (pp. 469-476). New York: John Wiley & Sons.

Basili, V., & Rombach, H. (1988). The TAME project: Towards improvement-oriented software environments. *IEEE Transactions on Software Engineering, 146*, 758-773.

Bayer, B., Marquardt, W., Weidenhaupt, K., & Jarke, M. (2001). A flowsheet centered architecture for conceptual design. In R. Gani & S.B. Jørgensen, (Eds.), *European Symposium on Computer Aided Process Engineering, 11* (pp. 345-350). Amsterdam: Elsevier.

Bayer, B., & Marquardt, W. (2003). A comparison of data models in chemical engineering. *Concurrent Engineering Research and Applications, 11*(2) 129-138.

Bayer, B., & Marquardt, W. (2004). Towards integrated information models for data and documents. *Computers and Chemical Engineering, 28*, 1249-1266.

Bechhofer, S., Harmelen, F. van, Hendler, J., Horrocks, I., McGuiness, D., Patel-Schneider, P., & Stein, L. (2004). *OWL Web Ontology Language Reference*. Retrieved from http://www.w3.org/TR/owl-ref/

Bergmann, R. (2002). *Experience management*. Berlin: Springer-Verlag.

Berners-Lee, T., Hendler, J., & Lassila, O. (2001). The Semantic Web: A new form of Web content that is meaningful to computers will unleash a revolution of new possibilities. *Scientific American, 17*.

Brandt, S., Schlüter, M., & Jarke, M. (2006a). A process data warehouse for tracing and reuse of engineering design processes. *Intl. Journal of Intelligent Information Technologies, 2*(4), 18-26.

Brandt, S., Schlüter, M., & Jarke, M. (2006b). Process data warehouse models for cooperative engineering processes. In *Proceedings 9ᵗʰ IFAC Symposium on Automated Systems Based on Human Skill And Knowledge*, Nancy, France.

Brandt, S., Morbach, J., Miatidis, M., Theißen, M., Marquardt, W., & Jarke, M. (2007). An ontology-based approach to knowledge management in design processes. *Computers and Chemical Engineering*.

Conklin, E. (1993). Capturing organisational memory. In *Readings in groupware and computer-supported cooperative work: Assisting human-human collaboration* (pp. 561-565). San Mateo, CA: Morgan Kaufman.

Dowson, M., & Fernström, C. (1994). Towards requirements for enactment mechanisms. In *3rd European Workshop on Software Process Technology (EWSPT-3)*, Villard de Lans, France (pp. 90-106).

EMC² (2007). Documentum. Retrieved from http://software.emc.com/products/product_family/documentum_family.htm.

Gao, J., Aziz, H., Maropoulos, P., & Cheung, W. (2003). Application of product data management technologies for enterprise integration. *Int. Journal Computer Integrated Manufacturing, 16*(7-8), 491-500.

Grabowski, H., Lossack, R., & Leutsch, M. (2001). A design process model. In *Proceedings of the 3ʳᵈ International Workshop on Strategic Knowledge and Concept Formation*, Sydney, Australia.

Humphrey, W.S. (1990). *Managing the software process*. Boston: Addison-Wesley.

Jarke, M., Gallersdörfer, R., Jeusfeld, M., Staudt, M., & Eherer, S. (1995). ConceptBase: A deductive object base for meta data management. *Journal of Intelligent Information Systems*, Special Issue on Advances in Deductive Object-Oriented Databases, *4*(2), 167-192.

Jarke, M., List, T., & Köller, J. (2000). The challenge of process data warehousing. In *Proceedings of the 26th International Conference on Very Large Databases—VLDB*, Cairo, Egypt.

Jarke, M., Lenzerini, M., Vassiliou, Y., & Vassiliadis, P. (2003). *Fundamentals of data warehouses* (2ⁿᵈ ed.). Berlin: Springer-Verlag.

Jarke, M., Miatidis, M., Schlüter, M., & Brandt, S. (2004). Media-assisted product and process traceability in supply chain engineering. In *37ᵗʰ Hawaii International Conference on System Sciences—HICSS*, Big Island.

Jarke, M., Miatidis, M., Schlüter, M., & Brandt, S. (2006). Process integration and media-assisted traceability in cross-organisational engineering. *International Journal of Business Process Integration and Management, 1*(2), 65-75.

Kim, Y., Kang, S., Lee, S., & Yoo, S. (2001). A distributed, open, intelligent product data management system. *International Journal of Computer Integrated Manufacturing, 14*, 224-235.

Marquardt, W.. & Nagl, M. (2004). Workflow and information centered support of design processes: The IMPROVE perspective. *Computers and Chemical Engineering, 29*, 65-82.

McGuiness, D., & Harmelen, F. van (2004). *Web Ontology Language (OWL) Overview.* Retrieved from http://www.w3.org/TR/owl-features/

Miatidis, M., & Jarke. M. (2005). Toward improvement-oriented reuse of experience in engineering design processes. In *Proceedings of the 1ˢᵗ International Workshop on Experience Management*, Melbourne, Australia.

Mesihovic, S., Malmqvist, J., & Pikosz, P. (2004). Product data management system-based support for engineering project management. *Journal of Engineering Design, 15*(4), 389-403.

Morbach, J., Yang, A., & Marquardt, W. (2007). OntoCAPE: A large-scale ontology for chemical process engineering. *Engineering Applications of Artificial Intelligence (EAAI)*, Special Issue on Applications of Artificial Intelligence in Process Systems Engineering, *20*(2), 147-161.

Münch, J., & Rombach, D. (2003). Eine Prozessplattform zur erfahrungsbasierten Softwareentwicklung. In M. Nagl & B. Westfechtel (Eds.), *Modelle, Werkzeuge und Infrastrukturen zur Unterstützung von Entwicklungsprozessen* (pp. 93-106). Wiley-VCH.

Nagl, M., Westfechtel, B., & Schneider, R. (2003). Tool support for the management of design processes in chemical engineering. *Computers and Chemical Engineering, 27*(2), 175-197.

Nonaka, I., & Takeuchi, H. (1995). *The knowledge creating company.* Oxford University Press.

Oberle, D., Volz, R., Motik, B., & Staab, S. (2004). An extensible ontology software environment. In S. Staab & R. Studer (Eds.), *Handbook on ontologies* (pp. 311-333). New York: Springer.

OMG. (2004). Unified Modeling Language (UML), version 2.0. Retrieved from http://www.uml.org/

Pentaho. (2007). Pentaho—Open Source Business Intelligence (homepage). Retrieved from http://www.pentaho.com/

Pohl, K., Weidenhaupt, K., Dömges, R., Haumer, P., Jarke, M., & Klamma, R. (1999). PRIME: Towards process-integrated environments. *ACM Transactions on Software Engineering and Methodology, 8*(4), 343-410.

PostgreSQL. (2007). *Homepage.* Retrieved from http://www.postgresql.org/

Raddatz, M., Schlüter, M., & Brandt, S.C. (2006). Identification and reuse of experience knowledge in continuous production processes. *9th IFAC Symposium on Automated Systems Based on Human Skill and Knowledge.*

Ramesh, B., & Jarke, M. (2001). Toward reference models for requirements traceability. *IEEE Transactions on Software Engineering, 27*(1), 58-93.

SAP. (2007). *SAP—Business Software Applications and Services (homepage).* Retrieved from http://www.sap.com/

Slide. (2007). *The Jakarta Slide project.* Retrieved from http://jakarta.apache.org/slide/

Stanford Medical Informatics. (2007). *The Protégé ontology editor and knowledge acquisition system (homepage).* Retrieved from http://protege.stanford.edu/

Szykman, S., Sriram, R., & Regli, W. (2001). The role of knowledge in next-generation product development systems. *ASME Journal of Computation and Information Science in Engineering, 1*(1), 3-11.

Yang, A., & Marquardt, W. (2004). An Ontology-based Approach to Conceptual Process Modelling. In A. Barbarosa-Póvoa & H. Matos (Eds.), *European Symposium on Computer Aided Process Engineering, 14* (pp. 1159-1164). Elsevier.

Sun. (2007a). Java Enterprise Edition at a Glance. Retrieved from http://java.sun.com/javaee/

Sun. (2007b). JSR-220: Enterprise JavaBeans™ 3.0 and the Java Persistence API (JPA). Retrieved from http://jcp.org/en/jsr/detail?id=220

W3C—World Wide Web Consortium. (1999). XSL Transformations (XSLT), version 1.0, W3C Recommendation. Retrieved from http://www.w3.org/TR/xslt

W3C—World Wide Web Consortium. (2006). Extensible Markup Language (XML) 1.0 (Forth Edition), W3C Recommendation. Retrieved from http://www.w3.org/TR/xml/

Chapter XII

Using Semantic Web Concepts to Retrieve Specific Domain Information from the Web

Rafael Cunha Cardoso, Federal University of Pernambuco and Tools & Technologies (HP-Brazil), Brazil

Fernando da Fonseca de Souza, Federal University of Pernambuco, Brazil

Ana Carolina Salgado, Federal University of Pernambuco, Brazil

Abstract

Currently, systems dedicated to information retrieval/extraction perform an important role on fetching relevant and qualified information from the World Wide Web (WWW). The Semantic Web can be described as the Web's future once it introduces a set of new concepts and tools. For instance, ontology is used to insert knowledge into contents of the current WWW to give meaning to such contents. This allows software agents to better understand the Web's content meaning so that such agents can execute more complex and useful tasks to users. This work introduces an architecture that uses some Semantic Web concepts allied to regular expressions (REGEX) in order to develop a system that retrieves/extracts specific domain information from the Web. A prototype, based on such architecture, was developed to find information about offers announced on supermarket Web sites.

Introduction

The WWW emerged by the end of the eighties, a time where the impact of this technology on society was unknown (Berners-Lee et al., 1994). The increasing use of the Web has caused a permanent growth in the amount of data available on it. Its specific characteristics have generated a crescent demand for tools specialized in performing efficient management and qualified data retrieval/extraction from Web contents (Baeza-Yates & Ribeiro-Neto, 1999). Efforts to overcome the obstacles created by this ample growth, associated with the desire of inserting some level of intelligence to the retrieval of documents disposed on the Web, have motivated the development of the new generation of the Web: the Semantic Web (Berners-Lee et al., 2001).

It can be thought of as an extension of the current Web where data gains its own meaning. The main objective of this new Web paradigm is to insert some level of knowledge into WWW resources so that software agents can be able to intelligently process Web contents (Hendler, 2001). The Semantic Web is a mesh of information linked up in such a way that can be easily processed by machines on a global scale (Palmer, 2001).

This chapter focuses on some Semantic Web concepts and technologies, particularly ontology and its languages such as DAML+OIL (DAML+OIL 2001) and OWL (OWL, 2004). An architecture that makes use of these concepts to build systems that are capable of retrieving specific domain information from the Web is introduced. A prototype that actually implements the ideas behind the architecture is also presented.

The main objective of such a prototype is to provide a mechanism that efficiently identifies and extracts relevant pieces of information from a set of data from specific knowledge domain. Other technologies are also presented and discussed through the subsections of the chapter to achieve this goal.

Information Description and Retrieval

The rapid growth of the Web has promoted a radical change in the lives of people who have access to it. It is difficult to imagine a modern society living without all of the advantages the Web has brought to mankind. The easy access to the Web allied to its increasing usage has significantly raised the amount of data available on it.

One of the problems caused by such growth is the lack of some kind of description associated to resources spread on the Web. Meaningless contents that populate the current Web have increased several of its problems. Amongst them are: the delay in the information location and the retrieval of a high number of unexpected resources, due to ambiguity problems (Lopatenko, 2001).

Inserting some level of intelligence to the documents disposed on the Web would allow software agents to act as midfielders between final users and services. An agent, containing a set of useful information about its users would be able to perform different tasks on their behalf. Examples are scheduling appointments, looking for the best price of a product, verifying the latest news about such users' interests, and so on.

For instance, in this scenario, where data without structure or meaning are predominant, tools specialized in collecting qualified information on the Web have been improved day after day. Their weakness is that their effective functionality is directly linked to the way the resources were described when published on the Web. Such tools may be classified into two main classes:

- **Research in directories:** Systems introduced when the Web was small enough to be collected in a non-automatic way. Documents are classified manually according to a taxonomy.
- **Search engines:** In these systems, software agents, known as spiders, which traverse the Web collecting relevant data, gather the resources. They valorize the database size instead of the information quality they retrieve.

These classes of software mechanisms are both guided by searches based on the meaning inlaid in the *keywords* provided by its users or contained in the text. These tools do not consider the semantic aspects involved in the keywords that were submitted to the search; they perform just a syntactic analysis. A complementary research area is information extraction (Adams, 2004). Its main objective is to extract relevant information from semi-structured documents, and present the extracted information in a user friendly format. NLP (Natural Language Processing), Wrappers Development and ontology-based methods are some techniques used to execute information extraction on semi-structured documents (Laender, 2002).

Integrated access to multiple data sources ranging from traditional databases to semi-structured data repositories is required in many applications. The need for integrating data from distributed, heterogeneous and autonomous data sources has received recently a great deal of attention (Ambite et al. 2001, Chawathe et al. 1994, Draper et al. 2001). It is necessary to provide a uniform view of these data sources in which the users can pose their queries to meet such a requirement.

Nowadays, we see the growth of Peer-to-Peer (P2P) applications for file sharing, and more recently for structured data sharing. Data management in P2P systems is a challenging and difficult problem considering the extreme number of peers, their autonomous nature and the potential heterogeneity of their schemas. A Peer Data Management System (PDMS) (Bernstein et al., 2002; Arenas et al., 2003; Ng et al., 2003) is an application that enables users to transparently query several heterogeneous and autonomous data sources. A PDMS is considered an evolution of the traditional data integration systems (Sung et al., 2005).

The Web

The original efforts to develop the Web as it is known today were done in the beginning of the nineties. Tim Berners Lee (Berners-Lee et al., 2001), the Web's idealizer, had faced several challenges before having its project understood and accepted by the scientific community. Such efforts however, were fully rewarded, once the Web had been consolidated as the means for information distribution having the faster growth in the worldwide history.

On the other hand, this fast expansion made the Web a data repository as huge as confused. The main factor that contributes to such scenario is the standard language used to create Web pages, the HTML (Hypertext Markup Language) (Ragget, 2005). This language does not specify any semantic related to the resource it formats; it is responsible just for the appearance of the Web document. Thus, a gap emerges between the information that is available to Web services and the one that is provided for human reading.

The lack of meaning in HTML documents makes it hard for software agents to process these kinds of documents in an intelligent way. Therefore, it is necessary to develop a way to allow us to insert "intelligence" into Web resources. XML (McLaughlin, 2001) includes some semantics on documents by allowing the definition of significant tags. Inserting meaning into Web documents may be summarized by only one expression: "Semantic Web" (Berners-Lee et al., 2001).

The Semantic Web

The Semantic Web (Berners-Lee et al., 2001) enables the evolution from a Web composed by documents to a Web composed by information. In this new scenario, all resources may contain a meaning, which can be interpreted and processed by both human and software agents to provide new possibilities for automatic Web information processing.

According to Shadbolt et al. (2006), agents can only flourish when standards are well established and the Web standards for expressing shared meaning have progressed steadily over the last five years.

In Sparck-Jones (2004), two Semantic Web views are depicted: the grand view and the modest view. The grand view is the one where Semantic Web is the core model of the world. It is expressed in a manner that supports reasoning about this world. On the other hand, the modest view is the one in which the Semantic Web is the

Figure 1. The Semantic Web architecture

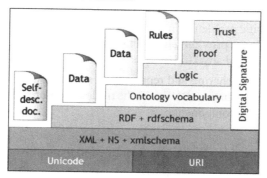

minimal apparatus of shared generic terminology that can be used to send some carrier pigeon messages from one universe of discourse to another.

To understand how the Semantic Web can be used to aid the information retrieval task, let us assume, for example, that one wants to use a search tool to look for information about a specific specie of bird, an eagle, for instance. Typing the word "eagle" in a search engine, a great variety of answers will be retrieved as a result. Besides the correct information about eagles, resources regarding the "War Eagles Air Museum," the American football club "Philadelphia Eagles" or the Country-rock band "The Eagles" can also be retrieved. This happens once the software responsible for performing the search just analyzes the keywords syntactically, and it is not able to discern the football club from the birds, the museum or the band. If these resources had been "marked" semantically, the software would be able to verify the intended word meaning amongst all possibilities. Of course this is a simple example, which could easily be corrected by adding other keyword (e.g., bird) to the search. But the objective of such a sample is just to illustrate how ambiguous a term may be in the actual Web.

In the Semantic Web vision, everything can be represented and addressed as an object. A person, a book, a car, a pet—everything—can be described as a resource. This brings other trade-offs that soon or later will have to be faced. For example, different users that did not know a previous existence of an object can represent a same resource more than once. But this is a discussion for the future.

An architecture, composed by several layers (see Figure 1), has been proposed by Tim Berners Lee (Berners-Lee et al, 2001; Studer, 2003) to support the Semantic Web.

The first two Semantic Web layers Unicode/URI (Uniform Resource Identifier) and XML, are aimed at providing a common syntax that may be widely adopted. While

UIR provides a standard way to reference entities, Unicode consists in standardization to symbols exchange. XML is a meta-language that allows the creation of languages to solve specific problems. In the Semantic Web vision, these two low-level layers are responsible for providing the syntax because they allow data structuring. However, they do not add any kind of semantics to these data.

RDF/RDFS allows both sharing and representing semantic data in the Web, while being able to relate information. RDF uses the triples to describe information. Each triple has the following components:

- **Resource:** Any object that may be identified in the real world
- **Property:** Aspects that characterize and describe a specific resource
- **Sentences:** Associate resources, properties and valid values for it

The use of these triples <resource, property, value>, guarantees the unique definition of concepts. However, it is still necessary to process and relate concepts that are ambiguously present in the Web. This is the role performed by the ontology layer.

The specification of ontology allows the communication between systems in an independent way by eliminating ambiguities that may exist among a set of words or terms. The logic layer currently is being treated along with the ontology layer.

The last two layers (Proof and Trust) follow the principle of validating the sentences that are described in Semantic Web documents. Amongst these layers, we would like to highlight the ontology vocabulary.

Ontology is a term well known in areas such as Philosophy and Epistemology denoting in that order, a "subject's existence" and a "knowledge to know" (Chandrasekaran et al., 1999). Recently, this term started being used in Artificial Intelligence (AI) to describe concepts and relationships used by agents. In the database (DB) community, ontology is a partial specification of a domain, which expresses entities, relationships between these entities and integrity rules.

Ontology also makes possible the communication between computer systems independently of the architecture and the information domain treated by eliminating ambiguities over a domain terminology (Bézivin, 1998). The main characteristics of ontology are:

- **Sharing:** It certifies that the several agents interacting over a theme possesses the same understanding of the domain concepts
- **Filtering:** It allows the modeled domain to take into consideration just the part of reality that interests to the application, discarding many unnecessary concepts

So, ontology provides a common/shared understanding about concepts of specific knowledge domains. This work uses domain ontology to support the extraction process execution defined by the system architecture presented in the section entitled "Retrieving Specific Information through ontology."

Some Existing Data Retrieval Systems

Several studies and works related to data retrieval/extraction from the Web can be found in literature (Laender et al., 2002). The importance of such areas, when acting together, is the possibility of handling the semi-structured data and traditional data structures (e.g., relational databases) alike, after the extraction process. There are several approaches to perform data extraction in Web documents: Natural Language Processing (NLP) (NLP, 2004), ontology-based mechanisms (Embley et al., 1999), Machine-Learning techniques (Soderland, 1999), among others. Some works are briefly addressed in the following.

WebQL (Arocena & Mendelzon, 1998) is a declarative query language capable of locating pieces of interesting data. HTML-generic *wrapper* analyzes the page sent as data entry, and creates a *hypertree*, an abstract tree that represents the HTML document that is being analyzed. Using the language, it is possible to write queries that searches for data represented in the *hypertree*, and the results are presented in a tabular form.

WHISK is a tool that uses NLP techniques for data extraction from text documents (Soderland, 1999). A set of extraction rules is induced from a collection of training documents. WHISK starts with an empty set of rules, which is filled at each interaction with the user. An interface is presented to users allowing them to add a tag for each attribute of interest from the instance. WHISK then uses the tagged instances to create rules and test the accuracy of the proposed rules.

ShopBot works with a set of URLs that addresses several online stores in the Web (Doorenbos et al., 1997). The ShopBot prototype operates in two phases:

- **Learning phase:** In this first phase, it applies a learning algorithm in the sites that will be analyzed. The learning stage examines the sites to "learn" a logical description of each one.

- **Comparison phase:** In this second phase an assistant of purchases uses the profiles to help the user to carry through purchases in real time.

The assistant uses the profiles to navigate each site, following the appropriate structure to discover the best price for a specific product desired by the user.

The Data Extraction Group at Brigham Young University (BYU) worked on extracting/retrieving information from Web resources using an ontology-based approach. In their tool (Embley et al., 1999; Jiang et al., 1999), ontology is previously constructed to describe the data of interest. By parsing a particular ontology, the tool is able to build a database by recognizing and extracting data from the input pages. To work properly, the tool requires a careful build of ontology. A specialist of the domain that is being analyzed shall do such work.

Swoogle prototype (Finin et al., 2005) consists in a crawler-based search engine that searches for RDF documents spread through the Web. Such a prototype allows users to retrieve indexed RDF documents based on the RDF classes and properties they use. The system has a database that stores metadata about documents marked with Semantic Web languages, and some crawlers that have the function of discovering such data.

The BlogVox (Java et al., 2007) is a prototype built to perform "opinion extraction" from *blog* posts. Retrieval is done over a special dataset exceeding three million posts collected from about 80,000 blogs. The prototype removes splogs, and eliminates content (blogrolls, advertisements, sidebars, headers, footers and so on) from the posts in order to significantly improve the results.

Infomaster (Genesereth et al., 1997; Kosala & Blockeel, 1997) accesses information stored in databases or ACL (Agent Communication Language) knowledge bases. The first information available in Infomaster is about renting of houses and apartments in San Francisco. Infomaster extracts ads from Web sites of several local journals that present rental information. These ads are separated in individual announcements, analyzed in a structured format and then loaded into a KIF (Knowledge Interchange Format) (KIF, 2004) knowledge base.

Besides the works previously commented, there are several other projects that deal with data retrieval/extraction that were not detailed in this text. Lixto (Baumgartner et al., 2004), Araneus (Atzeni & Mecca, 2000), Stalker (Muslea et al., 1999) e X-tract (Abascal & Sánchez, 1999) are some examples.

The prototype we have developed uses techniques adopted by some of the addressed works like ontology, tree-parsing and regular expressions. It uses the same premises of Infomaster and ShopBot to extract information from Web documents.

Retrieving Specific Information through ontology

A process to provide relevant information from the Web to meet users' expectations can be done by four main steps: (1) Web documents retrieval; (2) data analysis and extraction from the set of retrieved documents; (3) storage of the extracted information into a database; and (4) query the database. To achieve that, this section introduces a three-layered architecture (Figure 2) to perform specific information retrieval/extraction considering a given ontology. The layers are:

- **First layer:** This layer is related to user's browsers. It contains the Web interface to provide access to information extracted by the system.
- **Second layer:** It is responsible for information retrieval/extraction from the sources. Its modules are resource retrieval; data analysis/extraction; ontology parser. The ontology is part of this layer too.
- **Third layer:** It contains a database and provides all the functionalities related to database tasks (storage and querying tasks, for instance).

The layer components are detailed in what follows.

Resource Retrieval

Its main task is to retrieve from the Web the set of files belonging to the context related to the ontology. Software agents (bots) execute the first step in the information extraction architecture (Heaton, 2002) represented by phase A (sending the *bot* to the Web) and B (getting documents from the Web) in Figure 2. After this, the

Figure 2. Architecture layers and their components

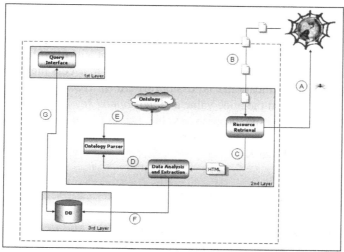

gathered data is submitted to a parser analysis. This process gets a set of pre-defined URLs, connects to the Web and downloads all HTML/XML files from these sites. The resources that were retrieved are then sent to a local folder to allow the data analysis/extraction process.

Data Analysis/Extraction

This module identifies and extracts relevant data from the HTML/XML files kept in the local folder. The analysis is done by parsers which provide an intermediate file representation, allowing an adequate resource examination.

This module enables navigation over the structures of the HTML/XML files and access to the words or expressions that are part of the document. Such expressions will be later compared to terms of a specific domain described by the related ontology. Three APIs to parse different formats of files, HTML, XML and specific ontology files, are used. Four steps are performed in the information extraction process, and they are detailed in the following.

Excluding Unnecessary Files

The first step executed by this module consists in removing data that will not be analyzed by the system. It must check the type of file it is dealing with to keep just HTML/XML files for further analysis. Data in other types of files are discarded.

Initial Analysis

This step is aimed at determining whether the HTML/XML files retrieved by the *bot* are related to the domain addressed by the system ontology. The objective of such verification is to avoid performing a complete analysis over files that are not in the scope described in the ontology. Parsers are used to access the HTML/XML nodes to perform this verification; it is possible to perform a *pattern matching* (Chng, 2001) operation between the node value and the *context keywords* (which are part of the ontology) by accessing each node value. If these *keywords* are found in the HTML/XML nodes, the file is considered valid and it is sent to the next phase. Otherwise the file is discarded.

Creating a Temporary File to Store HTML/XML Nodes Values

This step transposes the nodes that are part of the HTML files to a *XML temp file*. This is done to solve problems that may appear when we are dealing with HTML files. The creation of the *XML temp file* is executed internally using the HTML parser to access the nodes and the XML parser to create the *XML temp file*. This file contains all data belonging to the HTML file.

Identifying and Extracting Data from the Temporary File

This step is responsible for extracting the required information from the nodes of the temporary XML file. To do this, the system accesses the ontology through a specific parser getting the regular expression (REGEX) that was designed to extract the data from the analyzed site. Once identified, instances of the extracted data are inserted into a new XML file (called *XML final file*). Process D and E in Figure 2 represent the extraction process done through all these four steps. It also depicts the interactions with the ontology during the operations.

Storing and Querying Data

The extracted information shall be stored in a database. This process is represented by phase F in Figure 2. In order to accomplish this, the *XML final file* is read through the XML API and the extracted data populates a relational DB. After this, the DB is ready to receive queries from users, through a Web interface, delivering the required information about the domain that is modeled in the ontology. The querying process is done through a Web interface (Process G in Figure 2).

Domain Ontology

A domain-specific ontology is used to aid the identification and data extraction processes from HTML/XML files. The ontology is defined through three basic steps:

1. Domain definition
2. Graph modeling, that reflects the environment addressed by the application
3. Ontology creation using a specific language

The ontology shall model the knowledge domain so that the system can be capable of recognizing and extracting the desired information. The next step of the ontology development process is the ontology conceptual modeling. Ontology created from a Semantic Web viewpoint is modeled as graphs, since it may be seen as a set of elements related to each other. This modeling allows a direct mapping between the conceptual format and the formal definition of Semantic Web ontology.

Ontology Structure

The ontology shall be modeled by all necessary classes to keep relevant elements for modeling purposes. Amongst them, we can highlight two classes: one for maintaining instances of *context keywords* and the other one for the instances of the REGEX related to each element of interest.

Context keywords are specific to terms and will be useful to identify whether a certain file possibly contains the required information. They are used to determine the relevance of the documents that were retrieved to prevent totally out-of-context pages to be analyzed by the system.

REGEX are used later to identify the data that must be extracted from the Web document as described in the following subsection.

Regular Expressions

Once the architecture expects extracting information from XML/HTML files, it is important to consider two aspects of these types of files (especially applicable to HTML files):

- They do not have any semantic related to its tags
- The data presented by HTML files are usually written manually

These two aspects lead to the use of techniques that recognize data syntactically in the analyzed files. REGEX can be used to do this. It is a way to describe sets of strings, which permit to find relevant data inside texts through *pattern matching* operations. Using REGEX allows the definition of expressions representing a pattern that appears regularly in a text, which makes it possible to find the required data.

Creating the Specific Ontology

Once the ontology had been modeled, it can be represented by a Semantic Web development language such as OWL (OWL, 2004) or DAML+OIL (DAML+OIL 2001), for example. The access to data described in the ontology is done through Jena (McBride & Seaborne, 2003), a toolkit specifically developed to build Semantic Web applications.

Specific Parsers

Three different kinds of parsers to appropriately manipulate the files handled by the system are considered. They are presented in the following sections.

Ontology Parsing

Jena (2004) is used to allow the proper ontology analysis. It has an ontology API that makes it possible to navigate and to access the ontology elements. Such API allows creating an abstraction of the data model represented by the ontology. To distinguish XML from HTML files, two different APIs were used to provide access to those formats as detailed bellow.

XML Parsing

The DOM (Document Model Object) (DOM, 2004) model was proposed by the W3C (W3C, 2005) providing a standard to access data described in Web documents. This model uses a tree vision of the document that is being analyzed, and supplies a way to navigate in all nodes that are part of the file.

To analyze XML, the system uses JDOM (Java Document Object Model) (McLaughlin, 2001; JDOM, 2004) to parse the XML files that are retrieved by the bot. JDOM is an API that supports DOM in an optimized way in a Java language context. It behaves as Java, using Java collections, and provides a simple solution to create and examine XML files.

HTML Parsing

HTML pages are usually written without following rules established to XML documents creation. This implies in dealing with files with peculiar characteristics. Such characteristics motivated the use of a specific parsing API for HTML. The CyberNeko HTML Parser 0.8.1 (Clark, 2003) was used to provide HTML analysis. It consists in a HTML scanner and/or tag balancer that enable developers to examine HTML files and to access the data inside the file through a XML interface. Neko also reads the document fixing some common mistakes in HTML files such as missing end tags.

A Case Study

Our case study extracts information about offers announced by a set of supermarket Web sites. Such offers are presented in different ways varying from supermarket to supermarket. Such announcements are usually done using several techniques

Figure 3. The administrator interface

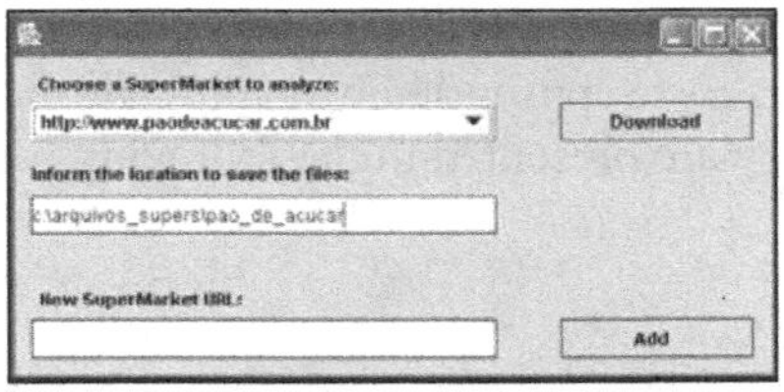

like images, animations, or pure HTML/XML files. This case study is limited to XML/HTML analysis, discarding other types of ads.

The *Resource Retrieval* module needs to be fed by the system administrator with a set of URLs from sites that shall be analyzed by the prototype. The administrator is able to execute such a task, using the administrator tool, developed in our project. Figure 3 presents the administration interface. The latter allows the administrator to insert new Supermarket URLs that one desires to analyze. A list of all supermarkets that may be analyzed using the prototype is presented in a select box. The Web retrieve/extract process is initialized by pressing the download button.

The *bot* connects these sites via HTTP (Hypertext Transfer Protocol) to download all files that are part of the sites. The tool also permits to cancel the operation; it undoes all operations performed before.

The Ontology

The second stage of the system performs *data analysis/extraction*. This stage uses the ontology built to this example. The ontology was modeled containing five classes: Regex, Promotion, Product, Promotional_term and Supermarket as it is shown in Figure 4. The classes Promotion, Product and Supermarket are used for data modeling purposes. The other two classes (Promotional_term and Regex) are as discussed in the previous section.

Context keywords are specific to terms that are useful to identify whether a certain file possibly contains announcements of products. In our ontology, examples of such keywords would be: "promotion," "offer," and so on.

Regular Expressions in the System

REGEX play an important role in this work since they permit to identify data from the HTML/XML files. For instance, let us consider the following REGEX developed to integrate the domain ontology used by the prototype:

Figure 4. The specific ontology modeled as a graph

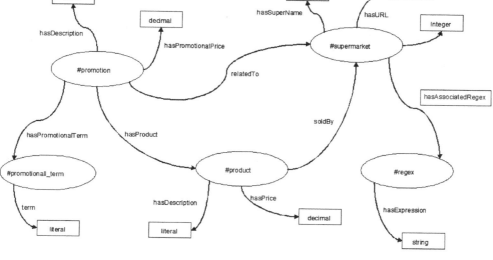

$(((r\backslash\$)\{1\})|((u|s)\backslash\$)\{1\}).*(\backslash d\{1,4\}).*((,\{1\}|.\{1\}).*(\backslash d\{2\})\{0,1\}))$

This expression is present in the ontology, and it is used to recognize any kind of price information. When it is used to execute the *pattern matching* over a string it returns information like: "R$1,99," "R$ 45,00," "R$8," "U$1,69," "US $ 190,00," and so on.

The current ontology contains five different REGEX, which allow recognizing syntactically the desired data inside HTML/XML files. Such number can rise once the REGEX have been properly developed and tested. The language used to create the ontology was the DAML+OIL (McGuinness et al., 2003; Carrol, 2002). DAML+OIL is a powerful Semantic Web language built on top of RDF (Resource Description Framework) (Lassila & Swick, 1999; Brickley & Guha, 2000; RDF, 2004) that can be seen as a vocabulary of properties added to RDF. The following code shows the definition of the Supermarket class in DAML+OIL:

```
<daml:Class rdf:about="#supermarket">
    <rdfs:label>
        supermarket
    </rdfs:label>
</daml:Class>
```

Properties are described separated from their classes in DAML+OIL. There are two types of DAML+OIL properties. The first one is represented by daml:DatatypeProperty tag. In this case, the property has its range attribute referencing a data type; literal or decimal values (leaf nodes in the graph model) are examples. The code below presents a definition of the property hasMarketName. Such an element is related to the SuperMarket class. The range tag determines which type of data this element accepts. In the example, it accepts the *string* datatype.

```
<daml:DatatypeProperty rdf:about="#hasMarketName">
    <rdfs:label>
name
</rdfs:label>
    <rdfs:domain>
<daml:Class rdf:about="#supermarket"/>
    </rdfs:domain>
    <rdfs:range>
<xsd:string/>
  </rdfs:range>
</daml:DatatypeProperty>
```

The relation between classes is made through daml:ObjectProperty properties. The definition of this kind of property is similar to Datatype element. The difference is the value of its range attribute that is a reference to another class that is defined in the data model. The code below represents that:

```
<daml:ObjectProperty rdf:about="#soldBy">
    <rdfs:label>
        soldBy
    </rdfs:label>
    <rdfs:domain>
        <daml:Class rdf:about="#product"/>
    </rdfs:domain>
    <rdfs:range>
        <daml:Class rdf:about="#supermarket"/>
    </rdfs:range>
</daml:ObjectProperty>
```

The code above relates the class product to the class supermarket through the soldBy property. The daml:ObjectProperty property provide a way to navigate over the graph model and consequently to access all property values present in the model.

Besides class definitions, there are also instance definitions of specific classes like REGEX and Promotional_term, which are used to discover the required information during the extraction process. The following code shows an example of the REGEX present in the ontology:

```
<regex rdf:about="#ID1">
        <hasExpression>
                (((r\$){1}).*(\d{0,4}).*((,{1}|.{1}).*(\d{2}){0,1}))
        </hasExpresion>
</regex>
```

Parsing

The prototype uses specific parsing tools to handle the files properly. When HTML pages arrive from a site, the first thing to do is to determine whether a page is relevant or not. Each node is individually analyzed by NekoHTML parser in the order of trying to find any ontology *context keyword*. If the document has one of the terms expressed in the ontology (one instance of Promotional_term), the HTML file is considered relevant. Otherwise it is discarded. A XML temporary file corresponding to such a HTML file is created when the file remains. The former will store all nodes that contain textual information in the HTML page. This is done to make handling the data easier through the XML parsing API.

The XML temporary file is then passed to the next step of the extraction phase. In this stage the prototype applies the REGEX that will be used to identify and extract relevant data from the file. Each site is analyzed by the REGEX that are part of the ontology. The REGEX are applied over all nodes of the XML files to recognize and extract data from each file. Once identified, data is extracted by the REGEX and the information is then structured in a new XML file, called XML final file. The following code presents a piece of such a file, which contains an extracted object.

```
...
<object_extracted>
<Product_description>
REFRIGERATOR ELECTROLUX F.F DFF35 BR 220V
</Product_description>
<original_price>null</original_price>
    <promotional_price>US$1.599,00</promotional_price>
    <supermarket>Wal Mart</supermarket>
    <url>http://www.walmart.com/offers.html</url>
<regex_applied>1</regex_applied>
  </object_extracted>
...
```

Figure 5. The Web interface

Once data are recognized and written to the XML final file, they are sent to the module that uses the information to populate the DB. The procedures that allow inserting data into the DB read the data from the XML final file, and create SQL statements to insert the information into the DB. Our project uses MySQL (MySQL, 2005) to store the data extracted from the Web files.

The DB is ready to be queried about supermarket offers by users through the Web interface after populated with the information recently extracted.

The interface, developed using JSP (Java Server Pages) technology (JSP, 2005), retrieves the extracted offers about products the user is interested in. It brings all information available in the DB in a friendly way. Figure 5 presents the Web interface currently in use. It presents all results that match the keywords submitted through the search option.

Conclusion

The Semantic Web is one of the W3C's long-term objectives. It is being developed in an environment of intelligent access to heterogeneous and distributed information. This work proposes a way of using some techniques related to the Semantic Web (RDF, ontology) together with techniques that allow syntactic analysis (Regular Expressions) to solve problems related to information extraction on the Web.

It introduces a general architecture that can be used to extract information from the Web on any domain. This can be achieved by the use of a specific ontology. A Java based prototype implementing the proposed architecture was developed.

A case study focusing on the knowledge domain of supermarket offers in the Web was presented. Its goal is to facilitate to get accurate information about products that are sold in supermarket Web sites without imposing tedious tasks to users, which would be needed otherwise.

Some tasks may be accomplished by future work. The ontology shall be specialized in order to explore concepts that were not fully addressed by this first version. The number of REGEX that are currently in use by the prototype shall also be increased aiming at recognizing different types of offer descriptions. Other ontology to be interconnected with the current one should be also developed in order to provide information exchange.

References

Abascal, R., & Sánchez, J. A. (1999). X-tract: Structure extraction from botanical textual descriptions. In *Proceedings of the String Processing & Information Retrieval Symposium and International Workshop on Groupware, SPIRE/CRIWG*, Cancún, Mexico (pp. 2-7).

Adams, K. C. (2004). *The Web as database: New extraction technologies and content management*. Retrieved from http://www.onlinemag.net/OL2001/adams3_01.html

Ambite, J., Knoblock, C., Muslea, I., & Philpot, A. (2001). Compiling source description for efficient and flexible information integration. *Journal of Intelligent Information Systems, 16*(2), 149-187

Arenas, M., Kantere, V., Kementsietsidis, A., Kiringa, I., Miller, R. J., & Mylopoulos, J. (2003). The Hyperion Project: From data integration to data coordination. *ACM SIGMOD Record, 32, 3.*

Arocena, G., & Mendelzon, A. (1998). WebOQL: Restructuring documents, databases and webs. In *Proceedings of the 14th International Conference on Data Engineering*, Orlandos, FL (pp. 24-33).

Atzeni, P., Mecca, G., Atzeni P., & Mecca G. (2000). Cut and paste. In *Proceedings PODS, 1997, Artificial Intelligence, 118* (pp. 1-2).

Baeza-Yates, R., & Ribeiro-Neto, B. (1999). *Modern information retrieval*. New York: ACM Press.

Baumgartner, R., Flesca, S., & Gottlob, G. (2004). *Visual Web information extraction with Lixto*. Retrieved from http://www.dia.uniroma3.it/~vldbproc/016_119.pdf

Berners-Lee, T., Cailliau, A., Luotenem, A., Nielsen, H. F., & Secret, A. (1994). The World Wide Web. *Communication of the ACM, 37*(8), 76-82.

Berners-Lee, T., Hendler, J., & Lassila, O. (2001). The Semantic Web. Internet. *Scientific American*, 34-43.

Bernstein, P., Giunchiglia, F., Kementsietsidis, A., Mylopoulos, J., Serafini, L., & Zaihrayeu, I. (2002). Data management for peer-to-peer computing: A vision. In *Proceedings of the WebDB Workshop*.

Bézivin, J. (1998). *Who's afraid of ontologies*. Retrieved from http://www.metamodel. com/oopsla98-cdif-workshop/bezivin1

Brickley, D., & Guha, R.V. (2000). *Resource Description Framework (RDF) Schema specification 1.0 27*, (1st.ed.). Retrieved from http://www.w3.org/TR/2000/CR-rdf-schema-20000327

Carrol, J. (2002). *Jena Tutorial: DAML+OIL—ontology description*. Retrieved from http://www.hpl.hp.com/semweb/doc/tutorial/DAML/

Chandrasekaran, B., Josephson, J., & Benjamins, V. (1999). What are ontologies, and why do we need them? In *IEEE Intelligent Systems, 1*(14), 20-26.

Chawathe, S., Garcia Molina, H., & Hammer, J. (1994). The Tsimmis Project: Integration of heterogeneous information sources. In *Proceedings of the 10th Meeting of the Information Processing Society of Japan (IPSJ)*, Tokyo, Japan (pp. 7-18).

Chng, B. (2001). *Matchmaking with regular expressions*. Retrieved from http://www.javaworld.com/javaworld/jw-07-2001/jw-0713-regex_p.html

Clark, A. (2003). *CYBERNEKO HTML PARSER*. Retrieved from http://www.apache.org/~andyc/neko/doc/html/index.html

DAML+OIL. (2001). *DAML+OIL reference description*. Retrieved from http://www.w3.org/TR/daml+oil-reference

DAML+OIL. (2004). *The DAML+OIL language*. Retrieved from http://www.daml.org/2001/03/daml+oil-index.html

DOM. (2004). *The DOM tutorial*. Retrieved from http://www.w3schools.com/dom/default.asp

Doorenbos, R., Etzioni, O., & Weld, D. (1997). A scalable comparison-shopping agent for the World Wide Web. In *Proceedings of the First International Conference on Autonomous Agents*.

Draper, D., Halevy, A., & Weld, D. (2001). The nimble XML data integration system. In *Proceedings of the 17th International Conference on Data Engineering (ICDE 2001)*, Heidelberg Germany (pp.155-160).

Embley, D., Campbell, D., & Smith, R. (1999). *Ontology-based extraction and structuring of information from data-rich unstructured documents*. Retrieved from http://www.cs.wisc.edu/~smithr/pubs/cikm98.pdf

Embley, D., Campbell, D., Jiang, Y., Liddle, S., Kai Ng, U., Quass, D., & Smith, R. (1999). Conceptual-model-based data extraction from multiple-record Web pages. *Data and Knowledge Engineering, 31*(3), 227-251.

Finin, T., Mayfield, J., Joshi, Cost, S., & Fink, K. (2005). Information retrieval and the Semantic Web. In *Proceedings of the 38th Annual Hawaii International Conference (System Sciences, 2005)*.

Genesereth, M., Keller, A., & Duschka, O. (1997). Infomaster: An information integration system. In *Proceedings of the ACM SIGMOD Conference*.

Heaton, J. (2002). *Programming spiders, bots and aggregators in Java*. Alameda: Sybex Inx.

Hendler, J. (2001). Agents and the Semantic Web. *IEEE Intelligent Systems, 16*(2), 30-37.

Java, A., Kolari, P., Finin, T., Mayfield, J, Joshi, A., & Martineau, J. (2007). BlogVox: Separating blog wheat from blog chaff. In *Proceedings of the Workshop on Analytics for Noisy Unstructured Text Data, 20th International Joint Conference on Artificial Intelligence (IJCAI-2007)*.

JDOM. (2004). *JAVA document model object*. Retrieved from http://www.ibiblio.org/xml/slides/extreme/jdom/

Jena. (2004). *Jena 2 ontology API*. Retrieved July 16, 2004, from http://jena.sourceforge.net/ontology/

Jiang, Y., Embley, D., & Ng, Y. (1999). Record-boundary discovery in Web documents. In *Proceedings ACM SIGMOD International Conference of Management of Data*, Philadelphia (pp. 467-478).

JSP.(2005). *JSP: Java Server Pages Technology*. Retrieved from http://java.sun.com/products/jsp/

KIF. (2004). *Knowledge interchange format*. Retrieved from http://logic.stanford.edu/kif/kif.html

Kosala, R., & Blockeel, H. (1997). Web mining research: A survey. In *Proceedings of the ACM SIGMOD Conference*.

Laender, A. Ribeiro-Neto B., da Silva, A., & Teixeira, J. (2002). A brief survey of web data extraction tools. *SIGMOD Record, 31*(2), 84-93.

Lassila, O. & Swick, R. (1999). *Resource Description Framework (RDF) model and syntax specification*. Retrieved from http://www.w3c.org/TR/REC-redf-syntax

Lopatenko, A. (2001). *Information Retrieval in Current Research Information Systems*. Retrieved from http://semannot2001.aifb.uni-karlsruhe.de/positionpapers/Lopatenko.pdf

McBride, B., & Seaborne, A. (2003). *Jena Tutorial for Release 1.4.0*. Retrieved from http://jena.sourceforge.net/tutorial/index.html

McGuinness, D., Fikes, R., Hendler, J., & Stein, L. (2003). *DAML+OIL: An ontology language for the Semantic Web*. Retrieved from http://dsonline.computer.org/0211/f/x5mcg.pdf

McLaughlin, B. (2001). *Java & XML* (2nd ed.). New York: O'Reilly.

MySQL. (2005). *MySQL: The world's most popular open source database*. Retrieved from http://www.mysql.com

Ng, W.,Ooi, B.,Tan, K., & Zhou, A. (2003). PeerDB: A P2P-based system for distributed data sharing. In *Proceedings of the19th International Conference on Data Eng. (ICDE)*.

NLP. (2004). *Natural language processing*. Retrieved from http://www.aaai.org/AITopics/html/natlang.html

OWL. (2004). *OWL: Web ontology language overview*. Retrieved from http://www.w3.org/TR/owl-features/

Palmer, S. (2001). *The Semantic Web: An introduction.* Retrieved from http://infomesh. net/2001/swintro/

Raggett, D. (2005). *Getting started with HTML.* http://www.w3.org/MarkUp/Guide/

RDF. (2004). *Resource Description Framework (RDF): Concepts and Abstract Syntax.* Retrieved from http://www.w3.org/TR/rdf-concepts/

Shadbolt N., Berners-Lee T., & Hall, W. (2006). The Semantic Web revisited. *IEEE Intelligent Systems, 21*(3), 96-101.

Soderland, S. (1999). Learning information extraction rules for semi-structured and free text. *Machine Learning 34,*(1-3), 233-272.

Sparck-Jones, K. (2004). What's new about the Semantic Web? Some questions. *SIGIR Forum, 38*(2). Retrieved from http://www.acm.org/sigir/forum/2004D/sparck_jones_sigirforum_2004d.pdf

Studer, R. (2003). The Semantic Web: Methods, applications and future trends. *The 3rd IFIP Conference on e-Commerce, e-Business, and e-Government,* Guaruja, São Paulo, Brasil.

Sung, L., Ahmed, N., Blanco, R., Li, H., Soliman, M., & Hadaller, D. (2005). *A survey of data management in peer-to-peer systems.* School of Computer Science, University of Waterloo.

W3C. (2005). *W3C: World Wide Web Consortium.* Retrieved from http://www.w3c.org

Chapter XIII

On the Problem of Mining Phrase Definition from Item Descriptions

Hung V. Nguyen, Arizona State University, USA

H. Davulcu, Arizona State University, USA

Abstract

Most search engines do their text query and retrieval using keywords. However, vendors cannot anticipate all possible ways in which shoppers search for their products. In fact, many times, there may be no direct keyword match between a search phrase and descriptions of products that are perfect "hits" for the search. A highly automated solution to the problem of bridging the semantic gap between product descriptions and search phrases used by Web shoppers is developed. By using scalable information extraction techniques from Web sources and a frequent itemset mining algorithm, our system can learn how meanings can be ascribed to popular search phrases with dynamic connotations. By annotating the product databases based on the meanings of search phrases mined by our system, catalog owners can boost the findability of their products.

Introduction

The World Wide Web has made a dramatic transition from its early beginnings as a distributed repository of information that you can browse into a dominant medium for conducting e-commerce. In particular, it has become a mainstream advertising medium for retail goods with online advertising reaching $16 billion in revenue in 2006. Because of this immense commercial power of the Web, the number of retailers, both large and small, who are setting up an online presence and subscribe to search advertising to generate leads to sell their goods through their Web sites, continues to proliferate.

In search advertising, vendors subscribe to triplets of the form < searchphrase, product − url, bid>. For example, a shoe store may subscribe to advertise its "NIKE Airmax 180" product as "running shoes" by specifying the triplet < runningshoes, NIKEAirmax180, $.50 >. This triplet indicates that whenever a Web site contains "running shoes" related information, this vendor would like to list its "NIKE Airmax 180" product and agrees to pay 50 cents per click. Nevertheless, vendors can not anticipate all possible ways in which to advertise their products. Advertising such as Google's AdSense utilize sense-disambiguation and keyword matching to place ads on highly relevant Web pages. However, there may be a semantic gap between the search phrases used by vendors and the way the relevant content is presented in the Web pages. For example, if a Web page mentions "stable light shoes," a smart advertising algorithm should be able to detect the relationship between "stable light shoes" and "running shoes," thus, relieving the advertiser from the burden of specifying ALL potential relevant search-phrases for "running shoes."

Keyword searching is the most common form of product search on the Web. Most search engines do their text query and retrieval using keywords. The average keyword query length is under three words (2.2 words) (Cutting & Douglas, 1997). Recent research (Andrews, 2003) found that 40% of e-commerce companies rate their search tools as "not very useful" or "only somewhat useful." Further, a review of 89 sites (Andrews, 2003) found that 75% have keyword search engines that fail to retrieve important information and put results in order of relevance; 92% fail to provide guided search interfaces to help offset keyword deficiencies (Andrews, 2003), and 7 out of 10 Web shoppers were unable to find products using the search engine, even when the items were stocked and available.

The defining problem: Vendors cannot anticipate all possible ways in which shoppers search for their products. In fact, many times, there may be no *direct keyword match* between a search phrase and descriptions of products that are perfect "hits" for the search. For example, if the shopper uses "motorcycle jacket," then, unless the publisher knows that every "leather jacket" is a "motorcycle jacket," it cannot produce all matches for the user's search. Thus, for certain phrases, there is a *semantic gap* between the search phrase used and the way the corresponding matching products are described. A serious consequence of this gap is that it results in unsatisfied customers. Thus *there is a critical need to boost product findability by bridging the semantic gap that exists between search phrases and product descriptions*. Closing this gap has the strong potential to translate Web traffic into higher conversion rates and more satisfied customers.

Issues in bridging the Semantic gap: We denote a search phrase to be a *"target search phrase"* if it does not directly match certain relevant product descriptions. The semantics of products matching such *"target search phrases"* is *implicit* in their descriptions. For phrases with fixed meanings, that is, their connotations do not change such as in "animal print comforter," it is possible to close the gap by extracting their meaning with a thesaurus and relating it to product descriptions, such as "zebra print comforter" or "leopard print bedding" and so forth. Where they pose a more interesting challenge is when their meaning is subjective, driven by perceptions, and hence their connotations change over time as in the case of "fashionable handbag" and "luxury bedding." The concept of a fashionable handbag is based on trends, which change over time, and correspondingly the attribute values characterizing such a bag also changes. Similarly, the concept of "luxury bedding" depends on the brands and designs available on the market that are considered as luxury and their attributes. Bridging the semantic gap, therefore, is in essence the problem of inferring the meaning of search phrases in all its nuances.

Our Approach: In this chapter, we present an algorithm that (1) finds products matching a "target search phrase" from Web documents by utilizing search engines, (2) extracts and structures product attributes and product descriptions for these products, and (3) uses an optimized frequent itemset mining algorithm to learn the "target phrase" definitions.

Our Contributions: We present a novel Web mining approach for inferring the meaning of search phrases from keyword matching product information. The mined rules can be used by a publisher or a search engine to boost the item findability. We present algorithms for:

- Automated item information extraction from heterogeneous Web sources.
- Automated techniques for extracting attribute-value pairs from descriptive item names.
- Optimized heuristic synthesis, on so-called 2-frequent itemset graph, for frequent itemset mining.

The next section discusses related work. In the third section, the architecture of the system is presented. Following that, we discuss the data extraction algorithms for collecting rich relevant product information from Web sources. In the fifth, we present the phrase definition mining algorithms from extracted data. With the sixth section, we present the experimental results, and Section 7 concludes the chapter.

Related Work

Definition Mining

In Liu (2000), linguistic analysis is employed to mine the description of phrases/queries. Specifically, that work is based on patterns such as *is a, or, such as, especially, including, or other, and other,* and so forth, in order to recognize the meaning of a phrase/query. This approach, however, cannot work well with domains where the target phrase does not associate within the context of the above patterns. Another related work is described in Len et al. (1997). In this work, the trends in text document are discovered based on sequential pattern mining in order to trace phrases. Then, each phrase is assigned an ID number and history of each phrase is tracked by partitioning documents into time intervals. From this, the trends of phrases are identified using trend queries. The output, however, is not the definition but trends of the usage of the phrases through a period. In Alohen et al. (1998), techniques called *generalized episodes* and *episodes rules* are used for Descriptive Phrase Extraction. *Episodes rules* are the modification of association rules and *episode* is the modification of frequent set. These concepts are used associated with some weighting measures in order to determine the (episode) rules that define a phrase. Because *episode* as described in Alohen et al. (1998) is a collection of features vectors with a partial order for that collection, authors claimed that their approach is useful in phrase mining in Finnish, a language that has the relaxed order of words in a sentence. In Nguyen et al. (2003), an algorithm that mines the definitions of hidden phrases from the Meta-Tags of Web documents was introduced. A phrase that frequently occurs in the meta-tags of Web pages but not in their body is called a "hidden phrase." We introduced a novel framework based on (1) sampling highly ranked documents that matches a hidden phrase by using a keyword search engine, (2) extracting frequent sets of highly co-occurring phrases from the pages using co-occurrence clustering and (3) use association rule mining for mining other phrases that co-occur with the hidden phrases. In this chapter, we attempt to mine the phrase definitions in terms of product information, whereas our previous work explores phrase definitions in terms of other phrases. By using the techniques developed in this chapter, it is possible to mine phrase definitions that connects "hidden phrases" to real product information in all its nuances.

Information Extraction

Information extraction from the Web is a well studied problem. But most of the work is wrapper- based. Wrapper is a small program that extracts the data from the Web sites. Wrapper is created either manually or semi-automatically after analyzing location of the data in the HTML page. These wrapper-based approaches are explained in Hammer et al. (1997) and Kushmerick et al. (1997). However, unlike our extraction techniques, wrapper-based approaches are site-specific, brittle, and not scalable.

A recent template-based approach is presented in the RoadRunner (Crescenzi et al., 2001) project. A template for a page is learned from a set of input pages and this template is used to extract the actual data. But this approach of learning the template may sometimes require many examples to effectively learn the schema. Instead, our information extraction technique relies on learning to effectively separate the static template instances from the dynamic information instances and it learns information paths with just two page instances.

Content Targeted Advertising

Recently, there has been a growing interest in the formal study of the content-targeted advertising techniques. The common goal of most of the papers in this area is to accurately find the relevant keywords from Web pages with respect to a given search phrase in order to populate the page with appropriate advertising entries and also to enhance the findability of items. Among them, this chapter and another recent paper (Jones et al., 2006) have relied on query substitution to achieve this common goal. Both works are different from prior research (Ruthven, 2003) in that they employ pseudo feedbacks, which can lead to query drift. These two works are also different from each other in the following way: In Jones et al. (2006), the authors use query logs with several other features to build an algorithm that combines the query pairs for substitution. In this chapter, we use a simple model and yield good results, asymptotically to human level. Another paper (Lacerda et al. (2006) uses genetic programming paradigm to develop the ranking algorithm for ads.

Frequent Itemset Mining

The frequent itemset mining problem is to discover a set of items shared among a large number of records in the database. There are two main search strategies to find the frequent items set. Apriori (Agrawal & Srikan, 1994) and several other Apriori-like algorithms adopt Breadth-First-Search model, while Eclat (Zaki, 2000) and FPGrowth (Han et al., 2000) are well-known algorithms that employ Depth-First manner to search all frequent itemsets of a database. Our algorithm also searches for frequent itemsets in a Depth-First manner. But, unlike the lattice structure used in Eclat or the conditional frequent pattern tree used in FPGrowth, we propose the so-called 2-frequent itemset graph and utilize heuristic syntheses to prune the search space in order to improve the performance. We plan to further optimize our algorithm and conduct more comparisons to above algorithms in our future work.

System Architecture

The architecture of the system, shown in the Figure 1, mainly consists of two components.

I. Data extraction: This component puts the target phrase into a search engine, fetches the results and extracts the data from the relevant pages. Finally, the extracted data is structured and labeled for mining the phrase definitions.

II. Mining search phrase definitions: In this phase, we divide the phrase definition mining problems into two sub problems (1) mining the parametric definition of product phrase. In particular, we obtain tabular dataset from the extraction engine and learn the rules that express the relations among attribute of product; (2) Based on the long description extracted by extraction engine, we learn the rules that express the textual description of the product phrase. Details are discussed in Section 5 and experimental results are shown in Section 6.

Data Labeling

This section presents the techniques for an e-commerce domain, for the sake of providing examples. Our techniques can be customized for different domains. The major tasks in this phase are *structuring and labeling* of extracted data. The readers are also referred to (Davulcu et al., 2003) for more information in details.

Labeling and Structuring Extracted Data

This section describes a technique to partition the short product item names into their various attributes. We achieve this by grouping and aligning the tokens in the item names such that the instances of the same attribute from multiple products fall under the same category indicating that they are of similar types. The motivation behind doing the partition is to organize data. By discovering attributes in product

Figure 1. System architecture

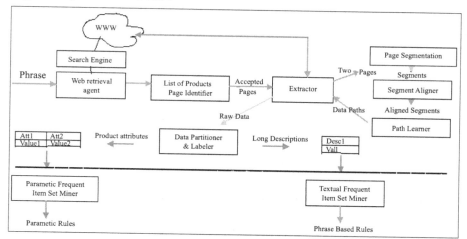

data and arranging the values in a table, one can build a search engine which can enable quicker and precise product searches in an efficient way.

The Algorithm

Before proceeding to the algorithm, it helps to identify item names as a sequence of *tokens* obtained when white-space is used as a delimiter. Since the sequences of tokens obtained from item names are all from a single Web page and belong to the same category, they are likely to have a similar pattern. As mentioned before, our algorithm is designed to process collections of such item names without any labeling whatsoever; so it can be performed on the fly as and when data is extracted from the Web sites. Following are the general properties of the data our algorithm can process:

- **Super-Tokens:** Any pair of tokens t_1, t_2 that always co-occur together and occur more than once belong to a multi-token instance of a type.

- **Context:** All single tokens occurring between identical attribute types belong to the same type. This means that if two tokens t_1 and t_2 from distinct item names occur in between same types T_L and T_R then they should be of the same type.

- **Anchor Type:** A token that uniquely occurs within all item names should belong to a unique type, which we call an *Anchor Type*.

- **Density:** Attribute types should be densely populated, which means that every type should occur within the majority of item names.

- **Ordering:** Pair-wise ordering of all types should be consistent within a collection.

- **Tokenization:** The item names are tokenized by using white space characters as delimiters. Tokens are stemmed so using the Porter Stemmer (Porter, 1980).

- **Super Tokenization:** The second step identifies multi-token attributes.

- **Initialization of Types:** To initialize, every item name is prefixed and suffixed with a *Begin* and an *End* token.

- **Context-Based Inference:** This step aligns tokens from different item names under a single type. This step takes advantage of tokens repeating across descriptions and operates based on the first assumption (Context) that tokens within similar contexts have similar attribute types.

If a token sequences t_x, t, t_y and t'_x, t, t'_y exist in D such that $t_x, t'_x \in T_p$ and $t_y, t'_y \in T_q$, then combine and replace the types of tokens t and t' with a new type $T_n =$ Typeof(t) U Typeof(t') .

Type Ordering: In this step, the set of inferred types T are sorted based on their ordering in the original item names. We utilize the Pair-wise Offset Difference (POD) metric to compare different types.

POD between types T_i and T_j is defined as:

$$POD_{ij} = \sum_{x \in T_i, y \in T_j} (f_x - f_y)$$

$$(1)$$

where f_x is the token offset of x from the start of its item name and f_y is the token offset of y. If this value is greater than zero, then the type T_i comes after type T_j in the sorted order.

Due to space constraints, tokens have been aligned such that those from the same type are offset at the same column. The type numbers the tokens belong to are indicated at the top.

Type Merging: A careful observation shows that some of the neighboring types are fillers for each other. This means that they are not instantiated together for any item name. Such types are candidates for merging and are called *merge compat-*

Algorithm 1. Item name partition

Input: D, a collection of item names D_0, D_1, ... D_n

Output: T, an ordered set of Types T0, T1, ... Tm where Ti is a bag of tokens that are instances of the same product attributes

```
 1: Tokenization(D)
 2: SuperTokenization(D)
 3: for each unique token t_i ε D_i  where D_i ε D do
 4:     create new type T_i
 5:     add t_i to T_i
 6:     add T_i to T
 7: end for
 8: repeat
 9:     ContextBasedInference(D, T)
10: until no inference is made
11: SortTypes(D, T)
12: repeat
13:     MergeTypes(D, T)
14: until no types are merged
15: repeat
16:     MergeConcatenateTypes(D, T)
17: until no types were merge-concatenated
```

---

ible. Merging at this point is logical because of our assumption that the types are densely populated.

Merge Concatenation: Finally, merge-concatenation is performed to eliminate sparsely populated types. Sparsely populated types are those with a majority of missing values. By our assumption, collections of item names should have dense attributes. This implies that the tokens of a sparsely populated type should be concatenated with the values of one of the neighboring types.

Experimental Results

To evaluate the algorithm, DataRover (Davulcu et al., 2003) system was used to crawl and extract list-of-products from the following five Web sites: www.officemax.com, www.officedepot.com, www.acehardware.com, www.homeclick.com and www.overstock.com.

Three metrics were used to measure the effectiveness of the algorithm. The first two evaluate the ability to identify fragments of the descriptions to the correct type and the last one indicates the correctness of the number of attributes.

Precision indicates how correctly type-value pairs are identified.

$$Precision = \frac{\text{type-value pairs identified correctly}}{\text{type-value pairs identified}}$$

Recall This quantity indicates if every existing type-value pair is being identified.

$$Recall = \frac{\text{type-value pairs identified correctly}}{\text{type-value pairs existing in the data}}$$

Attributes Error Rate indicates the error in the number of attributes described in the set of product names.

$$Error = \frac{|\text{actual attribute count} - \text{guessed attribute count}|}{\text{actual attribute count}}$$

Table 1. Summary of evaluation measures for different Web sites for the items name structuring algorithm

Web Site	Attribute Count Error Rate	Type-Value Precision	Type-Value Recall
www.officemax.com	0.07	0.89	0.94
www.officedepot.com	0.17	0.89	0.90
www.acehardware.com	0.06	0.92	0.94
www.homeclick.com	0.05	0.91	0.91
www.overstock.com	0.40	0.62	0.79

Mining the Definition of a Target Phrase

In this section, we introduce the problem of mining definitions of a phrase from product data extracted from the matching Web pages. Using extraction techniques discussed in Section 4, we can retrieve tabular parametric features of matching products as well as their long descriptions. Next, we apply frequent itemset mining algorithms to learn the parametric definitions and phrase-based definitions of target phrases from the above product data.

First, in Section 5.1 through 5.3, we introduce an algorithm that finds all frequent itemsets from a database. Section 5.5 discusses the problem of mining parametric definitions. In Section 5.6 textual definition mining is discussed. Since their introduction in 1994 by Agrawal et al. (1994), the frequent itemset and association rule mining problems have received a lot of attention among data mining research community. Over the last decade, many research papers (Agrawal & Srikan, 1994; Goeathal; Han et al., 2000; Zaki, 2000; Han & Kamber, 2001) have been published presenting new algorithms as well as improvements on existing algorithms to tackle the efficiency of frequent itemset mining problems. The frequent itemset mining problem is to discover a set of items shared among a large number of transaction instances in the database. For example, consider the product information database matching 'trendy shoes' that we extract from retail Web sites. Here, each instance represents the collection of product's <attribute, value> pairs for attributes such as brand, price, style, gender, color and description (see Figure 3). The discovered patterns would be the set of <attribute, value> pairs that most frequently co-occur in the database. These patterns define the parametric description of the target phrase 'trendy shoe.'

In this chapter, we present a mining algorithm with heuristic syntheses to find all itemsets, as well as itemsets with some internal structure.

The main features of our frequent itemset mining algorithm are as follows:

1.   It uses the vertical Boolean representation to encode the database into main memory. Specifically, in the database, each column is encoded as a Boolean array (bit vector) whose length is exactly the number of instances in the data set. Each element of the attribute vector represents the value of that attribute (occurs or not occur) in the corresponding record (instance).

2.   We define and construct the 2-frequent itemset Graph and search for all frequent itemsets by utilizing this Graph.

3.   We introduce two heuristic functions to prune the search space.

4.   We also discuss optimization techniques that exploit the internal structure of our itemsets.

Vertical Boolean Representation for the Database

In the database, each attribute is represented as a Boolean array (a bit vector) whose length is exactly the number of instances in the data set. Each element of the attribute vector represents the value of that attribute for the corresponding instance. In this representation, checking 2-frequent itemsets corresponds to an AND operation between two attribute vectors and counting the number of 1's in the resulting vector against the minimum support. We can similarly perform many other logical operations such as set subtraction, subset, superset, OR, XOR, and so forth, between any number of attribute vectors. Superset test operations are utilized frequently in our algorithm and can be executed extremely fast with bit-vector operations.

Constructing 2-Frequent Itemsets Graph

The set of 2-frequent itemsets plays crucial role in finding all frequent itemsets. This is because if a set is a frequent itemset, then all pairs of items in this set must be 2-frequent itemsets. Using this property of a frequent set, our algorithm will first create a graph that represents the 2-frequent itemsets among all items that satisfy the minimum support threshold. Finding all 2-frequent set takes $O(n^2)$ operations where n is the number of frequent single items.

The the 2-frequent itemset graph is the directed graph G(V,E) which is constructed as follows:

$V = I$; I is the set of items that satisfy the minimum support in database D.

$E = \{(v_i, v_j) \mid \{i,j\}$ is a 2-frequent itemset and i<j).

We sort the frequent single items into lexicographical order and for a 2-frequent itemset, we construct a directed edge from the node (item) whose index is lower to the node whose index is higher.

For this database, if minimum support δ is set to 25%, then the 2-frequent itemsets are $I_1 I_2$, $I_2 I_3$, $I_2 I_4$, $I_3 I_4$. The 2-frequent itemsets graph would be as in Figure 2.

5.3 Searching for Frequent Itemsets

The main idea of our algorithm is that, from the observation that if $\{I_i ... I_j\}$ is a frequent itemset, then all pairs of items in this set must also be a frequent itemset; the searching algorithm will traverse 2-frequent itemset graph to find all such frequent itemsets. Specifically, the algorithm iteratively starts from every node in the graph and recursively traverses depth-first to its descendants. At any step k (k>1), the algorithm will choose to go to a child node v of the current node so that the path from the beginning node to v forms a k-frequent itemset. If so, the algorithm will

Table 2. Database I

I_1	I_2	I_3	I_4
1	1	1	0
0	1	1	1
1	0	0	0
1	1	0	0
0	0	1	1
1	1	0	0
0	1	0	1
1	0	0	1

Figure 2. 2-frequent itemsets Graph for Database I

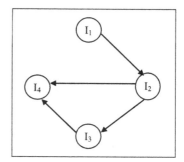

continue expand to v's children to search for (k+1)-frequent itemset and so on. There are several algorithms (Han et al., 2000; Zaki, 2000) that generate frequent itemsets in depth-first manner. In our approach, we introduce several heuristic syntheses in order to reduce the number of candidate set in each level of the depth first search algorithm. Like Eclat (Zaki, 2000), we also use vertical Boolean representation. A distinguishing feature of our algorithm is that it searches on the 2-frequent itemset graph.

Our algorithm utilizes the following heuristics to guide the search.

Heuristic 1: At step k, choose only children nodes of node v_{k-1} that have incoming degree greater than or equal to the number of visited nodes, counted from the beginning node.

Incoming degree of a node v, denoted as $\deg(v)$ is the number of nodes that point to v. The meaning of this heuristic is that, if $\deg(v)$ is smaller than the number of visited nodes (nodes in the path, then there exists at least one node among the set of previously visited k-1 nodes that does not point to v. In other words, there exists at least one node in the current path that does not form a 2-frequent itemset with v. Therefore, the k-1 nodes in the path (visited nodes) and v cannot form a k-frequent itemset, hence it is pruned out without candidate itemset generation.

Heuristic 2: At step k, choose only children nodes of node v_{k-1} that have the set of incoming nodes that is a superset of the set of all k-1 nodes in the visited path. This heuristic, which is applied after Heuristic 1, ensures that all previously visited nodes in the current path, must point to the node in consideration. This is also a necessary precondition that each visited node forms a 2-frequent itemset with the node in consideration.

Heuristic 1 is efficient since the 2-frequent itemset graph is already constructed and the degree of all nodes is stored before the search proceeds. Heuristic 2 superset testing operation can also be performed efficiently using the bit-vector representation. Consequently, by utilizing these heuristic estimates, we can prune a lot of nodes that cannot be added to the visited nodes to form a frequent itemset and eliminate a lot of candidate itemset generation.

Example: We consider the database in Table 2 and its 2-frequent itemset graph. The search algorithm starts from vertex I_1, I_1 has only one child, that is, I_2. Obviously, I_1 and I_2 form a 2-frequent itemset. The algorithm then goes on to I_2's children. I_2

Algorithm 2. Frequent itemset mining

Input: **D**, δ, **I**
Output: all frequent itemsets **F(I,δ)**
//main procedure
Construct all 2-frequent itemsets by counting the support of all pairs of single items
Construct the 2-frequent itemsets graph G(V,E)
F[I, δ]:= {}
for all **v** in **V** do
visited node list:= null
add v to list of visited node list
calculate_itemset (v)
endfor
end
Procedure calculate_itemset (v)
for each child v' of v **do**
// Heuristic 1
if deg(v') ≥ number of visited node **then**
// Heuristic 2
if the set of incoming nodes of v' is a superset of visited node **then**
if the set of visited node and v' has counting ≥ δ **then**
add v' to the list of visited nodes
add visited nodes list to F(I, δ)
calucalte_itemset(v')
//backtrack
remove v' from the visited node set
endif
endif
endif
endfor
end

---

has two children, that is, I_3 and I_4. Heuristic 1 tells the algorithm that $\deg(I_3) = 1$ is smaller than the number of visited nodes (so far, the algorithms has already visited I_1 and I_2 in this iteration). Hence, the algorithm does not consider the set $\{I_1, I_2, I_3\}$. In other words, the algorithm does not to create candidate set $\{I_1, I_2, I_3\}$. Now, the algorithm jumps to another child of I_2, i.e. I_4. We can see that $\deg(I_4) = 2$ but the heuristic 2 tells the algorithm that the set of incoming nodes of I_4 $\{I_2, I_3\}$ is not a superset of the set of visited nodes $\{I_1,I_2\}$, hence the algorithm does not have to consider the set $\{I_1,I_2,I_4\}$.

The algorithm then starts other iterations on vertices I_2, I_3, I_4 and ends up finding other frequent sets $\{I_2, I_3\}$, $\{I_2, I_4\}$ and $\{I_3, I_4\}$.

Data Preprocessing

In order to improve the performance of the algorithm, it is necessary to clean the data before running the algorithm. The cleansing preprocessing stage will eliminate all attributes columns that are infrequent as well as all instances that do not contain any frequent attributes.

Mining Parametric Definition of Phrases

Note that, since we extract data from the Web by posing a search phrase query to a Web search engine, all the instances in the data we get contain search phrase. Therefore, the association rule generation becomes simple by just putting the search phrase into the header of association rules and the body of rules is frequent itemsets. The support of obtained association rules equals to the support of frequent items set in their body since for a rule, the search phrase occurs in all instances that the frequent itemset (in the body of the rule) occurs.

Next, we would like to utilize the extracted product information to mine parametric phrase definition rules made up from conjunctions of distinct <attribute, value> pairs, like:

Trendy shoe ← brand = Steve Madden, Color = black, material = leather   (1)

Let us consider the extracted sample database represented in Figures 3 and 4. In order to facilitate the frequent itemset mining algorithm to mine frequent sets in the form of (1), we introduce a simple transformation to convert the database in Figure 3 into the form shown below in Figure 4.

Figure 3. Database II

ID	Brand	Style	Color	Material
01	Paul Green	oxford	Black	leather
05	Sesto Meucci	moc toe	Black	leather

Figure 4. Transformed database of Database II

b_1	b_2	s_1	s_2	c_1	m_1
1	0	1	0	1	1
0	1	0	1	1	1

The Database II and its transformed database are called *frequent itemset equivalent* databases. That means each frequent itemset of database II is equivalent to a frequent itemset in its transformed database. These two databases have the same number of instances but the number of items in the transformed database is much larger than the number of items in the original database. Specifically, the number of items in the transformed database is a polynomial of the number of items in the original database.

After the transformation, we can apply the frequent itemset mining algorithm to transformed database in Figure 4 to mine the frequent itemsets in the form (1) for the database in Figure 3. For the numeric parametric items, we adopt a discretization method to classify the values into discrete intervals to facilitate the mining algorithm. For example, for Price we have intervals C_1=[0-\$20], C_2 = [\$21-\$40] and so on. Furthermore, we observe that those items in the database in Figure 3 that fall into the same attribute class, for example, items m_1, m_2 and m_3 never occur pair-wise in the same frequent itemset. Therefore, we group items corresponding to the same attribute and during the construction of 2-frequent itemset graph, the graph never contains edges that connect any pair of items that fall into the same attribute group. This constraint reduces the search space and enhances the performance.

5.6. Mining Textual Definitions of Target Phrases

Another resource of rich phrase definitions is the long product descriptions of the matching products. In Davulcu (2003), authors described how to collect long product descriptions from product Web pages that matches a given target search phrase. In this section, we describe the proposed algorithm for mining phrase definitions that can connect hidden phrases to product descriptions themselves. An example of a long product description that matches "trendy shoe" is:

Get celebrity elegance, stylish look and luxury all in one with these Susan Lucci Suede Pumps with Lace-up Detail. You can choose from black or camel. The shoe's upper features suede and smooth leather with lacing detail at the center vamp. The lacing extends from the center top of the vamp to the side quarters. The pumps have a snip toe and rounded throat line. These shoes also have a manmade ribbed outsole to resist slippage and an approx. 3-1/4"H suede covered heel. Other features include: Susan Lucci™ couture-like, trendy apparel is inspired by her own personal collection and is designed for the fashion savvy woman who truly appreciates Hollywood glamour and style. Incorporating silk blends with stretch fabrics, her fashions give you the look of glamour with comfort and ease.

One can already identify phrases, such as "celebrity elegance," "stylish look," "Suede Pumps," "Lace-up Detail," "smooth leather," "fashion savvy woman" that could indicate "trendy shoe" status for a product. Hence, our first step is to identify frequently occurring phrases within long descriptions matching a hidden phrase. In order to generate candidate phrases, first, we perform part-of-speech (POS) tagging and noun and verb phrase chunking (Finch & Mikheev, 1997) on the long description to obtain a more structured textual description. Part-of-speech (POS) tagging and chunking the above description yields the structure illustrated in Box 1.

The phrases in between ([...]) corresponds to noun phrases. Next, we generate candidate words, and phrases of length two words, three words, and so forth, from the noun phrases in the matching long descriptions. For the above example, this would yield a list of words including "celebrity," "elegance," "stylish," and so forth, two words phrases such as "celebrity elegance," "stylish look," "couture-like

Box 1. POS tagging and chunking

```
: <TEXT>
    : <P>
        <S>((Get )) ([ celebrity elegance ]), ([stylish look]) and ([ luxury ]) all in one with ([
            these Susan Lucci Suede Pumps ]) with ([ Lace-up Detail ]).</S>
        <S> ...
        <S>([The shoe 's upper features suede ]) and ([ smooth leather ]) with ([ lacing
            detail ]) at ([ the center vamp ]).</S>
        <S> ...
        <S>([Other features ]) (( include )): ([ Susan Lucci ]) ([ s ]) ([ couture-like , trendy
            apparel ]) (( is inspired )) by ([ her own personal collection ]) and (( is designed
            )) for ([ the fashion savvy woman ]) who (( truly appreciates )) ([ Hollywood
            glamour ]) and ([ style ]).</S>
        <S> ...
    </P>
</TEXT>
```

apparel," "trendy apparel," and similarly three word phrases such as "couture-like trendy apparel," "fashion savvy woman," and so forth.

In the next step, we utilize the noun phrases as transaction instances and mine frequently used phrases from all the noun phrases of all the product descriptions that we have collected from the Web documents. This step yields frequently used phrases such as "stylish look" and eliminates not-so-frequent phrases such as "her own personal collection." Notice that the frequent phrases generated in this step are richer than frequent bi-gram, or n-gram models since we can create candidate phrases by selecting non-consecutive words such as "couture-like apparel" in the candidate phrase generation step.

Next, we use the mined frequent phrases as items and create transaction instances by marking all of the frequently used phrases matching anywhere in the long description. This would yield transaction instances made-up from frequently used phrases matching the product descriptions.

Example: The above long description might yield the following transaction instance:

{"celebrity," "elegance," "celebrity elegance," "luxury," "suede," "pump," "suede pump," "lace-up," "detail," "lace-up detail," "smooth," "leather," "smooth leather," "fashion," "savvy," "woman," "fashion savvy," "savvy woman," "fashion savvy woman"}

Next we mine the frequent itemsets among instances corresponding to the long descriptions to find the phrase definitions. Note that, due to our way to construct the items, all items are combinations of single words; therefore, there are items that subsume other items. As a subsequence, there are a lot of redundant final resultant frequent itemsets. For example, a long description might yield the following items: "suede," "pump," "suede pump," "fashion," "savvy," "woman," "fashion savvy," "savvy woman," "fashion savvy woman." Hence, we only want to mine the frequent itemset "suede pump," "fashion savvy woman" because these frequent itemsets subsume the former frequent itemsets. The frequent phrases by construction form a lattice.

In order to prune the redundant frequent itemsets and also to improve the performance of textual definition mining process, we integrated into the frequent itemset mining algorithm the component that makes use of the above lattice structure and visits the items by utilizing the partial order in the lattice, from larger to smaller phrases. The component will traverse top-down the lattice. If there are two items that form a 2-frequent itemset and one subsumes the other (one item is a superset of the other), for example phrase *"fashion savvy woman"* subsumes phrase *"savvy woman,"* then the 2-frequent itemset graph does not contain an edge that connects these two items. This pruning technique avoids producing redundant frequent item-sets, thus improving the performance of the long description miner.

Experimental Results

In this section, we show the experimental results for several target phrases from three different product categories. The extraction engine and the frequent itemset mining algorithms that we develop in previous sections are used to perform experiments for the following product categories: *shoes, handbags* and *beddings*, for the target phrases: *discount shoes, trendy shoes, fashion handbags, luxury bedding* and *sport beddings*. After extracting parametric tabular data and long descriptions from Web sites for each of the target phrases, we used parametric frequent itemset mining algorithm and textual frequent item set mining algorithm to perform the experiments. The tables below show some of the definitions that were mined. According to our retail expert the quality of mined parametric rules is between 60%-80% and the quality of the mined phrase definitions were deemed high. We expect that a richer collection of product information would yield even higher quality definitions.

Table 3.

	Parametric Rules	Support
Trendy shoes	Brand=Steve Madden, gender=woman, style=oxford ➔ trendy shoes	3%
	Brand = American Eagle, material=leather, color=black ➔ trendy shoes	3%
	Brand=Kenneth Cole, color=black, type=dress, price in [$60-$80] ➔ trendy shoes	7%
	Brand = Guess, material = leather, type = casual ➔ trendy shoes	3%
Discount shoes	Style = porcelain, price < $20➔ discount shoes	10.25%
	Brand = Donald J Pliner, gender = men, price in[$60-$80] ➔ discount shoes	15%
	Style = high heel, color = black, price in [$40-$60] ➔ discount shoes	3%
	Brand = Bacco Bucci, gender = men, price in[$60-$80] ➔ discount shoes	6.5%
	Style = pump, price in [$20-$40] ➔ discount shoes	3%

Table 4.

	Parametric Rules	**Support**
Fashion-handbags	Brand = Jil Sander, material = leather, type = clutch ➔ fashion handbags	4.25%
	Brand = Carla, design = mancini, material = leather ➔ fashion handbags	2.4%
	Brand = Butterfly, design =beaded ➔ fashion handbags	2.4%
	Brand = Sven, material = leather ➔ fashion handbags	10.2%
	Design = beaded, color = pink ➔ fashion handbags	2%
	Design = beaded, color = blue, type = tote ➔ fashion handbags	3.2%

Table 5.

	Parametric Rules	**Support**
Luxury beddings	Design = Baffled box, material = cotton ➔ luxury beddings	5%
	Design = Waterford, material = linen ➔ luxury beddings	6%
	Material = silk ➔ luxury beddings	3%
	Design = Sussex, material = polyeste ➔ luxury beddings	6%
Sport beddings	Design = All American, material = polyeste ➔ sport beddings	6%
	Design = All star, material = polyeste ➔ sport beddings	9%
	Design = Big and bold ➔ sport beddings	17%
	Design = sports fan ➔ sport beddings	45%

Table 6.

	Textual Rules	**Support**
Trendy shoes	casual, leather ➔ trendy shoes	6%
	trendy sneaker ➔ trendy shoes	7%
	Wedge edge ➔ trendy shoes	5%
	trendy sandal ➔ trendy shoes	6%

Table 7.

	Textual Rules	**Support**
Luxury beddings	Satin, embroidery ➔ luxury beddings	1.1%
	Egyptian cotton mate-lass ➔ luxury beddings	0.6%
	Silk, smooth, King set ➔ luxury beddings	0.75%
	Piece ensemble ➔ luxury beddings	0.75%
Sport beddings	Addition pillow ➔ sport beddings	0.4%
	American sport ensemble ➔ sport beddings	0.4%
	Paraphernalia sport ➔ sport beddings	0.6%

Table 8.

	Textual Rules	Support
Fashion-handbags	Leather, Handcraft ➜ fashion handbags	0.55%
	Magnet snap closure➜ fashion handbags	0.32%
	Black handbags ➜ fashion handbags	0.3%
	Leather adjustable strap➜ evening handbags	0.3%
	Italian handbags ➜ fashion handbags	0.2%

Comparison to Relevance Feedback Method

In order to compare the performance of our definition miner to standard relevance feedback retrieval method (Salton & Buckley, 1990), we mined a large database of shoes (33,000 items) from a collection of online vendors. Next, we keyword queried the database with the target exemplary search phrase "trendy shoe." From the 166 keyword matching shoes, we mined rule-based phrase definitions for "trendy shoes" yielding rules such as fashionable sneaker, platform shoes and so forth, that were validated by a domain expert. These mined rules matched 3,653 additional shoes. Alternatively, we also computed the relevance feedback query vector using the above 166 matching shoes. We also identified a similarity threshold by finding the maximal cosine theta, Θ, between the relevance feedback query vector and all of the 166 shoe vectors. Retrieval using the relevance feedback vector with this threshold yields more than 29,000 matches out of 33,000. The light colored bars in Figure 5 illustrate the histogram plot of the 29,293 instances that falls into various similarity ranges. Similarly, the dark colored bars plots the similarity ranges of the 3,653 shoes that were retrieved by matching with our mined definitions. As can be seen from the distributions in the above chart, the items retrieved with our mined definitions have a very uniform similarity distribution (with around 300 of these being below the threshold), as opposed to having a skewed distribution towards the higher values of similarity. Since dark colored bars correspond to relevant "trendy shoes" matching our rules, which were validated by an expert, most of these items should have ranked towards the higher end of the similarity spectrum. However, relevance feedback measure failed to rank them as such; hence, it performed poorly for this task, and it can be concluded that, our rule-based method yields high precision compared to even relevance feedback method.

Figure 5. Similarity histogram for rule-based and relevance feedback based matches

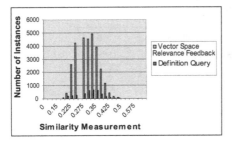

Figure 6. Similarity histogram for relevance feedback and relevance feedback with LSI

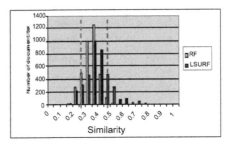

Comparison to Relevance Feedback with LSI

We go further by comparing our method with relevance feedback combined with latent semantic indexing, LSI (Deerwester et al., 1990). The plot of similarity ranges obtained by ranking the 3,653 shoes, retrieved with our mined rules, using relevance feedback with and without LSI technique is shown in Figure 6. The light colored dashed line represents the cosine theta threshold Θ for the relevance feedback ranking; similarly the dark colored dashed line represents the cosine theta threshold for the relevance feedback with LSI. The recall for relevance feedback is nearly 93%. However, since it matches 88% of a random collection of shoes, its precision is lower. On the other hand, even though the ranking of relevance feedback with LSI falls onto a higher similarity range, it appears to have a much lower recall (of 25%) for this experiment with exemplary target phrase "trendy shoes."

Conclusion and Future Work

Our initial experimental results for mining phrase definitions are very promising according to our retail domain expert who is a webmaster at an affiliate marketing Web site. We plan to scale up our experiments to hundreds of product categories and thousands of phrases. Also, our current data labeling techniques require a domain expert to label the extracted attributes so accurate classifiers can be trained. We propose to do future research for mining the data labels themselves from the vendor Web sites whenever they are available, hence reducing the manual labeling. Also, we would like to perform experiments to determine how precisely our algorithm learns the definitions of phrases that changes their meaning over time.

Through the analysis of outcomes, we believe there is much room for extending this work, both in phrase definition mining and information retrieval. For example, derived rules can be used in a new paradigm of relevance feedback in which system and users interact in a new way.

References

Agrawal, R., & Srikant, R. (1994). Fast algorithms for mining association rules. In *Proceedings 20th International Conference VLDB* (pp. 487-499).

Aholen, H., Heinonen, O., Klemettinen, M., & Verkamo, A.I. (1998). Applying data mining techniques for descriptive phrase extraction in digital collections. *Proceedings of ADL'98*, Santa Barabara, USA.

Andrews, W. (2003). *Gartner Report: Visionaries invade the 2003 search engine magic quadrant.* White Paper. Retrieved from http://click.atdmt.com/DSM/go/ btppnv101500006dsm/direct/01/2003 04 24

Baeza-Yates, R. A., & Ribeiro-Neto, B.A. (1999). *Modern information retrieval.* Boston: Addison-Wesley.

Crescenzi, V., Mecca, G., & Merialdo, P. (2001) Roadrunner: Towards automatic data extraction from large Web sites. In *Proceedings of the 2001 International Conference on Very Large Data Bases.*

Cutting & Douglas, R. (1997). Real life information retrieval: Commercial search engines. In *Panel Discussion at SIGIR 1997: Proceedings of the 20th Annual ACM SIGIR Conference on Research and Development on Information Retrieval.*

Davulcu, H., Vadrevu, S., Nagarajan, S., & Ramakrishnan, I., V. (2003). OntoMiner: Bootstrapping and populating ontologies from domain specific Web Sites. *IEEE Intelligent Systems, 18*(5).

Deerwester, S., Dumais, S., Landauer, T., Furnas, G.W., & Harshman, R. A. (1990). Indexing. Latent semantic analysis. *Journal of the Society for Information Science, 41*(6), 391-407.

Steve Finch, S., & Mikheev, A. (1997). A workbench for finding structure in texts. *Applied Natural Language Processing.* Washington, DC.

Goethals, B. (2003). Survey on frequent pattern mining. *Department of Computer Science,* University of Helsinki, Finland. Retrieved from http://www.cs.helsinki.fi/u/goethals/publications/survey.pdf

Hammer, J., Garcia-Molina, H., Cho, J., Crespo, A., & Aranha, R.(1997). Extracting semistructure information from the Web. In *Proceedings of the Workshop on Management of Semistructured Data.*

Han, J., Pei, J., Yin, J., & Mao, R. (2000). Mining frequent pattern without candidate generation. In *Proceedings of the ACM SIGMOD International Conference on Management
of Data*. Reading, MA: ACM Press.

Han, J., & Kamber, M. (2001). *Data mining: Concepts and techniques*. San Francisco:
Morgan Kaufmann.

Jones, R., Rey, B., & Madani, O. (2006). Generating query substitutions. In *Proceedings of
the 15ᵗʰ WWW Conference* (pp. 387-396).

Lacerda. A., Cristo. M., Goncalves, M. A., Fan, W., Ziviani, N., & Ribeiro-Neto, B. (2006).
Learning to advertise. In *SIGIR '06: Proceedings of the 29th ACM SIGIR Conference*
(pp. 549-556). New York: ACM Press.

Liu, Y.K. (2000). *Finding Description of Definitions of Words on the WWW*. Master's thesis,
University of Sheffield, England. Retrieved from http://dis.shef.ac.uk/mark/cv/publi-
cations/dissertations/Liu2000.pdf

Nguyen, Hung.V., Velamuru, P., Kolippakkam, D., Davulcu, H., Liu, H., & Ates, M. (2003).
Mining "hidden phrase" definitions from the Web. *APWeb*. (LNCS 2642, pp. 156-165).
Xi'an, China: Springer-Verlag.

Porter, M.F. (1980). An algorithm for suffix stripping, *Program, 14*(3), 130-137.

Ruthven. I. (2003). Re-examining the potential effectiveness of interactive query expansion.
In *SIGIR '03: Proceedings of the 26ᵗʰ annual international ACM SIGIR Conference*
(pp. 213-220). New York: ACM Press.

Salton, G., & Buckley, C. (1990). Improving retrieval performance by relevance feedback.
Journal of the American Society for Information Science, 41(4), 288-297.

Zaki, M.J. (2000). Scalable algorithms for association mining. *IEEE Transactions on
Knowledge and Data Engineering, 12*(3), 372-390.

Chapter XIV

Improved Privacy:
Preserving Techniques in Large Databases

K. Anbumani, Karunya University, India

R. Nedunchezhian, Sri Ramakrishna Engineering College, India

Abstract

Data mining techniques have been widely used for extracting non-trivial information from massive amounts of data. They help in strategic decision-making as well as many more applications. However, data mining also has a few demerits apart from its usefulness. Sensitive information contained in the database may be brought out by the data mining tools. Different approaches are being utilized to hide the sensitive information. The proposed work in this article applies a novel method to access the generating transactions with minimum effort from the transactional database. It helps in reducing the time complexity of any hiding algorithm. The theoretical and empirical analysis of the algorithm shows that hiding of data using this proposed work performs association rule hiding quicker than other algorithms.

Introduction

Experts say that data mining in the wrong hands will end up in destruction. The main threat of data mining is to privacy and security of data residing in large data stores (Clifton & Marks, 1996; Atallah, Bertino, Elmagarmid, Ibrahim, & Verykios, 1999; Agrawal & Aggarwal, 2001; Muralidhar, Krishnamurty, Sarathy, Rathindira, Parsa, & Rahul, 2001; Oliveira & Za¨ıane, 2003a, 2003b; Verykios, Elmagarmid, Bertino, Saygin, & Dasseni, 2004; Ashrafi, Taniar, & Smith, 2005). Some of the information considered as private and secret can be brought out with advanced data mining tools; this is a real concern of people working in the field of database technology. Different research efforts are under way to deal with this problem of preserving security and privacy.

Sensitive information contained in a database can be extracted with the help of non-sensitive information. This is called the *inference problem* (Clifton et al., 1996; Marks, 1996; Verykios et al., 2004). Different concepts have been proposed to handle the inference problem. The process of modifying the transactional database to hide some sensitive information is called *sanitization*. By sanitizing the original transactional database, the sensitive information can be hidden. In the sanitization process, selective transactions are retrieved and modified before handing over the database to a third party.

Modification of transaction involves removing an item from a transaction or adding an element to the transaction. In some cases, transactions are either added to or removed from the database as suggested in Clifton et al. (1996). The modified database is called *sanitized database* or *released database.*

Several approaches have been proposed to hide sensitive data with good accuracy. The efficiency of a privacy-preserving algorithm is measured based on (1) the time taken to hide the data, (2) the number of new rules introduced as a result of the hiding process, and (3) the number of legitimate rules lost or which cannot be extracted from the released database.

The task of locating a transaction for sanitization from a massive amount of data is not a trivial process and it is certainly a time consuming one. In many research efforts, the highly time consuming process of retrieving the transactional database is not taken into account efficiently. This chapter proposes two methods to hide sensitive association rule in a faster manner. The first method uses the advantages of *frequent pattern growth tree (FPT)* to identify and retrieve the generating transactions directly from the transactional database without exhaustive search. An array is used to keep track of the identifiers of the required transactions for sanitization. The second method proposes another approach to hide rules using a partitioning approach.

This chapter is organized as follows: the subsequent section discusses the existing related works. The proposed approach is discussed in third section. The performance of the algorithms is discussed in the section "Performance Evaluation,",, and the final section presents a summary.

Related Work

Typically, the hiding process involves two steps: (1) generation of association rules and (2) hiding of association rules. Association Rule Mining is one of the functionalities of data mining. The process of producing association rules consists of (1) the frequent itemsets generation and (2) the rule generation. Frequent itemsets generation is a tedious process because it performs the time consuming task of the generation of candidates and pruning of unnecessary itemsets.

A number of Apriori derivative algorithms are available to improve the efficiency of association rule mining (Agrawal, Imielinski, & Swami, 1993; Agrawal & Srikant, 1994; Hidber, 1999; Webb, 2000; Han & Kamber, 2001; Lin & Kedem, 2002). The algorithms for mining association rule differ in the approaches they use. Bottom-up (Agrawal et al., 1993; 1994), top-down or combination of both the approaches (Lin et al., 2002) is used for generating frequent itemsets. The approaches differ in terms of how the transactions of database are scanned. A few algorithms generate frequent itemsets without the costly candidate generation (Han, Pei, & Yin, 2000; Han et al., 2001; Lee & Shen, 2005). The frequent pattern growth tree (FPT) generates the frequent itemsets without candidate generation (Han et al., 2000; 2001). The tree is constructed based on the occurrence of the frequent items. Each transaction in the database is reordered before adding the items of the transaction to the FPT. It proposes a novel frequent pattern structure. The entire database is compressed

Table 1. A transactional database

TID	List of items
T100	I1,I2,I5
T200	I2,I4
T300	I2,I3
T400	I1,I2,I4
T500	I1,I3
T600	I2,I3
T700	I1,I3
T800	I1,I2,I3,I5
T900	I1,I2,I3

Figure 1. Frequent pattern growth tree (FPT) for the database of Table 1

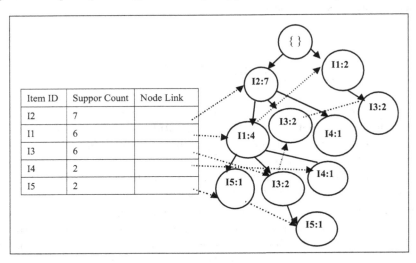

Item ID	Suppor Count	Node Link
I2	7	
I1	6	
I3	6	
I4	2	
I5	2	

into a small data structure and eliminates the unnecessary scans over the database. It reduces the number of scans over the database to only two passes irrespective of the size of the database. Figure 1 depicts the structure of FPT for transactional database of Table 1 (Han et al., 2001).

Many techniques have been suggested to hide sensitive data in large databases. Clifton et al. (1996) suggest different possible solutions to protect the sensitive data such as limiting access to the data, fuzzing the data, and augmenting the data. In Lee et al. (2004), a sanitization matrix is proposed according to the sensitive patterns and non-sensitive patterns.

In Oliveira et al. (2003a), two algorithms, namely, 1) Round-robin algorithm and 2) Random algorithm are proposed. Oliveira et al. (2003b) propose an algorithm called *sliding-window* algorithm which is introduced to hide data. It applies a look-ahead procedure to verify whether that transaction has been selected as sensitive transaction for other rules to be hidden. In Agrawal et al. (2001), the authors discuss an *expectation maximization* (EM) algorithm for distribution-reconstruction, which is more effective than the currently available methods in terms of level of information loss. Specifically, it proposes that the EM algorithm converges to the maximum likelihood estimate of the original distribution based on the perturbed data. In Verykios et al. (2004), various assumptions are followed to hide association rules. Five algorithms have been proposed. They hide rules by considering the antecedent part of the rule or consequent part of the rule or the entire rule to sanitize the generating transactions of the transactional database. While the above mentioned approaches are moderately successful in hiding sensitive data, they are computationally inten-sive and time consuming. Hence, for practical applications, there is a great need for faster algorithms and approaches for sensitive information hiding.

Problem Formulation

Let   D be the Database of transactions.

t ∈ D be the transaction with unique identifier, TID.

$I = \{I1, I2, ..., In\}$ is the set of all the items. So, $t \subseteq I$.

t supports itemset $X \subseteq I$ if $X \subseteq t$.

The itemset X is said to have support s if $s\%$ of transactions contains X.

$$\text{Support of an itemset} = \left\{ \frac{|X \cup Y|}{|D|} \right\} * 100, X, Y \subseteq I \tag{1}$$

Support shows the frequency of occurrence of the itemset.

Association rules show the inter-relationship between attributes of the database. This rule is said to have a minimum confidence c if:

$$\left\{ \frac{|X \cup Y|}{|X|} \right\} * 100 > c, X, Y \subseteq I \tag{2}$$

Confidence shows the strength of the relation. Association rules with above mini-mum support and minimum confidence are only mined. Let the set of association rules mined be R from D. Let R_H be the subset of R, the set of rules to be hidden. The problem is to convert D into D' in such a way that the rules in R_H cannot be mined from D' which is the released database.

The Proposed Approaches

This section elaborates on the two new techniques proposed in this chapter for reducing the time complexity of the hiding process.

Method 1

This method proposes an approach to hide sensitive association rule in a faster manner. It takes advantage of the *frequent pattern growth tree* (FPT) to construct an array called *generating-transaction identifiers*, which helps to retrieve the necessary transactions directly. Since the proposed approach attempts to hide rules quickly, any sanitization method which directly deals at the transaction level for hiding rule can be used with the proposed approach to reduce the time complexity.

Each node of the FPT contains the name of the element and its corresponding number of occurrences. In the modified FPT, besides those two values, a list is maintained for keeping the transaction identifiers. The list is called *transaction locator*. The transaction locators provide the identifiers of the generating transactions to facilitate direct retrieval of the respective transactions from the database without an exhaustive search. It will be kept in the secondary storage when the size is large. Hence, the time to retrieve the generating transactions is only about the total number of identifiers available in the respective transaction locators. In order to reduce the time for traversing the tree, an array called the *generating transaction count* (GTC) is created. The GTC array is of maximum size $|L_l|$ x $|L_l|$, where $|L_l|$ is the number of frequent items. The rows are assigned according to the frequency of items. The item with maximum occurrence in the database occupies the first row and so on and so forth. The columns in the array specify the different levels and the positions of a particular item in the FPT and the transactions of the database respectively. Using the array, either the number of partially or fully generating transactions can be found without traversing the tree.

Figure 2. Modified FPT (MFPT)

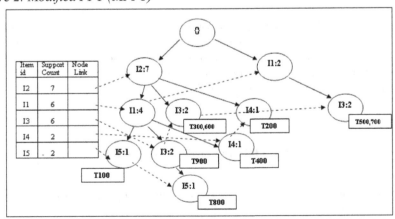

Table 2. Generating Transaction Count array (GTC)

Items	Levels				
	1	2	3	4	5
I2					
I1					
I3		T300, T500, T600,T700	T900		
I4		T200	T400		
I5			T100	T800	

In the proposed approach, the sorting of generating transactions is not done since the array is already constructed based on the occurrence of these items. It is easier to refer to the respective transactions with the help of the GTC array.

For example, the modified FPT (MFPT) is shown in Figure 2 and the equivalent Generating Transaction Count array is shown in Table 2 for the data in Table 1.

For example, the transaction T100 in Table 1 contains three frequent items. The item with minimum occurrence among those three items is I5. Hence, the transaction identifier T100 is stored in the GTC array in the fifth row and third column position. The remaining generating transactions identifiers are stored onto the array in the same manner. The following sequence of steps gives an overview of the approach.

The process of hiding association rules rapidly is depicted in Figure 3. The proposed method can be applied for any sanitization algorithm, which openly deals with items in a transaction. For comparison, we have considered the algorithms *1.a* and *2.c* in Verykios et al. (2004). The algorithm *1.a* sanitizes a set of transactions that partially supports the antecedent of the rule to be hidden. The algorithm *2.c* sanitizes

Figure 3. Association rule hiding process

General algorithm:

Input: Minimum support, Minimum confidence, Database D,

           Database size |D|, a set of rules to be hidden R_H

Output: Released Database D'

   1.   Construct a GTC array for the database D.

   2.   Using the GTC array,

        i) for each rule to hide, find out which transactions are to be retrieved for sanitization.

        ii) using the transaction identifiers available in GTC, retrieve the respective generating transactions from the database.

   3.   Apply the sanitization process

---

the transactions that fully support the large itemsets to be hidden in a round-robin fashion. A rule can have many generating transactions; finding all those transactions requires $|D|$ scans. The proposed approach deals with this problem and minimizes the amount of time required.

Verykios et al. (2004) requires $O(|R_H| * |A_D|)$ time to hide the rules in R_H. For each rule to be hidden, first it scans the database to collect the generating transactions of the antecedent. The generating transactions are selected for sanitization by the number of antecedent items they contain. The transaction with a larger number of items of antecedent is considered for sanitization first. As a second step, it counts and sorts the generating transactions depending on the number of items of antecedents they contain. Then it chooses the transaction with the largest number of antecedent items for sanitization. The algorithm *1.a* hides the sensitive rule by increasing the support of the antecedent of the rule. Therefore, it reduces the confidence of the rule below the minimum confidence threshold.

The algorithm *2.c* requires $O(|R_H|*|A_D|)$ time for hiding a set of L_H large itemsets. In the proposed algorithm, the generating transaction can be located directly without exhaustive search with the help of GTC array. This requires a time of only $O(2|D|)$.

In this approach, an attempt is made to improve the processing time of the hiding algorithms. The sanitization methods recently prescribed by Verykios et al. are followed without any modification (2004). Thus the other two factors, rules lost and new rules introduced, which measure the performance of any hiding algorithms, are the same as in those algorithms. These two factors are not changed.

Figure 4. Proposed algorithm

1.	In the 1st scan, identify frequent items and their supports.
2.	In the 2nd scan, construct the GTC array
	In a cell of the GTC array, we assign transaction identifiers having the original level as row and different occurring levels as columns. (Size of the GTC array is $\| L1 \| * \| L1 \|$)
3.	For each rule *r* in R_H
3.1	Determine *K*, the number of generating transactions to be modified.
3.2	Retrieve the items of the antecedent one by one from the last.
3.3	For each item extracted from the antecedent, retrieve the cell value from the GTC array with the row as the original value of the item and column as (*lr-i*), *i* varies from positional *i* to (*lr-1*). It gives the list of transaction identifiers.
3.4	Retrieve and sanitize the transactions from the dataset directly using the transactions identifier. *K=K-* (number of transaction modified)
3.5	Repeat 3.3 until *K* <= 0.

The algorithm in Figure 4 explains our approach. Here:

- K is the number of generating transactions to be modified
- R is the set of association rules mined from D
- R_H is the set of rules to be hidden
- l_r is antecedent of the rule r, to be hidden

After constructing the GTC array, the array is checked for getting the identifiers of generating transactions with the maximum number of antecedent elements of the rule to be hidden. For instance, to hide a rule *antecedent*→ *consequent*, according to algorithm 1.a, transactions with *n-1* elements of the antecedent are processed for hiding where n is the total number of elements in the antecedent. Then transactions with *n-2* elements of the antecedent are processed and if some more transactions are still required, it will consider the transactions with *n-3* elements and so on.

The GTC array in the proposed approach directly gives the transactions with the corresponding number of supporting elements. If an identifier is at the nth row and an entry at the nth level in the array, it means that the MFPT is having a path containing all the first n frequent items. Suppose the item is at some other lower level in the tree; it means that the particular path does not have one or more frequent items whose support is greater than the current item under consideration. For example, if an item is at the fifth row as well as at the fifth column, it means that the path containing all of the first five frequent items are in the sequence. Suppose the item is at level 1; it means that the first four frequent items are not in that path.

Method 2

This section proposes another novel method to hide essential association rules quickly. The generating transactions of the rules to be hidden can be located from the transactional database with minimum effort. Hence, it saves the unnecessary time spent for exhaustive search over the database. The method proposed here tries to reduce the time and space complexities of hiding process.

The given database is divided into a number of segments. Each segment is associated with a new data structure called item support vector (ISV), which contains the support of each individual item in that segment. The structure of an ISV is given in Table 3.

For example by segmenting the database given in Table 1 with each segment size=3, the ISV for segment1 is given in Table 4.

Table 3. Item support vector (ISV)

Item	I_1	I_2	...	I_n
Count				

Table 4. Item support vector for segment 1

Item	I_1	I_2	I_3	I_4	I_5
Count	6	7	6	2	2

It keeps the counts of individual items of a particular partition of the database. The number of locations in the vector is equivalent to the number of items in I, where I is set of items. The value of first location of the ISV denotes the occurrence of item $I1$ in that partition. Similarly, the last location specifies the count of the item In. Based on the minimum support, the massive database is partitioned into equivalent blocks (P_i). For each block, an ISV is maintained (in the main memory) to record the occurrence of individual items in that particular block. From the content of ISV, the exact frequency of individual items and approximate incidence of itemsets can be estimated.

Illustrative Example

The transactional database given in Table 1 is partitioned into equivalent blocks as shown in Table 5. Each block is assigned with an ISV. Table 6 represents ISVs for the partitions *P1, P2,* and *P3*.

When the number of rules to be hidden increases, the frequency of revisiting the entire database also proportionately increases. Using the proposed method, the frequency of

Table 5. A transactional database

TID	List of elements	
T100	I1,I2,I5	P1
T200	I2,I4	
T300	I2,I3	
T400	I1,I2,I4	P2
T500	I1,I3	
T600	I2,I3	
T700	I1,I3	P3
T800	I1,I2,I3,I5	
T900	I1,I2,I3	

Table 6. Partition-wise itemsupport vector

Partitions	Items				
	I1	*I2*	*I3*	*I4*	*I5*
P1	1	3	1	1	1
P2	2	2	2	1	0
P3	3	2	3	0	1

revisiting the database can be considerably minimized. The existing works scan the database entirely and repeatedly to locate the generating transactions of the rules to be hidden. For instance, to hide a rule *I1→I3* in the database *D*, using the proposed method, itemsupport vectors of different partitions only are referred to rather than revisiting the database again and again. Since the occurrences of *I1* and *I3* are more in partition *P3*, there is a possibility to have these combinations together in a few transactions. Hence, it is sufficient to limit the scanning to *P3* alone. Similarly, to hide the set of rules R_H, the itemsupport vectors only are referred.

The proposed technique is given in the following algorithm, *HideRule*.

Algorithm *HideRule*

Input: D, R_H, min_sup

Output: D'

1. Identify among the rules R_H, a rule with the largest support and assign its support value to s (maximum support).

2. Divide the database into blocks of size

$$\frac{|D|}{af * (s - min\_sup)} \qquad (3)$$

where *af* is block adjustment factor, $1 \leq af \geq 0$.

3. For each partition, fill up the itemsupport vectors.

4. For $i \leftarrow 1$ to $|R_H|$

    4.1   Pick a rule r_i of $|R_H|$

    4.2   Determine a partition of database which is having more occurrences of rule antecedent and consequent (antecedent $\cup$ consequent)

    4.3   Visit that partition and collect the generating transactions

    4.4   Sanitize those transactions one by one until the support or confidence value is less than the threshold value.

5. $R_H = R_H - r_i$

Step 1 in the algorithm finds a rule with largest support among R_H rules and assign to the variable s.

Step 2 divides the database into blocks of size

$$|P_i| = \frac{|D|}{af * (s - \min\_sup)} \qquad (4)$$

The block adjustment factor, *af* decides the size of the partition. The value of *af* can be large for dense datasets and small for the sparse datasets.

For example, to hide a set of rules R_H in a given dataset *D*:

r_1 with support   30
r_2 with support   20
r_3 with support   10

with the block adjustment factor, *af* = 1.

the dataset size, |D| = 100 transactions

the maximum support, s = 30 (the maximum support of a rule in R_H)

the block size is determined as:

$$\text{Block size} = \frac{|D|}{af * (s - \min\_sup)}$$

$$= \frac{100}{1 * (30 - 20)}$$

= 10 transactions.

Similarly, to hide the same rules with the block adjustment factor, *af* = 0.5.

$$\text{Block size} = \frac{|D|}{af * (s - \min\_sup)}$$

$$= \frac{100}{0.5 * (30 - 20)}$$

= 20 transactions.

From the example, it is known that the value of *af* mainly decides the number of transactions in a block.

Some algorithms consider the transactions supporting the antecedent, consequent or both. The search time for generating transactions increases when *af* decreases. The rest of the steps are for constructing the itemsupport vector and retrieving the generating transactions.

Performance Evaluation

This section gives details of the experimental evaluation of the performance of the proposed algorithms.

Experimental Setup

The experiment was conducted on a Pentium IV computer with a CPU clock rate of 2.8 GHz, 256 MB of main memory running Windows Operating System. The datasets for the experiment were generated synthetically as suggested by Agrawal et al. (1994). Three databases T5.I3.D5K, T5.I3.D10K, and T5.I3.D50K were generated. In each dataset, the average transaction length (ATL) and the maximal frequent itemset size were kept at 5 and 3, respectively. The sizes of the three datasets, |D|, are 5K, 20K, and 50K, respectively.

Input for the association rule hiding algorithms were either a set of frequent itemsets or a set of association rules. Hence, to generate the required inputs, the *Apriori* and *Pincer* algorithms were used. Other effective association rule mining algorithms can also be used.

Time Complexity of the Proposed Algorithms

Method 1

The process of hiding an association rule requires exhaustive scan over the transactional database to identify the necessary generating transactions of a rule. The time taken for this process will be more when the number of rules to be hidden is large.

Due to the hiding process, there is a chance to lose some of the valuable rules already existing in the transactional database. New rules may also be introduced. These are the side effects of any hiding process. Thus, these three points, namely time taken for hiding a set of association rules, rules lost and new rules introduced are considered as parameters to measure the performance of any hiding algorithm. This work attempts to reduce the time complexity alone. As this work uses the hiding technique given by Verykios et al., the side effects of our approach on the database are also the same as those algorithms of (2004a).

In an association rule hiding algorithm, the time required to identify and sanitize the necessary generating transactions of a rule is central to the hiding process. The time for revisiting the database for each and every rule to be hidden is a major time consuming process. The proposed approach suggests an effective method suitable for real-time applications. It tries to minimize the time complexity substantially with the help of the GTC array.

The time complexity of our approach is compared with all the five algorithms given in Verykios et al. (2004a). The comparison is depicted as graphs in Figure 5.

Figure 5. Performance evaluation

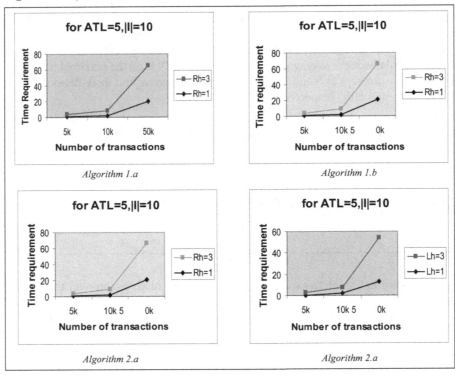

continued on following page

Figure 5. continued

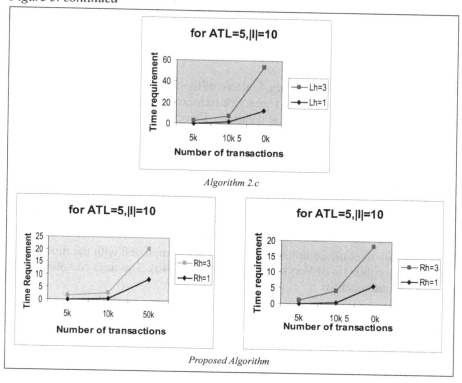

Algorithm 2.c

Proposed Algorithm

A theoretical expression for the time complexity is derived below. The time required to hide a set of rules R_H, by the proposed approach is:

$$2*|D| + \sum_{i=1}^{|R_H|} K_{ij}$$

Since the approach requires two scans of the database, the time required to construct the GTC array is $O(2*|D|)$ which includes the generation of frequent items, L1 and filling of cell values of the array. The variable K_j is the number of generating transactions that needs to be retrieved and sanitized to hide a rule r_i of R_H. It may be noted that:

$$\sum_{i=1}^{|R_H|} K_{ij}$$

values will always be very much smaller than |D|. For example:

$$\sum_{i=1}^{|R_H|} K_{ij}$$

may be a few tens while |D| may be a few tens of thousands. The GTC array simplifies this process by providing the respective transaction identifiers, TID to enable direct access from the transactional database. Therefore the exhaustive scan over the transactional database for locating the generating transactions of each rule is prevented. In other approaches, the database is repeatedly and completely scanned for the same purpose.

Of the five algorithms 1.a, 1.b, 2.a, 2.b, and 2.c of Verykios et al., the algorithm 1.a takes $O(|R|*A_D + C)$, the algorithms 1.b and 2.a each take $O(|R|*A_D)$, and the algorithms 2.b and 2.c each take $O(|D|*|L_H|)$ to perform the hiding process (Verykios et al., 2004a; Verykios, Elmagarmid, Bertino, Saygin, & Dasseni, 2004b).

Let us compare the time complexity of the proposed approach with the time complexity of algorithm 1.a of Verykios et al (2004a, 2004b). The time complexity of the proposed approach is:

$$O\left(2*|D| + \sum_{i=1}^{|R_H|} K_{ij} \right) \tag{5}$$

where, j is the number of transaction to be sanitized for hiding a rule, r_i.

$$\approx O(2*|D|) \tag{6}$$

since, $\sum_{i=1}^{|R_H|} K_{ij}$ is very much negligible compared to $2*|D|$.

The first term of Equation (1.5), $2*|D|$ is for constructing the GTC array. The second term

$$\sum_{i=1}^{|R_H|} K_{ij}$$

is the number of generating transactions to be retrieved from the transactional database for sanitization, which varies from 1 to $|R_H|$.

The time complexity of algorithm 1.a of Verykios et al. (2004a; 2004b) is:

$$= O(|R_H| * A_D + C) \tag{7}$$

$$\approx O(|R_H| * A_D)$$
$$\approx O(|R_H| * |D| * ATL) \tag{8}$$

since C is negligible compared to the other terms.

Thus the ratio of complexity of this work compared to the time complexity of algorithm 1.a of Verykios et al. (2004a) and Verykios, Elmagarmid, Bertino, Saygin, and Dasseni (2004b) is:

$$2 * |D| \ : \ |RH| * |D| * ATL$$

that is,

$$1 \ : \ \frac{(|R_H| * ATL)}{2} \tag{9}$$

Proceeding along the similar lines the ratio for the other algorithms are:

$$1 \ : \ \frac{(|R_H| * ATL)}{2} \tag{10}$$

for algorithms 1.b and 2.a and

$$1 \ : \ \frac{(|L_H|)}{2} \tag{11}$$

for algorithms 2.b and 2.c.

From perusal of equations (9),(10) and (11), it is seen that the time complexity of the proposed technique is less—ranging from:

$$\frac{(|L_H|)}{2} \ \text{times to} \ \frac{(|R_H| * ATL)}{2}.$$

For the experimentation conducted here:

$$|R_H| = 3$$
$$|L_H| = 5$$
$$ATL = 5$$
$$|L_H|/2 = 2.5$$

$$\frac{(|R_H|*ATL)}{2} = 7.5$$

Therefore the reduction in time is 2.5 times to 7.5 times.

Method 2

As in section a), the experiments were conducted on the same three databases T5.I3. D5K, T5.I3.D10K, and T5.I3.D50K. In each dataset, the average transaction length (ATL) and the maximal frequent itemset size were 5 and 3, respectively. The sizes of the three datasets, |D|, are 5K, 10K, and 50K, respectively.

The process of hiding an association rule requires extensive search over the database to locate the necessary generating transactions of a rule. The time consumption for this process will be more when the number of rules to be hidden is large.

Time taken for hiding rules, number of rules lost and number of new rules introduced, because of the hiding process, are normally considered as factors to measure the performance of any hiding algorithm. The proposed method tries to reduce the time complexity alone. As this work uses the hiding technique given in Verykios et al. (2004a), the side effects of the proposed approach on the database are also the same as algorithms of Verykios et al. (2004a).

An expression for the time complexity of the proposed approach is derived along the following lines. To construct the itemsupport vectors (ISVs), scanning of the entire database is required. This requires |D| number of I/O operations. Then with the help of ISVs, the search is limited to a particular partition of the database. The partition that has to be brought from the disk to the main memory is decided as in Step 4 of the algorithm *HideRule*. This requires $|P_i|$ number of I/O operations.

Checking ISVs values and checking for the generating transactions in the selected partition involve only memory access. Since memory access takes much smaller time than a disk access, memory access times are ignored in the derivation of the time complexity of the algorithm. The time to transfer the transactions in the selected partition from the disk to the main memory requires |P| number of I/O operations.

Hence, the total I/O operations required:

$$= |D|+|P| \tag{12}$$

$$= |D| + \frac{|D|}{af*(s-\text{min\_sup})} \tag{13}$$

$$= |D| * \left(1 + \frac{1}{af * (s - \text{min\_sup})} \right) \tag{14}$$

$$\approx |D| \tag{15}$$

Since $\left(\dfrac{1}{af * (s - \text{min\_sup})} \right) << 1$ in practical situations.

Of the five algorithms 1.a, 1.b, 2.a, 2.b and 2.c of Verykios et al. (2004a), the algorithm 1.a takes $O(|R_H| * A_D + C)$. The proposed technique is compared with the algorithm 1.a to evaluate the time complexity. The values of other two factors (number of rules lost and number of new rules introduced) are the same as the algorithm 1.a because the hiding strategy mentioned in the algorithm is followed without any modification.

Let us compare the time complexity of the proposed approach with the time complexity of algorithm 1.a of Verykios et al. (2004a, 2004b). The time complexity of algorithm 1.a of Verykios et al. (2004a, 2004b) is:

$$= O(|R_H| * A_D + C) \tag{16}$$

$$\approx O(|R_H| * A_D)$$

$$\approx O(|R_H| * |D| * ATL) \tag{17}$$

Since C is negligible compared to the other terms (Verykios et al., 2004b).

Thus, the ratio of complexity of this work compared to the time complexity of algorithm 1.a of Verykios et al. (2004a, 2004b) is:

$$|D| \; : \; |R_H| * |D| * ATL$$

i.e., $1 \; : \; |R_H| * ATL$ $\tag{18}$

Proceeding along the similar lines the ratio for the other algorithms are:

$$1 \; : \; |R_H| * ATL \tag{19}$$

Figure 6. Performance evaluation

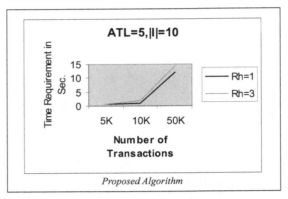

Proposed Algorithm

for algorithms 1.b and 2.a, and

$$1 \; : \; |L_H| \tag{20}$$

for algorithms 2.b and 2.c.

From perusal of Equations 18, 19, and 20, it is seen that the time complexity of the proposed technique is less – ranging from $|L_H|$ times to $|R_H| * ATL$.

For the experimentation conducted here,

$|R_H| = 3$
$ATL = 5$
$|L_H| = 5$
$|R_H| * ATL = 15$

Therefore the reduction in time is 5 times to 15 times.

Time complexities of the algorithms of Verykios et al. (2004a) and the proposed technique are shown in the Figure 6.

Summary

In this chapter, two novel approaches are presented to hide association rules on a large transactional database in a faster manner. The first approach reduces the time for hiding association rules by as much as 2.5 times to about 7.5 times. It is found that the time to revisit the transactional database has been reduced with the help of the data structure, generating transaction count (GTC). This work can be incorporated to any hiding algorithm to enhance their response time. The space complexity of the algorithm has also been drastically reduced.

In the second method, a novel approach is proposed to hide association rules on a large transactional database with the help of the data structure, item support vector (ISV). This approach reduces the time for hiding association rules by as much as 5 times to about 15 times. This work can be integrated into any hiding algorithm, which directly deals with transactions in order to enhance their response time. The space complexity of the algorithm has also been considerably minimized.

The effectiveness of the proposed approaches is demonstrated using synthetic data. As future work, the techniques given in this chapter can be suitably extended for hiding association rules in multiple data sources.

References

Agrawal D., & Aggarwal, C. (2001). On the design and quantification of privacy preserving data mining algorithms. In *Proceedings of the 20th ACMSIGACT-SIGMOD-SIGART Symposium on Principles of Database Systems*, California, USA.

Agrawal, R., Imielinski, T., & Swami, A. (1993). Mining association rules between sets of items in large databases. In *Proceedings of the 1993 ACM SIGMOD International Conference on Management of Data*, Washington, DC (pp. 207-216).

Agrawal, R., & Srikant, R. (1994). Fast algorithms for mining association rules. In *Proceedings of the 20th VLDB Conference*, Santiago, Chile (pp. 487-499).

Ashrafi, M., Taniar, D., & Smith, K. (2005). Privacy-preserving distributed association rule mining algorithm. *International Journal of Intelligent Information Technologies*, *1*(1), 46-69.

Atallah, M., Bertino, E., Elmagarmid, A., Ibrahim, M., & Verykios, V. (1999). Disclosure limitation of sensitive rule. In *Proceedings of the Workshop on Knowledge and Data Engineering Exchange*.

Clifton, C. (1993). Protecting against data mining through samples. In *Proceedings of the 13th IFIP WG11.3 Conference on Database Security,* Washington (pp. 193-207).

Clifton, C., & Marks, D. (1996). Security and privacy implications of data mining. In *Proceedings of the ACM SIGMOD Workshop on Data Mining and Knowledge Discovery*, Montreal, Canada (pp.15-19).

Han, J., & Kamber, M. (2001). *Data mining: Concepts and technique*. San Francisco: Morgan Kaufmann.

Han, J., Pei, J., & Yin, Y. (2000). Mining frequent patterns without candidate generation. In *Proceedings of the ACM SIGMOD International Conference on Management of Data*, Texas (pp. 1-12).

Hidber, C (1999). Online association rule mining. In *Proceedings of the ACM SIGMOD International Conference on Management of Data*, Philadelphia (pp. 145-156).

Lee, C. & Shen, T. (2005). An FP-split method for fast association rules mining. In *Proceedings of the 3rd International Conference on Information Technology: Research and Education, ITRE 2005* (pp. 459-463).

Lee, G., Chang, C.Y., & Chen, A.L.P. (2004). Hiding sensitive patterns in association rule mining. In *Proceedings of the 28th Annual International Computer Software and Applications Conference (COMPSAC'04)*.

Lin, D. & Kedem, Z. (2002). Pincer-search: An efficient algorithm for discovering the maximum frequent set. *IEEE Transactions on Knowledge and Data Engineering, 14*(3), 553-566.

Marks, D.G. (1996). Inference in MLS database. *IEEE Transactions on Knowledge and Data Engineering, 8*(1), 46-55.

Muralidhar, Krishnamurty, Sarathy, Rathindira, Parsa, & Rahul (2001). An improved security requirement for data perturbation with implications for e-commerce. *Decision Science, 32*(4), 683-698.

O'Leary, D.E. (1991). Knowledge discovery as a threat to database security. In *Proceedings of the First International Conference Knowledge Discovery and Databases*, (pp. 507-516).

Oliveira, S., & Za¨ıane, O. (2003a). Protecting sensitive knowledge by data sanitization. In *Proceedings of the Third IEEE International Conference on Data Mining (ICDM'03)* (pp. 613-616).

Oliveira, S., & Zaïane, O. (2003b). Algorithms for balancing privacy and knowledge discovery in association rule mining. In *Proceedings of the Seventh International Database Engineering and Applications Symposium (IDEAS'03)* (pp. 54-65).

Verykios, V., Elmagarmid, A., Bertino, E., Saygin, Y., & Dasseni, E. (2003). Association rule hiding. Retrieved December 2004, from http://dke.cti.gr/CODMINE/TKDE_Verykios-et-al.pdf.

Verykios, V., Elmagarmid, A., Bertino, E., Saygin, Y., & Dasseni, E. (2004). Association rule hiding. *IEEE Transactions on Knowledge and Data Engineering, 16*(4), 434-447.

Webb, G.I. (2000). Efficient search for association rules. In *Proceedings of the ACM SIGKDD International Conference on Knowledge Discovery and Data Mining* (pp. 99-107).

About the Contributors

Vijayan Sugumaran is professor of management information systems in the department of Decision and Information Sciences at Oakland University, Rochester, Michigan, USA. His research interests are in the areas of ontologies and Semantic Web, intelligent agent and multi-agent systems, component-based software development, knowledge-based systems, and data & information modeling. His most recent publications have appeared in *Information Systems Research, ACM Transactions on Database Systems, IEEE Transactions on Engineering Management, Communications of the ACM, Healthcare Management Science, Data and Knowledge Engineering, The DATABASE for Advances in Information Systems,* and *Information Systems Journal*. Besides serving as the editor-in-chief of the *International Journal of Intelligent Information Technologies*, he also serves on the editorial board of seven other journals. Sugumaran is the chair of Intelligent Information Systems track for the Information Resources Management Association International Conference (IRMA 2001-2002 and 2005-2007) and the Intelligent Agent and Multi-Agent Systems in Business mini-track for Americas Conference on Information Systems (AMCIS 1999-2007). He served as chair of the E-Commerce track for Decision Science Institute's Annual Conference, 2004. He also regularly serves as a program committee member for numerous national and international conferences.

* * *

K. Anbumani obtained his bachelor's degree from the Madras University, his master's degree from the Pune University, and his PhD from the Indian Institute of Science, Bangalore, all in India. After working in the industry for 2 years, he took up engineering teaching in various capacities—lecturer to principal. Presently he is the director of the School of Computer Science and Technology, Karunya Deemed

University, Coimbatore, India. Anbumani's current interests include data mining, information security, image processing, and Internet technology.

Patricia Anthony obtained her PhD from the Department of Electronics and Computer Science, University of Southampton, United Kingdom. She is currently attached with the faculty of Engineering and Information Technology, Universiti Malaysia Sabah. Her research interests are in the application of agent technology in e-commerce and e-learning. Her main research projects now are mostly focused on online auctions in which she uses agent technology to develop strategy for bidders as well as for sellers. She is also looking at applying agent technology in e-learning to assist students in their learning. She has published more than 20 papers in journals and conference proceedings.

Elarbi Badidi received his PhD in computer science in July, 2000 from Université de Montréal, Canada. He received his master's degree in computer science (1995) and his bachelor's degree in electrical engineering (1987) from École Mohammedia des Ingénieurs (Morocco). Badidi joined the College of Information Technology (CIT) of United Arab Emirates University as assistant professor of computer science in September, 2004. Before joining the faculty at CIT, he was the bioinformatics group leader at the Biochemistry Department of Université de Montréal. His research interests lie in the areas of Web services, middleware, distributed systems, bioinformatics, and distance learning.

Abdelghani Benharref is preparing a PhD in electrical and computer engineering, Concordia University, Montreal, Canada. His interest domains include: Web services, Web services composition, management of Web service, QoS of Web services.

Sebastian C. Brandt has been working on process integrated modeling environments since 1997. After receiving his degree from RWTH Aachen University in 2003, he started as a doctoral candidate in the Collaborative Research Centre 476, focusing on the support of information flows in chemical design processes. To improve the users' information retrieval processes, he developed and realized the concept of a process data warehouse where process and product artifacts from the design processes are managed. In this context, he works on the integration and extension of enterprise document management and resource planning systems for application in the early phases of these creative design processes.

Ramón F. Brena is a full professor at the Center of Intelligent Systems, Tech of Monterrey, Mexico, since 1990, where he is head of a research group in distributed knowledge and multi-agent systems. Brena holds a PhD from the INPG, Grenoble, France, where he presented a doctoral thesis related to knowledge in program synthesis. His current research and publication areas include: intelligent agents and multi-agent systems, knowledge management, representation and distribution, Semantic Web, and artificial intelligence in general. Past research includes: program synthesis and software reuse, as well as automated reasoning. Brena is a member of the SMIA (AI Mexican Society), the AAAI and the ACM, and is recognized as an established researcher by the official Mexican research agency, CONACyT.

Ralf Bruns is a professor of computer science at the Fachhochschule Hannover (University of Applied Sciences and Arts). His research interests include: software architecture, distributed systems, and Internet technologies. He received a degree and a PhD in computer science from University of Oldenburg, Germany. He is a member of the German Computer Science Society.

Rafael Cunha Cardoso is currently a system engineer working at Hewlett-Packard Brazil, located in Porto Alegre, Brazil. He obtained his master's degree in computer science from the Universidade Federal de Pernambuco--UFPE--Brazil in 2004. His undergraduate studies in computer science were completed in 2001 at Universidade Católica de Pelotas--UCPel--Brazil. His main research interest areas are databases, Semantic Web and Information Retrieval Systems. He has published three papers in international conference proceedings. Currently, he started researching themes he may use to develop his future doctorate.

Hasan Davulcu (Hasan.Davulcu@asu.edu) has been an assistant professor in the Computer Science and Engineering department at Arizona State University since 2002. He received his PhD in computer science from the University of New York at Stony Brook. His research interests include Web mining and information integration.

R. Dssouli is professor and a director of CIISE, Concordia University. She received the Doctorat d'Université degree in computer science from the Université Paul-Sabatier of Toulouse, France in 1981, and a PhD in computer science in 1987 from the University of Montréal, Canada. She has been a professor at the University Mohamed 1er, Morroco, from 1981 to 1989, assistant professor at the University of Sherbrooke from 1989 to 1991, and full professor at the University of Montreal until May 2001. Her research area is in communication protocol engineering, requirements engineering and multimedia applications. Ongoing projects include incremental specification based on scenario languages, QoS and multimedia applications, design for testability, conformance testing based. She served as a member of committee program of many conferences (IWPTS, IWTCS, FORTE, CFIP, MMNS, MMM, FIW, NOTERE), and she organized several international conferences (IWPT'93, CFIP'93, FORTE'95, CFIP'96, NOTERE'98, SDL Forum'99, NOTERE'04, and TESTCOM'05).

Jürgen Dunkel is a professor of computer science at the Fachhochschule Hannover

(University of Applied Sciences and Arts). He received a degree in computer science from University of Hagen and a PhD from the University of Dortmund, Germany. His research interests include software architecture, distributed systems, and agent technologies. He is a member of the German Computer Science Society.

Stéphane Faulkner is an associate professor in Technologies and Information Systems at the University of Namur (FUNDP). Faulkner is also an invited professor with the Universitary Faculties, St. Louis of Brussels. His interests of research evolve around requirements engineering and the development of precise (formal) modeling notations, systematic methods and tool support for the development of multi-agent systems, database and information systems. His publications include more than 40 international refereed journals or periodicals and proceedings papers.

Fernando da Fonseca de Souza is currently an associate professor at Centro de Informática of Universidade Federal de Pernambuco (UFPE), Brazil and head of University Extension at Centro de Informática. He earned his PhD in computer science from the University of Kent at Canterbury, England in 1992, his master's degree in computer science (1982) and bachelor's in Civil Engineering (1976) from UFPE, Brazil. His main research interests are in the areas of databases and informatics on education. de Souza has published over forty five technical articles in conference procedures, journals and book chapters. In his academic carrier he has advised twenty-four graduate students and four PhD theses. He is a member of the Brazilian Computer Society. He also was head of the Computer Science undergraduate course at UFPE.

Mohamed Salah Hamdi was born on April 1, 1967 in Sidi Bouzid, Tunisia. He received a degree (Diplom-Informatiker Univ.) in computer science from the Technical University of Munich, Germany in 1993 and a PhD (rer. nat.) in computer science from the University of Hamburg, Germany in 1999. From 1994 to 1999, he was a lecturer at the Department of Computer Science of the University of Hamburg, Germany. In September 1999, he joined the National Institute of Applied Sciences and Technology of the University of Tunis, Tunisia, as an assistant professor. From 2001 to 2005, he was working as an assistant professor at the Department of Mathematics and Computer Science of the United Arab Emirates University in Al Ain. Since September 2005, he has been an assistant professor at the University of Qatar in Doha. His research interests are focused on intelligent autonomous agents, e-learning, information customization, machine learning, and artificial intelligence in general.

Igor Hawryszkiewycz is the research leader in the area of collaborative systems at UTS. He earned a BA and a MA in electrical engineering at the University of Adelaide, and a PhD from the Massachusetts Institute of Technology. His early research covered the design of databases and information systems for business. Since 1987, his work has focused on collaborative work including the design of collaborative systems with emphasis on knowledge management, including small business networks, or research planning at the World Health Organization (WHO). His team has developed the prototype LiveNet workspace system, which supports collaborative applications. He has over 150 publications and three text books.

Matthias Jarke is professor of Information Systems at RWTH Aachen University and director of the Fraunhofer FIT Institute for Applied Information Technology in Sankt Augustin, Germany. Jarke studied computer science and business administration at the University of Hamburg and held faculty positions in New York University and the University of Passau prior to joining RWTH in 1991. His research interest is information systems support for cooperative applications in engineering, business, and culture. Jarke served as chief editor of *Information Systems* from 1993-2004 and is currently president of GI, the German Informatics society.

Ivan J. Jureta is currently pursuing his PhD at the Information Management Research Unit, University of Namur, under the supervision of Stéphane Faulkner. In 2005, he received a master's degree in management from Université de Louvain and a master's degree in international management from the London School of Economics and Political Science and Université de Louvain. His doctoral research focuses on the specification and analysis of adaptive and open service-oriented systems.

Manuel Kolp is associate professor of computer science at the Université catholique de Louvain, Belgium where he is head of the Information Systems Research Unit and coordinator of the Center of Excellence in Management and Information Technology. Kolp is also an invited professor with the University of Brussels and the Universitary Faculties, St. Louis of Brussels. His research work deals with agent architectures for ERP II systems. He was previously adjunct professor at the University of Toronto. He has been involved in the organization of international conferences such as CAiSE 2002 and VLDB 2004 and is co-chair of workshops like AOIS. His publications include more than 50 refereed journals or periodicals and proceedings papers as well as three books.

Xining Li is a professor of computing and information science at the University of Guelph and the director of the IMAGO Lab. His research interests include mobile agent system, logic programming, and virtual machine implementation. Li received a PhD in computer science from the University of Calgary.

R. Nedunchezhian is currently head of the Department of Information Technology, Sri Ramakrishna Engineering College, Coimbatore. He received his bachelor's degree in computer science and engineering from the Bharathidasan University, his master's degree in computer science and engineering from the Bharathiar University and is pursuing his PhD at Bharathiar University. His research interests are knowledge discovery and data mining, distributed computing, and information security. He is a life member of the Advanced Computing and Communication Society and Member of Computer society of India.

Hung Viet Nguyen (hung@asu.edu) is a PhD candidate in the Department of Computer Science and Engineering, Arizona State University working with Hasan Davulcu. He affiliates with the Cognitive Information Processing Systems Laboratory. His interests center data mining, statistical learning in information retrieval and text/Web mining, machine learning (graphical models, SVM, clustering) and applications. He earned his BS in computer science and engineering from Vietnam National University, Hanoi and his MS in computer science from the University of Cambridge, UK.

Weidong Pan is currently doing PhD research at UTS, Australia. Prior to the PhD research, he was an associate professor at the Department of Computer Sciences of Jiangsu Radio and Television University, PRC. He earned a master's degree in computer science at Nanjing University of Aeronautics and Astronautics, PRC. He has published more than 50 research papers and ten text books. His research interests include artificial intelligences, database and their applications in teaching and learning.

Eduardo H. Ramírez holds master's degree in information technology from the Tech of Monterrey, México, where he collaborated as a research assistant and staff engineer at the Center of Intelligent Systems. He is involved in the development and enterprise implementation of the JITIK Project. He is co-founder and CTO of Ensitech, S.C., a high-tech startup with consultancy and research activities on distributed computing and Web technologies. His current research work and interests involve agent-oriented software engineering, Web services and service-oriented architectures, Semantic Web, rich Internet applications and collaborative knowledge management.

H. Sahraoui is associate professor at the Department of Computer Science and Operations Research (software engineering group) of University of Montreal. His research interests include the application of artificial intelligence techniques to software engineering, object-oriented metrics, software quality, software visualization, and software reverse- and re-engineering. He has published around 100 papers in conferences, workshops, and journals and edited three books. He served as steering, program and organization committee member in several major conferences (ECOOP, ASE, METRICS, ICSM...) and is a member of the editorial boards of two journals. He was the general chair of the IEEE Automated Software Engineering Conference in 2003.

Ana Carolina Salgado is currently an associate professor at Centro de Informática of Universidade Federal de Pernambuco--UFPE--Brazil. She obtained her doctorate in computer science from the University of Nice, France in 1988, her master's degree (1983) and bachelor's degree (1980) in computer science from UFPE. Her main research interests are in the areas of databases, information integration on the Web and cooperative systems. Salgado has published over 90 technical articles in conference proceedings and journals. In her academic activities, she has advised 29 master's and five PhD theses. She is member of the ACM and of the Brazilian Computer Society. She also was head of Centro de Informática and head of the Computer Science undergraduate course at UFPE.

Marcus Schlüter studied mechanical engineering at RWTH Aachen University. He received his degree in 1998 before starting as a researcher at the Institute of Plastics Processing IKV in Aachen, working on the Collaborative Research Centre IMPROVE. His research interests include the field of requirements engineering in plastics and chemical engineering, especially the computer-based support of the design processes of compounding extruders. In 2003, he received his PhD in mechanical engineering. From 2003, he worked at Fraunhofer FIT as a senior researcher on innovative information systems in plastics and process engineering. Since 2005, he is CEO of the aiXtrusion GmbH company, developing automation control and information systems for plastics extrusion processes.

Simon Schwingel is a consultant at busitec GmbH in Muenster, Germany. He has obtained a degree in information systems from the University of Muenster. His research interests include Web services and security architectures for Web-based platforms.

Alexander Serenko is an assistant professor of management information systems in the faculty of business administration, Lakehead University, Canada. He holds a master's degree in computer science, an MBA in electronic business, and a PhD in management information systems. Serenko's research interests pertain to intelligent agents, user technology adoption, knowledge management, and innovation. Alexander's articles appeared in various refereed journals, and his papers received awards at Canadian and international conferences.

Lei Song is a senior software engineer in 724 Solutions Inc. His research interests include distributed systems, mobile agents, information retrieval and search engine technology. Song received an master's degree in computing and information science from the University of Guelph.

Mohamed Adel Serhani is assistant professor at the College of Information Technology U.A.E University, U.A.E. He received his master's in computer science (2002) from University of Montreal, Canada, and his PhD in electrical and computer engineering (2006) from Concordia University, Canada. His research area is on Web services engineering that includes service selection and discovery, service lifecycle, QoS integration in SOA, End-to-End QoS management for Web services, QoS and Web services composition. He also worked on the application of artificial intelligence techniques mainly fuzzy logic to software engineering, object-oriented metrics, and software quality. He served as member of committee program and/or reviewer in the following conferences (IIT'05, ISWS'05, IIT'06, IRMA'06, IA'2006, CSA'06, WCNC'07, IASIS'07, ICOMP'07 and GCA'07).

Gottfried Vossen is a professor of computer science in the Department of Information Systems and a director of European Research Center for Information Systems at the University of Muenster in Germany. He is the European editor-in-chief of Elsevier's *Information Systems--An International Journal*. His research interests include conceptual as well as application-oriented problems concerning databases, information systems, electronic learning, the Semantic Web as well as Web 2.0. Vossen has been a member in numerous program committees of international conferences and workshops. He is an author or co-author of more than 120 publications, and an author, co-author, or co-editor of 20 books on databases, business process modeling, the Web, e-commerce, and computer architecture.

Peter Westerkamp is currently an IT-product manager at WGZ Bank AG in Düsseldorf, Germany. Until November 2006, he worked as a research assistant at the Department of Information Systems of the University of Muenster, Germany. He has received a bachelor's degree as well as a diploma in information systems from the University of Muenster. In 2005, he earned a PhD from the University of Muenster for his work on service-oriented e-learning platforms.

Index

W

Web component 157, 159, 164
Web container 157, 160
Web mining 61, 64, 71, 72, 73, 90
Web service 3, 5–6, 7, 8, 9, 13, 19
Web service agent 157, 166

Web services composition 197, 206, 208
Web service security (WSS) 16–17
Web services programming stack 199

X

XML 262, 263, 264, 265, 268, 269